The squandered dividend

The free market and the environment
in Eastern Europe

Roger Manser

EARTHSCAN

Earthscan Publications Ltd, London

First published in 1993 by
Earthscan Publications Limited
120 Pentonville Road, London N1 9JN

A catalogue record for this book is available from the British Library

ISBN: 1 85383 174 3

Typeset by DP Photosetting, Aylesbury, Bucks
Printed and bound in Great Britain by
Biddles Ltd, Guildford and King's Lynn

Earthscan Publications Limited is an editorially independent subsidiary
of Kogan Page Limited and publishes in association with the
International Institute for Environment and Development and the
World Wide Fund for Nature.

N. 81. 7. £11.95.

>oP S
(Man)

The squandered
dividend

CONTENTS

LIST OF ILLUSTRATIONS

BOXES

FIGURES

MAPS

TABLES

ACKNOWLEDGEMENTS

Many people have helped me write this book and I cannot thank them all individually. A few cannot be named. Others who provided me with new concepts, documents or interesting case histories, or who painstakingly explained their ideas or practices, or who nudged me into fresh ways of thinking, include Grzegorz Peszko, Ruth Bell, Tom Kolaja, Katarzyna Klich, Maroš Silný, Tsvetana Dimitrova, Ivan Matejović, Iza Kruszewska, Miroslaw Dakowski, Michal Holoubek, Ewa Dubik, Tim Jenkins, Marek Gruchelski and Wojciech Stodulski.

I have also had encouragement at difficult times in Gdańsk, Warsaw and Sydenham from Ania Marzec and our children Julian and Tomas, Janusz Marzec (who kept me in cigarettes and vodka during my times in Warsaw), Iwona Braniewska, Witek Żylicz and Hania and Ryszard Szarpak.

Roger Manser

THE QUIET REVOLUTIONS OF 1989

THE SULPHUR DRAGON

The expectations of ecological improvement which helped bring on the quiet revolutions in Central and Eastern Europe (CEE) in 1989 and 1990 remain today, almost as far from realization as they did then. This book analyses why. It focuses on the failure of the nascent free market to bring the economic gains upon which substantial environmental improvements could have been built. Progress depends on a sea-change in attitudes in Western Europe, and as Michal Holoubek of the Czech environmental group Brontosaurus has said, the CEE governments learning how to build on the environmentally positive aspects of the free market.[1]

Take Kraków, Poland's former capital (see Map 1.1): it is a historic city, listed by UNESCO as one of the world's most historic sites; it is part of the country's cultural make-up, much like York or Canterbury in England and Venice or Florence in Italy. Unlike most of Poland's other towns, it escaped destruction during the Second World War. But more or less since then it has been under continuous attack from air pollution, particularly sulphur dioxide emissions from the massive steel works built after the war by the communists, from two nearby power stations, and from local heating systems as well as from acid rain from further afield. In this it shared the fate of many other cities in Poland, the Czech Republic, Slovakia, the former East Germany and to a lesser extent Hungary and the Balkans.

In one of Poland's most famous legends, set in the mists of time, sulphur mined near Kraków saved its residents from being devoured by a marauding dragon. According to the myth, a shepherd boy eventually killed the beast by placing tar and sulphur inside a sheepskin, which it then ate. With the fire in the dragon's belly having ignited the explosive mixture, it drank from the waters of the nearby river Vistula, to quench

Map 1.1 *Central and Eastern Europe*

its thirst, and burst. And, as in most fairy tales, the shepherd boy married the princess in the castle and lived happily ever after.

This time the impact of sulphur and other pollutants has been pernicious. The decision of the communist government in the early 1950s to site the steel works close to the city ignored the wider geographical and commercial realities of the area, and bequeathed Poland's new government with an environmental bill which still has to be paid. Over the last 30 years, heavy metals, sulphur dioxide and dust from the Sendzimira steel works, particulates from the small and large district heating plants, nitrogen oxides from the growing volume of traffic, and pollutants from the nearby chemical industry have all contributed to the city's air pollution. Its more than 700,000 inhabitants were threatened daily by the air they breathed. Atmospheric acids have eaten away the finer details of various historical buildings including the splendid Sukiennice – the Renaissance cloth hall at the centre of the city's enormous market square. A fifth of the Huta Sendzimira's 30,000 steel workers were said by the Polish Ecological Club (PKE), which has its headquarters in the town, to leave their jobs every year due to ill-health. Others, though, attributed this high figure to the generous disability pensions for those who have worked in heavy industry.

Meanwhile untreated sewage and excessive water emissions from the local chemical industry have dirtied the river Vistula. In and around the city of Kraków, it was classified as 'substandard', which meant it was too polluted even for industrial use. In fact the upper Vistula, along with its tributaries in Silesia, was 'the most polluted river in Poland', according to Professor Jerzy Kurbiel of the Kraków University of Technology.[2] Cleaner water for drinking had to be transported to the city over great distances.

One of PKE's top priorities in the 1980s was the closure of the steel works: during this period, the threat from industry to the natural environment was part of the public's case against communism. But with the recession after 1991, attitudes went into reverse. The steel workers in Kraków were typical of this change: the major rallying cry suddenly became jobs. In 1990, employment in the country's 25 or so steel mills was around 136,000 and moves to reduce capacity and employment by over half were widely resisted. After considerable lobbying, the Polish government announced in 1992 that, though other plants were to be closed, Sendzimira was not. However, steel making would in due course be stopped, and, as part of a national plan to restructure the steel industry, the Kraków mill would be merged with Katowice, 60 kilometres away.

The restructuring of Poland's steel industry was primarily intended to make it fit to compete in the free market at home and abroad. The estimated cost was $4.5 billion over ten years. But it is unclear to what extent the plan would lead to a reduction in industrial emissions. In the late 1980s, the Katowice steel mill was also a very large source of air pollution. If financing for the plan from Western banks becomes available, emissions at Katowice may be reduced. If it does not – and the primary aim of the investment component of the plan is improved productivity and not reduced emissions – the higher output of raw steel from Katowice to supply its own and Kraków's needs could result in increased pollution. Lower discharges would require consistently applied environmental laws and a reliable enough market for the restructured companies to accumulate the resources necessary for the new technology.

In 1990, some economists and most politicians believed that within a few years Central and Eastern Europe would be on the same economic and environmental level as the West; three years on, the official view is that this process could instead take several decades. Certainly since 1989 and 1990, the pace of change has been much slower than expected. Few questioned the underlying assumption that capitalism would ultimately be able to achieve this goal. Indeed, for most commentators the failure of communism was taken to mean the success of capitalism.

Throughout the 40 years of the cold war, the West vaunted the superiority of free enterprise. But in the early 1990s, when it had the opportunity to show the advantages of capitalism, it could only come up with a mish-mash of aid programmes and a niggardly level of foreign direct investment. The deficiencies of the free market transplant adopted by the region stymied fundamental economic improvement and hindered government moves to repair the environmental fabric of the region. While a detailed analysis of the situation is for academic economists to make, the day to day consequences included increased poverty, and rising social tensions and crime. As governments and the consultants slowly found out, the free market's invisible hand was by no means the automatic purveyor of ecological balance that they once envisaged.

THE 'SECOND WORLD'

Prior to the fall of the Berlin Wall, eight countries made up East and Central Europe. These were Albania, Bulgaria, Czechoslovakia (CSFR), East Germany (officially known as the German Democratic Republic, or GDR), Hungary, Poland, Romania and Yugoslavia (see Table 1.1). Czechoslovakia, Hungary and Poland were sometimes referred to as Central Europe, and Albania, Bulgaria, Romania and Yugoslavia as the Balkans. In 1990, the GDR merged with the Federal Republic, in a move that many saw as historic, while in 1991 and 1992 Yugoslavia disin-

Table 1.1 *Selected social and economic data, by country, 1990*

	Population in millions mid-1990	Urban population as % of total 1990	Approx GDP per capita 1990 ($)	Phones per 1,000 inhabitants 1987	% private enterprise in NMP/GDP mid-1980s
Albania	3.3	35.2	645	na	na
Bulgaria	8.8	67.7	2,250	248	9
Ex-CSFR	15.7	77.5	3,140	246	3
Ex-GDR	16.8	77.2	na	na	na
Hungary	10.6	61.3	2,780	152	15
Poland	38.2	61.8	1,690	122	15
Romania	23.2	52.7	1,640	111	4
Ex-Yugoslavia	23.8	56.1	3,060	na	na
Total/average	140.4	na	2,280[1]	155[2]	9[2]
OECD	832.0[3]	na	17,390[3]	542	70–80

Notes [1] excluding Albania and ex-GDR; [2] excluding Albania, ex-GDR and ex-Yugoslavia; [3] 1989; na not available

Sources Basic indicators, Table 1, *World Development Report 1992*, World Bank, OUP; Economic and social indicators, Tables 1 and 2, *Reforming the economies of Central and Eastern Europe*, OECD, Paris, 1992; and others

tegrated into at least three if not four or five countries or entities. In January 1993, the velvet divorce followed the velvet revolution and Czechoslovakia split into Slovakia and the Czech Republic.

In the post-war years many in the West lumped all Central and Eastern Europe together. Though their similarities were often fewer than their historical and socio-political differences, political scientists in the '60s categorized the communist bloc as the 'second world', intermediary between the industrialized first and the developing third world. The second world was typecast as a strong Soviet Union surrounded by a dozen or more 'satellites', formed in its image. These countries, which included others such as Cuba, Mongolia (and China at one time) outside Eastern Europe, were certainly under Soviet political and economic influence. The communist party (which went under different names in the various countries) controlled political life, as well as their economies, which were broadly linked through Comecon – the Council for Mutual Economic Assistance or CMEA.

Following World War II, growing economic differences in the standards of living between East and West were initially masked by the rapid reconstruction of towns and industries throughout the continent. But during the '60s and '70s, the economic development of the two halves of the continent became visibly asymmetrical. The West granted loans to nearly all East European governments after the first oil crisis to revitalize their industries but, as the projects were often either ill conceived or poorly implemented, their overall impact was ultimately negative.

Furthermore, as the first world Western countries restructured in the 1980s, incorporating computers, robots and other high technology into industry and their increasingly large service sector, poor quality manufactured goods from Central and Eastern Europe could no longer compete in the West. Their economies spiralled downwards. It must have become clear to the region's leaders that communism could not continue as before and, once Mikhail Gorbachev became preoccupied with the consequences of the USSR's own economic and political debacle, the region had no one to turn to for political support and economic subsidies. It was only a matter of time before the system imploded, unloved except by a few diehards.

Communism left pockets of CEE in an ecological mess. There were disaster areas such as the so-called black triangle (see page 22) as well as a greater number of smaller 'hot-spots', such as Copşa Mică in Romania, Bor in Yugoslavia and Elbasan in Albania. In these localities, factory emissions had poisoned the soil and air and both ground and surface water. Poor environments contributed to the ill-health of many, especially young children: in East Germany the incidence of bronchitis among children increased by a half between 1975 and 1989. In some areas one in every two children suffered from respiratory diseases. One estimate made in Poland suggested that in 1985 the value of production lost due to such sicknesses and other environmental causes was equivalent to over 25 per cent of the national income,[3] though this is now seen as an exaggeration.

Since the revolutions of 1989 and 1990, when a hammer destroyed the ideological sickle, the region has been in economic turmoil. The political impetus of German reunification, together with the enormous resources made available by Western Germany, gave the ex-GDR a jump start down the road to capitalism and environmental restructuring. In this it was an exception. More cash was being put into the former GDR, which had a population of 17 million in the late '80s, than into all the other seven countries combined. Said Jürgen Möllemann, Germany's Federal Minister of Economic Affairs at the time, 'From the middle of 1990 to the end of this year [1991], more than DM100 billion [just over $60 billion] has been provided for the economic, social and ecological upswing.'[4] As the decade wore on, the numbers multiplied.

Even with this massive input of outside resources, it was unclear how long the economic and environmental rejuvenation of the new German Bundesländer (or states) would take. In spite of a well organized privatization programme, in early 1993 a quarter of the country's former state owned enterprises remained in state hands and another quarter was in the process of being liquidated. Progress in tackling environmental degradation in the centre of the country – around Halle and Leipzig, where the

6

chemical industry had been based – was slow. Conditions also remained bad in the south and east, where there were a number of large lignite fired power stations.

Poland had few of the advantages of Eastern Germany and most of the disadvantages. In this book, the Polish experience is used to illustrate the major trends in the region. With a population of nearly 40 million, it is by far the largest country in East and Central Europe, and in addition has some of the best statistics. It was also among the first to begin restructuring, ostensibly setting something of a pattern of liberalization, stabilization and gradual structural adjustment, which most of the others have followed to a greater or lesser extent.

Today, with capitalist restructuring in vogue, Poland like the other countries further south has become a mixture of the first, second and third worlds: first world cultural and consumer aspirations for videos, cable TV and cars, second world public housing and nationalized industries, and third world telecommunications and wage levels. In 1991, average wages in Poland were around $150 a month, and unemployment levels close on 10 per cent as mines and factories were on short-time work; the production of food by both state and private farms fell while poverty increased. The contradiction between expectations and reality manifested itself in a soaring crime rate.

In terms of environmental degradation, Poland vied with Czechoslovakia and the GDR in the late 1980s as the worst polluter. In all three countries, the generation and consumption of coal-based electrical energy was the principal cause. The area where all three met – dubbed the black triangle – was the vortex. For instance, much of the air pollution in Poland's Upper Silesia came from either the southern and eastern parts of the former GDR, or neighbouring Bohemia in the Czech Republic. Chorzow and Bytom to the north of Katowice were among the most blighted parts of the area.

In Poland, lignite was used in several large domestic power stations in the centre and west of the country. The power industry produced not only sulphur dioxide and dust, but salt water, which was pumped from the mines into the rivers. The high volume of untreated sewage flowing into the Vistula and Oder rivers made Poland the worst polluter of the Baltic Sea, with most of the country's beaches unfit for bathing.

In Czechoslovakia, in the late 1980s, according to Dr Jan Cerovsky, chief scientist of the State Institute for Nature Conservation, 'mining activities, particularly open cast lignite mines in north-west Bohemia, have caused grave devastation of the countryside'. Air pollution was endemic in the area. 'The severe environmental consequences and the great energy consumption of lignite mining itself, on the one hand, and its economic importance on the other, poses a dilemma that will be very hard to solve.'⁵ The production of fuel and energy reportedly consumed more than a fifth of the electricity generated, while a third of the country's forests were damaged, some irreparably, by acid rain.

In both the Czech and Slovak Republics, nuclear energy is the other main source of power. Its initial development pre-dated the Chernobyl disaster of 1986, which forced the communist government to halt the construction of further nuclear power stations. In early 1993, the crisis was deemed over and the new Czech government gave Westinghouse the go-ahead to complete the nuclear power plant at Temelin. It justified this decision on the grounds that three thermal power stations could then be closed.

Czechs from Bohemia and Moravia made up two thirds of the former federal republic's population. Their advantages included a skilled work-force and relatively low unemployment, as befitted an area with a strong industrial tradition. In contrast, Slovakia was born with 10 per cent or more unemployment, an intensive agriculture and a heavy and largely military industrial base left over from the cold war. While foreign investors favoured the Czech Republic, both divorcees, like Poland, lacked the capital to restructure their factories, mines and agriculture.

Though Hungary was an agricultural country, the communists tried hard to industrialize it. The Gabčikovo-Nagymaros barrage system on the Danube was part of this trajectory. Opposition to the project from 1984 onwards eventually resulted in 'one of the most impressive political victories ever achieved in eastern Europe.'⁶ Thousands of protestors working with the Hungarian environmental group, Danube Circle, were a major factor in the collapse of the communist Hungarian government. In 1989 the country withdrew from the project, leaving first the Czechoslovak government in Prague and then from January 1993 the Slovak government in Bratislava to continue its construction. Industrial environmental degradation was largely caused by out of date and badly managed factories.

Political and economic relaxation during the 1970s and 1980s helped create a small but significant private sector which since 1990 has given the country an edge in attracting foreign investment. However the fashionable centre of Budapest belies the real state of the country. The country's debts are high and much of the physical infrastructure outdated and run down; progress in privatizing the economy has actually been quite slow, particularly when compared with its northern neighbours.

Bulgaria was similar to Hungary in that it was essentially an agri-cultural country after the Second World War; industrialization came only in the 1960s – much later than elsewhere. Communism collapsed as a political force following the failure of its attack on the country's Turkish minority. Since then economic and political instability have hindered the development of a market economy. In the early 1990s, Sofia lacked both the bourgeois appeal of central Budapest and the tourist crowds of Prague.

Though the Bulgarian environmental group Ekoglasnost successfully publicized the country's widespread agricultural and industrial, air and water pollution in the late 1980s, since then the environmental movement has disintegrated. Ekoglasnost has become a shadow of its former self. In its place, the Green Patrols have assumed the activist mantle, and the Independent Club of Ecological Experts or Green Future has taken up the intellectual challenge. One of their main targets is the aged nuclear power plant at Kozloduy on the Danube, which many still see as the most dangerous in Europe.

In Romania, to the north of the Danube, Ceaucescu fathered a grandiose population growth policy, which left most Romanians in dire poverty. Moreover, his totalitarianism meant a virtual absence of environmental infrastructure. 'The lack of pollution control technology and the outdated industrial plant are the main reasons for the scale of Romania's air pollution problems', according to Dr Angheluta Vadineanu, Romania's Secretary of State for the Environment in 1990. His priority was to gain widespread acceptance within the country for the policy 'that protection of the environment is of fundamental importance to the long term and sustainable development of Romanian society.'[7]

In the last few years, hardly a month has gone by without one of the region's ecological trouble spots popping up in the Western press. The Bulgarian nuclear plant at Kozloduy, the Gabčikovo dam on the Danube, the Temelin nuclear power station in the Czech republic, toxic waste imports into Poland or Romania, the tailings dam on the Tara river in Montenegro, as well as Chernobyl in Ukraine have all fleetingly filled newspaper columns. They were reminders both of the communists' abuse of the physical environment, and the new governments' failure to address environmental recovery with the same enthusiasm as economic growth.

ECONOMIES FOR SALE

The transition which the region is now undergoing constitutes a test of the flexibility of the capitalist system. For economic change to succeed in the eyes of the local population, it should bring higher real incomes; in contrast, for environmental success it would have both to clean up those areas which were polluted by the communists, and to stop the exploitation of the environment, upon which the industrial growth was and is based.

The achievement of the latter is in turn dependent on the fulfilment of four demanding conditions. The first two are basically economic – restructuring both the national economies and the individual businesses in the region, while the second two are principally environmental – passing and enforcing stringent laws on emissions and waste disposal, and having appropriate policies and finance to steer the transition towards clean production and low waste technology.

The principal tool used by the new governments to restructure their economies and enterprises was foreign investment. Their goals were privatization and the removal of state controls. Their success depended on overcoming five constraints:

1. The absence of an economic model of how to move from a state owned to a privately owned economy; the region has consequently become a live experiment.
2. The legacy of communism – the social habits and economic structures of the last 40 years were more permanent than many had thought.
3. The lack of appropriate infrastructure and resources – capital, management skills, and professionals in a number of areas.
4. Heavy indebtedness.
5. The politicians' lack of experience and consequent mismanagement of government.

On top of these, there were three other obstacles faced by the new governments. They were:

1. The shortage of foreign capital: not only was the West in recession, for many of its firms the risk of investing in the region was not worth the candle.
2. The dearth of official aid: in spite of the political acclaim that greeted the new regimes, most Western governments were rather mean in their practical assistance.
3. The deep recession brought on in the region by the stabilization policies of the International Monetary Fund (IMF) and the move to international hard currency trading within Comecon in January 1991; factories selling to the USSR and Eastern Germany were particularly badly hit.

With hindsight it can also be seen there was a conflict between political expectations and economic reality. In general decision-makers and their advisors in 1989 overestimated capitalism's positive impact on the economy. The politicians thought that once inflation was cured then the 'magic of the market' would foster foreign interest, restructure lame duck industries, and encourage local entrepreneurs to start new light manufacturing and service industries.

One reason for the misplaced optimism was that the region was not as strong economically as had been believed. In a letter to the IMF in early 1991, Leszek Balcerowicz, the Polish Deputy Prime Minister and architect of the country's switch to capitalism said, 'Poland has emerged from communism with a badly depleted capital stock, an inadequate infrastructure and widespread environmental devastation. As a result, there is a vast need for capital accumulation and replacement, successfully to accomplish structural adjustment and raise living standards on a sustainable basis.'[8] A World Bank official commented later the same year that 'Forty years of the command economy had led to a totally ill adapted and inadequate capital stock, and to totally different management and work practices.'[9] Additionally in 1990 there was quite insufficient acknowledgment of the free market's intrinsic weaknesses. In particular, governments and the multilateral banks seem to have disregarded the risks of investing in a region undergoing radical transformation.

Moreover as the decade wore on, the economic policy options for CEE governments became more limited. Not only did nationalism influence attitudes towards privatization and foreign investment, but with the deepening recession the availability of local finance was reduced. The advent of the free market increasingly allowed the region's economy to be invaded by the turbulence of global competition for capital and labour, as well as goods and services. Local companies thus sought a safe haven for their profits outside the country rather than investing in local manufacturing, while skilled and professional workers wherever possible emigrated. The balance of payments deteriorated with the inward flow of goods and service, mainly from the European Community (EC), greater than the region's exports.[10] Furthermore privatization and restructuring were not succeeding in the way the IMF and World Bank's laboratory technicians had thought they would.

Also in the early 1990s, other than in Eastern Germany, economic aid from outside was small. The World Bank provided some help for improvements to infrastructure, while the European Bank for Reconstruction and Development (EBRD) focused on selected bankable projects, such as food processing, telecommunications, and property. The EC, in spite of a lot of talk and some aid, refused to more than half open its doors to CEE exports.

In the face of these impediments, it was hardly surprising that the economic results of the transition were disappointing. The reform programmes of Central and East European governments stumbled and in some cases stalled. Impoverishment worsened. The decline in demand brought on by the sudden advent of the market economy and the collapse of sales to the USSR and elsewhere pushed up unemployment to unheard-of levels, and living standards, particularly in the countryside, down to below the poverty line. Inflation hit those, such as pensioners, on fixed incomes and the impact of rising real prices meant that even those in full-time work often had to moonlight to make ends meet.

Yet politically most electorates did not want a return to communism and the system of central planning, which had provided for full employment. Though images such as Lech Walesa's vault over the Gdańsk shipyard fence and the fall of the Berlin Wall may have suggested communism collapsed for political reasons, economic factors were probably more important – communism had not brought the lifestyle which most people wanted. Comparisons with Western Europe through magazines, television and individual visits had become more and more unfavourable. People felt they were being excluded from a Western-style prosperity which was theirs almost by right.

Thus nearly all the new governments, armed with their bevies of Western consultants, forced the pace towards a privately owned economy, unencumbered with state controls. Their approach reflected the views of Sir William Ryrie of the World Bank's International Finance Corporation that 'economic man cannot be far beneath the surface. One has to believe that a decontrolled environment with the right incentives will lead to the emergence of entrepreneurs.'[11]

Though privatization was the most obvious of the changes initiated by governments, other elements included reform of the banking system, bankruptcy laws, the removal of subsidies and fostering foreign investment. Economic cooperation with the West was doubly welcome. Politically, it was a sign that Winston Churchill's iron curtain had been pulled back, and economically it helped cash-strapped governments. Throughout the region, West European and particularly German investment was the dominant commercial driving force. At least 80 per cent of the private capital being invested in both Eastern Germany and Czechoslovakia was German. In Poland and Hungary, German investors were important, though companies based elsewhere – the USA, Sweden and Austria – were also active.

The structure of economic activity in the region has begun to shadow that of other middle income developing countries, in which the state often had a majority stake in heavy industry. Most new investment was in trading, particularly in supplying branded consumer goods to the local market. With wages often only 10 per cent of West European levels, the region also had an advantage in labour intensive operations such as vehicle assembly for the local and export markets.

THE ECONOMIC AND ECOLOGICAL JIGSAW

Immediately following the revolutions, there was a brief period when it had seemed environmentalists might succeed in shifting their countries' economies on to a path favouring sustainable development. Fundamental environmental issues such as resource depletion and global survival were on the agenda. It was believed that foreign investment would help restructure the economy and in so doing reduce emissions and improve the efficiency of the antiquated units inherited from the communist era. Fiscal and other policies aimed at reducing pollution and turning communism's industrial monsters into effective resource-efficient companies were proposed and sometimes even accepted by governments. The activists sought to leapfrog the environmental delinquency of the West by integrating their countries' programmes for economic development and environmental recovery at both national and local levels.

Their brave attempt was soon however swamped by the difficulties of introducing a free market in the region, the pressures for economic growth and the enormous cost of the necessary environmental investments. In 1990 and 1991, environmental expenditure rose significantly, but thereafter it could be said that the opportunities offered by the quiet revolutions for environmental restructuring were squandered. More or less unnoticed, the great flood of concern for the environment in 1989 evaporated into a cloud of one-upmanship among the aspiring middle classes and the struggle for survival by most others.

The full cost of restructuring economic activity to meet reasonable local environmental standards was estimated at approximately $600 billion. Though this was to be spread over two decades, it was at least double the region's combined 1990 gross domestic product (GDP). The total included cleaning up the worst of the mess left by the communists' pollution economy, improving the efficiency with which energy and other raw materials were used, wherever possible reducing the impact of economic activity on the global environment, and conserving biodiversity.

In order to pay for environmental improvements, the economy had to grow, and at the same time industry had to feel the watchful eye and threatened arm twist of a government committed to environmental protection. In fact, more or less the opposite happened. The economy declined and though environmental user fees, emission charges and fines were increased, they increasingly went unpaid, as enterprise debts rose and bankruptcy loomed. Public opinion often turned a blind eye where jobs were at stake. Surplus capital, if any, was used to finance survival or at best to switch production to more profitable lines. It was rarely used to meet environmental targets.

The energy and heavy industrial sectors, which included some of the most polluting plants in simple volume terms (but not necessarily the most threatening to health) faced the hardest problems in restructuring. In the case of energy, state owned enterprises were unable to provide budgetary support, while most of the markets for the goods produced by heavy industry had vanished with the collapse of Comecon.

A few factories were able to take advantage of the weaker free market rates of exchange, currency convertibility and lax implementation of environmental laws briefly to boost exports to the West. Steel exports from Czechoslovakia to the EC rocketed in 1992, but were then subject to extra restrictions to protect the Community's own steel industry. For most of the power utilities and heavy industrial plants, there was little support for new investment from the multilateral banks or foreign companies, which opted instead for shorter term, less risky gains in other sectors. Communism's industrial dinosaurs were set to become extinct, but in the meantime to pollute, albeit at a lower level than in the past.

In autumn 1990, Bronislaw Kaminski, then the Polish Minister of Environmental Protection, gave his view of the future link between economic development and the environment in a statement to the World Conservation Union. 'The activities of all government bodies will be planned so as to assure continued economic use of the natural environment, whilst actively protecting it in order to raise the quality of life of the entire nation and, in turn, help the Polish economy.'[12] Other countries' ministers in their statements to the Union recognized there could be a dissonance as well. The Hungarian Minister for Environment and Regional Policy, Sandor Kerestes, noted that his government 'wishes to develop the economy and the environment together in a sustainable way with the reservation that in the case of a conflict between these two areas, it will place short range economic interests after those of ecological stability.'[13] In 1990, in the pleasant atmosphere of the conference room, giving the environment a positive priority was fine.

By 1993, such views had largely been overtaken by the twin policies of privatization and reducing controls, in which the limited number of multinationals which had invested in the region were given a central role. Few of them, on the one hand, were directly involved in environmental scams, though where they could negotiate a beneficial deal, they did. This was particularly the case where governments were irresolute, or for ideological reasons did not wish to control incoming investment. On the other hand, their operations encouraged consumerism, crafting Central and Eastern Europe in the only brand name image they knew (and many in the region wanted). It was no coincidence that Pepsi Cola and Coca Cola were usually among the first to invest in any country. The results may have been acceptable for the government, or even for the individual workers who kept their jobs, but the environment was the loser.

Since 1989, moreover, some Western companies have negotiated contracts with governments and/or joint venture partners, which would not have been tolerated in the West. For example, they sought ways to avoid paying environmental fines, to obtain subsidized sulphur dioxide polluting power or to set up operations which were firmly regulated elsewhere, such as the processing of toxic waste. During the very early 1990s, the number which succeeded was not large. However, as the decade wore on, the state increasingly became too weak to dictate firm environmental conditions for foreign investment. Faced with rising unemployment, and colossal foreign debts as well as political instability in a number of cases, governments began to welcome foreign investment, more or less irrespective of its activity.

Low labour costs combined with the weak administration of environmental laws attracted marginal investors in ecologically threatening industries, such as chemicals and waste processing. Iza Kruszewska, who campaigns for Greenpeace International against the waste trade in Central and Eastern Europe, believed that by 1993 the region was well on the way to becoming 'Europe's dumping ground for obsolete technologies, withdrawn products and waste.'[14]

This is different, but not a lot different from the communists in the 1970s and 1980s. Both they and the new governments in practice based their decisions on a narrow definition of economic activity, which excluded from the costs of production both environmental damage and the use of non-renewable resources. Though the polluter pays principle (PPP) was theoretically accepted by most of the new governments, under communism and to a lesser extent under the free market, the real operative principle was that pollution paid.

Though communism was a materialistic ideology, it often contained a puritanical streak; everyone was meant to have sufficient and the wealthy were supposedly penalized. In reaction to this in the early 1990s, the Adam Smith model of capitalism found a new home, in which the governments of Central and Eastern Europe played second fiddle to Western companies.

OBJECTIVES OF THE BOOK

The central purpose of this book is to describe and analyse the impact of the economy on the environment, both under the communist system, and more especially today, as Central and Eastern Europe moves towards a mixed or capitalist economy and a democratic system of government. Its pessimistic theme is the likely failure of the free market to bring substantial improvements to the environment. This is principally due to the failure of economic restructuring, the shortage of funds for environmental investments and the lack of public support for firm environmental legislation.

In examining the way the free market was established or re-established, the book disputes the views of some of the more naive commentators who in 1990 claimed that it would be self-developing. They believed that the invisible hand would soon replace the tall belching smokestacks with clean sunrise industries. Three years later, a more detached view suggests an interventionist approach would have been more effective in restructuring industry and there are some signs that this is now beginning to happen. In an ecologically aware world, industrial restructuring and environmental needs would have gone hand in hand at all times.

On environmental issues governments were willing to take a hands-on approach in 1990, but after then other priorities became more pressing and their enthusiasm waned. The book examines some of the ways in which they, industry and non-governmental organizations (NGOs) have been and are trying to make environmental improvements. The book's message is that these should be taken further.

Structure of the book

The book starts by looking at the past 40 years. In the communist era, with political life and the economy held in irons, the contradiction between economic growth and the environment left battle zones of ecological destruction. This is discussed in Chapters 2 and 3; the former describing the environmental legacy, and the latter analysing the reasons for it.

The headlong rush from communism into a free market in the early 1990s had a positive potential in that it introduced greater flexibility into economic life. While there are dangers in comparing 1980s communism with late twentieth century capitalism, the passage to a free market economy was expected to bring both harm and benefit to the environment.

These issues are taken further in the next two chapters. Chapter 4 describes the economic upheaval currently taking place in the region, describing the progress and difficulties of privatization, restructuring and the introduction of a free market. Chapter 5 looks in detail at the environmental consequences of the free market, analysing both the positive and negative trends.

Chapter 6 examines some of the economic measures being undertaken to establish an environmentally sustainable economy. It examines issues such as the polluter pays principle, environmental liability, trading pollution permits and debt for nature swaps. Chapter 7 focuses on energy as the underlying cause of much of the region's environmental degradation. It discusses the potential for energy saving and the way it has been displaced by policies geared to energy generation, including nuclear power and the Gabčikovo-Nagymaros dam project on the Danube.

The final chapter describes some of the other responses of governments and the international community to the economic and environmental turmoil. It also outlines some of the policy improvements that could be made on both the economic and environmental fronts. These include the banking system, the EBRD, and the introduction of cleaner technology.

2

THE SCARS OF STALINISM

A BLACK PICTURE?

In 1989, it was easy though misleading to paint a completely black picture of Eastern Europe. The region contained several large heavily polluted districts and a fair number of polluted cities and towns, rivers and streams. Both within and without them, there were also smaller zones where the natural habitat had been or was being totally destroyed. However, between these areas as well as sometimes within them, there were stretches of unspoilt forest, secondary growth and clean water. These included protected areas – national parks, nature reserves and the like, with varying restrictions on human activity.

Katowice voivodeship (or province) in Upper Silesia was often said to be one of the most polluted areas in the region, yet it illustrates the diversity of conditions. In the late 1980s, some 7.4 per cent of its land was 'visibly damaged by coal, zinc, lead and sand mining', about 3 per cent was 'degraded by mining excavations, tunnels, subsided land, damps and flooded areas', but about a quarter was covered by forest. Moreover just under half its land was agricultural, supplying 70 per cent of the food eaten by the local population.[1]

While it would be charitable to believe that the casual visitor in the late 1980s was misled into thinking that the city she or he was visiting was a microcosm of the whole region, it would be more accurate to say that the image of black billowing clouds and dilapidated buildings was one of the last propaganda coups of the cold war. Some parts of both the Western media and the local opposition overstated the extent of the ecological disaster in order to condemn and if possible bury communism and central planning. In reality, the picture should have been pepper and salt. There were certainly a number of urban patches of very unhealthy dusty black surviving under a pall of irritating charcoal grey and a few completely blank areas. Much more visible though were the swathes of green and brown.

Living in some towns and cities was certainly risky. Aerial photographs of Upper Silesia register not only the urban chaos, but also the layers of smoke and gases escaping from the high rise chimneys of its smelters and power plants.[2]

A report by German dissidents on the uranium mines in the former East Germany published in the late 1980s told how they were initially at least run by the ex-USSR as a state within a state. The dangers of working and living in the area were kept quiet for security reasons. In the early post-war years, the mines attracted workers as wages were higher and food more plentiful. In the 1970s, the level of mining activity declined, but for those still working underground and living above ground there was radioactive dust in the air, and radioactive water from underground sources and from the run-off from the large slag heaps.[3]

Together with the tailings from metal mining in the same area, the area affected is about $1,500 \text{ km}^2$ – about 1 per cent of the ex-GDR's land surface. While uranium mining stopped in Eastern Germany soon after unification, it continued for up to several years in parts of Hungary, the Czech Republic and Bulgaria.

This chapter identifies some of the key statistics on emissions and other abuses of the environment in selected sectors and areas in the late 1980s. It also describes some of the consequences for human health. (The next chapter analyses the reasons for the region's environmental degradation.)

USE AND ABUSE OF THE ENVIRONMENT

During the 1980s, sulphur dioxide was seen by many as the quintessential industrial pollutant, the principal cause of acid rain, which was in turn one of the main environmental issues in industrialized Western Europe. For some it was a paradox that the so-called first world industrialized countries actually emitted less sulphur dioxide per head of population than the second world countries of Central and Eastern Europe. Lignite burning East Germany and Czechoslovakia were probably the world leaders in emissions per head, and Romania and Bulgaria in emissions per unit of GDP (see Table 2.1). Once this became known, it was easy to characterize the region as a polluters' paradise. The main source of the sulphur dioxide was industry and in particular coal-fuelled power generators.

In fact dust was probably just as or more detrimental to human health than sulphur dioxide. As Table 2.2 shows, in the late 1980s dust emissions from Central and Eastern Europe were also high, in comparison with

Table 2.1 *Sulphur dioxide emissions, by country, 1985 and 1988/9*

Country	Total (000 tonnes SO_2) 1985	1989	Per head 1989 (kg)	Per km^2 1989 (kg)	Per $1m GDP + (tonnes)	Per TOE energy use + (kg)
Albania (est)	50	50	17	2	na	na
Bulgaria	1,140	1,030	114	9	70	50
CSFR	3,150	2,800	179	22	30	19
E Germany	5,000	5,210	306	48	na	27
Hungary	1,420	1,218	115	13	19	20
Poland	4,300	3,910	103	13	33	16
Romania	3,600	4,800+	104	20	70	34
Yugoslavia	1,500	1,650	70	6	na	na
For comparison						
Canada	3,704	na	148*	na	na	na
UK	3,676	3,552	62	15	4	9
USA	21,100	20,700	83	2	na	na
W Germany	2,400	1,500	24	6	–	2

Notes * for 1985; + 1988; ... less than 1; TOE tonne oil equivalent; est estimated; na not available

Sources *The environment in Europe and North America*, Annotated Statistics 1992, United Nations, New York, 1992; and others

those of Western Europe. As with sulphur dioxide, the main source was coal-fuelled power generation. Other industrial emissions in specific locations included carbon disulphide, fluoride (particularly around aluminium smelters), and chlorine. Emissions of vehicle linked pollutants – nitrogen oxides (NO_x), lead, carbon dioxide (CO_2) and hydrocarbons – were low in absolute terms compared with the West. Relative to GDP,

Table 2.2 *Emissions of various air pollutants, by country, 1988 (000 tonnes, except where stated)*

Country	Dust	NO_x (fixed source)	NO_x (moving source)	Lead	CO_2 (10^6 tonnes)	Hydro-carbons
Bulgaria	808	336	52	0.2	na	164
CSFR	1,245	655	310	na	na	313
E Germany	2,200	408	300	na	360	500
Hungary	na	124	120	0.5	88	na
Poland	1,615	1,060	490	1.6	440	1,000
Romania	785	na	na	0.8	127	na
For comparison						
Canada*	1,710	na	na	na	471	2,316
UK	533	1,264	1,378	3.1	585	2,013
USA	na	na	na	na	na	na
W Germany	530	1,000	1,850	3.0	710	2,650

Note * for 1985; na not available

Sources *The environment in Europe and North America*, Annotated Statistics 1992, United Nations, New York, 1992; and others

however, they were quite high, reflecting in part the old age and lack of maintenance of the relatively small number of vehicles on the roads.

Industrial air emissions are initially highly concentrated and then dispersed by wind action. Katowice with 2.1 per cent of Poland's land area generated a quarter of the country's gaseous and dust emissions in the late 1980s. However, some 60–70 per cent of the sulphur dioxide (SO_2) air pollution in the town originated outside the area. Indeed about half the sulphur dioxide received by Poland came from neighbouring countries, particularly Czechoslovakia and East Germany.

Comparative information on water emissions by country was patchier, but it would seem all countries had a considerable problem with underground drinking water quality around their urban centres. In former East Germany, some 20 per cent of waters could be drunk after being treated with normal technology; 45 per cent was unusable. In Poland in the late 1980s, less than 5 per cent of the rivers were class I – fit to drink; around 40 per cent was unclassified chemically, and double that biologically. Saline discharges from the coal mines at Czeczott, Piast and Ziemowit were a particular problem, as they were large and had very low unit mining costs.

Though the trends in Hungarian surface water varied, the quality of ground water 'has consistently deteriorated.'[4] Most ground water used for drinking was distributed 'with little or no treatment.'[5] An estimated four-fifths of Romania's rivers were unable to supply drinking water. In the Czech Republic, class I water represented 17 per cent of water flow length, and the poorest quality 22 per cent, while in Slovakia, about half the water flows were class IV. 'The ground water contamination [was] increasing, mainly because of nitrates, pesticide and fertilizer residues, and chlorinated hydrocarbons.'[6]

Transboundary rivers such as the Elbe and Danube were particularly polluted. An analysis by Greenpeace of the Elbe where it left Czech territory showed high levels of organochlorine pesticides, heavy metals, aromatic compounds and other solvents.[7] Discharges of untreated sewage and non-point pollution (particularly of phosphate and nitrate fertilizers) resulted in increased biological oxygen demand (BOD) in the rivers and receiving seas. Strong eutrophication in coastal areas of the Baltic Sea became 'disastrous'[8] in the later 1970s, though since then there has been some improvement. The Adriatic and the Black Seas also had severe quality problems in the 1980s due to tourism.

Solid wastes can be classified according to their source (for example, mining, other industrial or municipal wastes), their toxicity, their dispersion, and their reuse. During the 1980s, mining and coal ash (particularly brown coal ash) wastes mounted in Poland, the GDR, and Czechoslovakia. In Czechoslovakia they reached around 35–40 tonnes per person per year. It is usually assumed that the volumes of industrial waste generated in the East were greater than in the West, but this may not always have been the case. For example, Polish mining waste was officially estimated to be about half that of the UK.[9] Agricultural liquid wastes accumulated in Hungary, Bulgaria and Slovakia.

One of the biggest concerns was hazardous or potentially hazardous waste. During the 1960s and 1970s, Poland buried at least 40,000 tonnes of 'highly toxic agricultural waste' – pesticides (DDT), organochlorides and used pesticide containers.[10] Some of this was placed in hundreds of concrete tombs, many of which were ill sited in respect of water supplies. Some was just encased in steel drums and put in shallow graves, and some illegally buried without any form of containment. Today it is suspected that even that officially stored may soon pose a health danger. There is evidence that both the concrete tombs and steel drums may be disintegrating, allowing the seepage of their contents into a local water supply.

Nuclear wastes from power stations were officially sent to the ex-USSR for reprocessing, but it is not clear to what extent this actually happened. It is known however that wastes from uranium mining and treatment plants remain unprotected in several countries. The end of the cold war saw the departure of Warsaw Pact and in particular ex-USSR troops. Their vacated army depots were often contaminated with oil, which in places had seeped into the ground water.

Geographically, the overlapping concentration of pollution and heavy industry led the media to coin graphic terms such as the black triangle. This was the worst polluted part of the region. At its core were parts of Lower Silesia, northern Bohemia and Saxony. Others termed it the sulphur triangle.[11] In reality it was neither a triangle nor a rigidly defined area: other nearby districts, equally degraded, included Cottbus and the Halle-Leipzig district in Eastern Germany and the Ostrava/Katowice/Kraków area in Moravia and southern Poland. It should have been called a polygon and not a triangle, and grey and not black.

Dotted throughout the region, there were numerous other 'hotspots', where the ecological problems were concentrated on a town or a particular industrial site. In Poland, official figures claimed that in the late 1980s some 35 per cent of Poland's population lived in 80 towns and 27 areas which faced severe ecological threats.[12] Within the black triangle, in the south west of the country the worst affected areas were Upper Silesia, the copper mining and smelting area around Glogów and Legnica in Lower Silesia, and the Kraków district. Other seriously threatened areas included Gdańsk Bay and its literal, the sulphur mining areas around Tarnobrzeg and Tarnów, and Łódź.

In other countries, the pattern was similar. Czechoslovakia's disaster zones outside the black triangle included Prague and Bratislava as well as parts of eastern Slovakia. Between the north and south banks of the Danube, Romania and Bulgaria waged a war of words over chlorine from the Giurgiu chemical works drifting over the Bulgarian town of Ruse. Copşa Mica in central Romania was one of Europe's worst ecological hotspots due to air emissions from the Carbosin chemical plant and the two imperial smelting furnaces for processing lead and zinc concentrates. Organika-Zachem in Bydgoszcz was reportedly the only factory in Poland to issue warning instructions to local residents: among other substances, it emitted chlorine and phenols. The list could go on – the number of towns in the region with similar problems could easily have been extended to several hundred.

In addition at certain industrial sites, the soil was heavily contaminated by wastes, particularly heavy metals and chemicals. At the Borsod chemical works in Hungary, 500–1,000 tonnes of mercury from the production of chlorine was said to have seeped into the soil. At Wolfen in Germany, chemical wastes from the film factory containing phenols, volatile hydrocarbons, and carbon disulphide were dumped in a nearby old coal mine.

In urban areas, it was not only industry which caused air and water pollution. Non-point sources were also substantial generators. East Germany's two-stroke Trabants and Wartburgs as well as coal and wood burning stoves contributed to the smog hazard. The diesel fuel used by antiquated buses and trucks was rarely desulphurized.

In rural areas, agriculture was in many ways as destructive as industry in the towns. There was widespread non-point water pollution arising from the use of chemical fertilizers and animal slurry, as well as pesticides. Farming marginal land contributed to soil erosion, extensive monocropping to reduced soil fertility and irrigation to falling water tables and saline soils. Second homes and allotments ate into habitats. Everywhere biodiversity was under pressure.

The above description is a snapshot of the region just before the quiet revolutions. In the course of the '80s, while many emissions fell, their cumulative impact on the environment grew. In Katowice 'total gaseous emissions decreased by over 30 per cent between 1980 and 1988,'[13] but the area's trees were 'weakened by industrial air pollutants (especially SO_2, NO_x, ozone, fluorine, and particulate matter)', which made them more susceptible to disease and insect attacks. 'The environmental impact of this tree loss included a shortening of the snow melting period, the appearance of erosion channels in forests ... and higher acidity and sulphur in the soil.'[14] In places by the late 1980s the industrial abuse of the environment over 30–40 years had far exceeded any assimilative capacity, with a seriously deleterious impact on natural habitats and human life alike.

ILL-HEALTH AND LIFE EXPECTANCY

Under the communists, little environmental research work was done and even less was published, for political reasons. Nevertheless broad brush statistics highlighted the deteriorating health of the region's people. In the late 1980s, life expectancy was three to four years less than in the West and infant death rates some two to three times higher. Some of this data is shown in Table 2.3.

Much of the evidence of the environmental impact on ill-health is circumstantial given the importance of other factors such as cigarette smoking and diet. In Poland, for instance, life expectancies in rural areas surpassed those in urban areas in recent years, 'a highly unusual demographic trend', associated, said World Bank analysts, 'with the fact that environmental pollution is concentrated in urban areas.'[15]

Urban life expectancy in Katowice voivodeship was said to be the shortest in Poland – a full year less than the national average for both men and women – reflecting the higher mortality rates from heart diseases, cancers and digestive tract illnesses among people aged over 60 years.[16] Emissions of dust, sulphur dioxide and other gases in 1987 in the voivodeship were 285 tonnes/km^2, compared with around 1 tonne/km^2 in some of the rural provinces.

While average infant mortality rates in the province in the late 1980s were 18.5 per 1,000 live births, marginally higher than the Polish

Table 2.3 *Basic health indicators, by country, late 1980s*

Country	Life expectancy at birth 1985–90	Infant death rates[1] 1985–90
Albania (est)	72.1	40
Bulgaria	72.6	15
CSFR	72.0	14
E Germany	74.5	10
Hungary	71.3	17
Poland	72.4	17
Romania	71.1	23
Yugoslavia	71.7	25
For comparison		
Canada	76.3	8
Mexico	67.2	47
Turkey	64.1	76
UK	74.5	9
USA	75.0	10
W Germany	74.5	9

Note [1] Infant deaths per 1,000 live births

Source Health and Nutrition, *World Resources 1988–89*, World Resources Institute, Basic Books Inc, New York

average, in several parts of the conurbation, such as Bytom they were close to 30 per 1,000.[17] In Rozbark, a small area of Bytom, in 1987 they even exceeded 40 per 1,000,[18] a figure close to Mexican levels, in spite of Poland's 'first world' medical service. This high figure was thought by the vice-chairwoman of Bytom's town council, Dr Ewa Dubik, to reflect the high level of heavy metals in the air around the 'White Eagle' lead smelter and the generally high levels of benzapyrene in the town.[19] The Katowice voivodeship also suffered from the highest incidence of premature births (8.5 per cent), genetic birth defects (10.1 per cent of all live births) and spontaneous miscarriages in Poland.[20]

In early 1993, a more detailed study prepared by the World Bank, OECD and others for the environmental action programme for Central and Eastern Europe (see Chapter 8) identified and grouped individual places associated with environmental health problems in the 1970s and 1980s into nine broad categories.[21] These were locations where there were:

- Over-exposures to lead among children
- Acute respiratory diseases associated with air pollution
- Chronic respiratory diseases associated with air pollution
- Reasonably strong associations between mortality and air pollution
- Documented associations between abnormal physiological development and air pollution
- High levels of nitrates in the drinking water so as to require the provision of bottled water to protect infants against blue baby syndrome
- Problems with arsenic
- Contaminated supplies of drinking water
- Other problems.

In most of the places listed, the problems continued into the early '90s. Areas which were mentioned in several categories were the hot spots such as: the Legnica-Glogów area, Katowice and Kraków in Poland; central and northern Bohemia in the Czech Republic; parts of Slovakia including Bratislava and Ziar nad Hronom; Devnya, Plovdiv, Asenovgrad, Vratsa, Srednogorie and Pernik in Bulgaria; Borsod, Dorog and Ajka in Hungary; and Copşa Mică and Bucharest in Romania. The study did not cover Germany, Yugoslavia or Albania.

The towns and districts included in these nine categories were estimated to cover between a tenth and a fifth of the region's population. In the urban areas of south-west Poland and Bohemia, the main causes of the environmental ill-health included the emissions of heavy metals, dust and sulphur dioxide and the accumulation of heavy metals in the soil, which was then used for agriculture. Water pollution was less of a problem.

In parts of Slovakia, Hungary, Romania and Bulgaria, the leaching of nitrate fertilizers and animal wastes into local water supplies posed a hazard for infants. For instance in the mid-1980s in Hungary, of the country's 3,000 towns and cities, 800 reportedly had to use bottled water or piped water from neighbouring areas, because their wells were contaminated with nitrate compounds, to such an extent that the water was unfit for human consumption.[22] In the towns, particularly in Romania, point sources including chemical plants, smelters and power stations were major risks.

A COMPLEX ISSUE

Ill-health in general is often seen as reversible. Recent research has however indicated that those living permanently in the smog of Upper Silesia may suffer from genetic damage. The cause, according to the Marie Sklodowska-Curie clinic in Gliwice, was aromatic hydrocarbons produced by burning coal.[23] The research left unclear whether such defects were being passed from parent to child.

Towards the end of the 1980s, the loosening grip of the communist party combined with the rising concern with environmental health spurred public opinion to campaign for the closure of particular plants. Several of the groups such as Ekoglasnost in Bulgaria and the Danube Circle in Hungary achieved national prominence at the time when communism fell. Others such as Poland's PKE were equally effective but took less political limelight. Though they all succeeded in raising environmental questions, the ultimate target of their campaigns and analysis was the monolithic communist party. As the next chapter shows, the issues were often more complex than the groups claimed.

3

THE DEVELOPMENT OF A
POLLUTION ECONOMY 1945–89

NO SINGLE ANSWERS

'Pollution in Eastern Europe in the years up to 1989 was a function of the
age and location of its industry',[1] said Bernard Brentnall, Chairman of
British Sulphur Consultants, a UK firm with long experience of working
with the region's chemical industry. Though a snap comment, it contained more than a grain of truth. Much of the industry was old and
poorly maintained and it was often located in areas that made little sense
in terms of economic geography.

Yet it has to be stressed there are no single answers as to why and how
the central planners made Central and Eastern Europe into one of the
world's largest sources of pollution. While it is true communist governments frequently failed to take the environment as seriously as their
own propaganda suggested they would, accusing communism was often
more of a political riposte than serious economic analysis.

Some of the ways in which the governments ruined the environment
were in fact just as capitalist as communist: both economic systems, for
example, heavily exploited raw materials, the former less visibly in
developing countries and the latter at home. Before the Second World
War in a number of Central European countries, the state worked with
private capital. In the years immediately after it, indicative planning and
state ownership were taken up by many of the nominally capitalist West
European countries, and though economic planning became less popular
in the '50s and '60s, state ownership was retained by most as a means of
meeting both social and economic goals. Moreover, both systems tended
to look for short term rather than longer term solutions to their environmental problems.

This chapter analyses the main causes of the region's environmental degeneration after the Second World War. The reasons were in one sense economic: they included the misallocation of resources due to the priority given by Stalinism to heavy industry, and its subsequent misdirection by the system of economic planning. But in addition, they were also political and psychological: the region was for many years in self-imposed isolation from the major trends in the world's economy, with individuals often too frightened to speak their minds. As the bureaucracy ballooned, individual motivation eventually became marooned in a sea of dispirited complacency.

BEFORE THE SECOND WORLD WAR

In the nineteenth and early twentieth centuries, the region was essentially agricultural and rural. Economic conditions ranged from exploitation in the Russian part of Poland to nodes of advanced engineering in Czechoslovakia. Germany and to a much lesser extent Russia (pre-1914) dominated the north, the Austro-Hungarian empire the middle and the Ottoman empire the south and east.

Though Poland was traditionally an agricultural country, its industrial revolution began just before it was finally dismembered in the late eighteenth century. The first steam pump was installed in 1788 in Upper Silesia in the mining town of Tarnowskie Gory, which 'allowed shafts to be sunk to a greater depth ... which naturally enabled a handsome increase in extraction of zinc, lead and iron ores'.[2] During the nineteenth century, Silesia was developed by Prussia as an industrial frontier colony, something akin to Siberia today. Heavy industry (coal, steel and non-ferrous metallurgy) predominated, essentially because of the distance to the major markets in Berlin and beyond. Following the end of the First World War, newly reborn Poland acquired the textile centre of Łódź and the steel works at Dąbrowa, both of which had been under Russian control until 1914. After 1921, it also took in large chunks of Silesia from Germany. These contained coal mines, lead and zinc mines, and steel works.

The GDR had of course been part of the German Reich before 1945, though it was not as industrial as the western three-quarters. Chemical factories had begun to be developed in the late nineteenth century; for example in 1895 Chemische-Fabrik Griesheim began the electrolysis of brine in Bitterfeld, using local deposits of lignite and salt for the production of indigo as a textile dye. Within a few years, the company concentrated all its chlorinated hydrocarbon activities there, making the area the centre of the German electrochemical industry. Meanwhile at nearby Wolfen, Agfa established in 1896 its own manufacturing arm for dyes and photographic materials.

When Czechoslovakia became independent in 1918, it was the world's tenth largest industrial power, having inherited 70–80 per cent of Austro-Hungary's industry. Bohemia was the most advanced area of the joint empire, while Moravia gained from its position at the edge of the Upper Silesian coalfield. Between 1920 and 1939, the country further developed its metal and machinery industries, and in electrical products particularly it was a major European force. However, the country's development was very uneven – by the late '30s, only 8 per cent of its total industrial output came from Slovakia.

Other than in Bohemia and Moravia, industrial development in the Austro-Hungarian empire was isolated. For example in 1854 the world's first oil well was reportedly sunk near Krosno, in what is now south-east Poland. There were also coal mining and iron working areas, linked primarily with the development of the state railways, such as Jesenice in Slovenia, Reschitza (Reşiţa) now in Romania, and Vitkovice in Moravia. In the inter-war period, other centres of mineral-based heavy industry grew up. These included non-ferrous mining at Bor and Trepča in Serbia, iron and steel at Zenica (just north of Sarajevo) in Bosnia, and methane gas at Copşa Mică in Romania.

THE STALINIST MODEL OF INDUSTRIALIZATION

After the communists took over, they expanded the region's existing industrial base with a vengeance, taking the USSR as their economic model. Under Stalin, industrialization in the Soviet Union was based on an abundance of natural resources, cheap labour, and coercive politics. This was the so-called command economy, with state-owned industry run administratively from the centre. From the late 1940s, it was also applied throughout Central and Eastern Europe.

There is no Marxist theory of industrialization. Karl Marx analysed how nineteenth century capitalism developed as an economic system. Moreover, if there had been a Marxist theory of industrialization, it would probably have taken the grime and dust of Engel's *Condition of the Working Class in England* as its starting point. Manchester in 1844 was probably the very opposite of the picture of communism in Marx's mind when he wrote *Das Kapital*.

Furthermore in the world at the time of Marx, most capital was held by wealthy private individuals, who invested in their own or possibly another's business for the economic return they hoped to receive. Little thought was given to the whys and wherefores of investment and growth.

After the 1917 revolution this changed. The bulk of investment capital in Russia was suddenly in the hands of the state, rather than individuals, and how to use it became a matter for the party economists/planners and the politicians. All the Soviet politicians believed in some industrialization, but after 1926 the faction giving the priority to heavy industry gained the upper hand. It was believed this strategy would contribute to maximum growth, beget a socialist industrial sector and create a political goal for the party rank and file. The emphasis on heavy industry was a political decision, which matured into a theory and then into conventional wisdom. Billowing chimney smoke came to be seen as a symbol of national virility.

The Second World War disrupted all the economies of Eastern Europe, and destroyed great swathes of Poland and East Germany. By the late 1940s all eight countries were controlled by communist governments, of which seven took their lead, both politically and economically, from Moscow. Yugoslavia followed similar economic policies. The Stalinist ideology of the period up to the late 1950s prescribed a diet of state or municipal economic self-sufficiency, alongside heavy industry. Conventional wisdom disallowed light industry, and in any case there was little capital available for such 'follies'.

Mirroring the Soviet Union, much of the industry built up in these years was based on the exploitation of natural resources – coal mining and power generation, more iron and steel, fertilizers, pulp and paper, and chemicals. The construction of around ten integrated steel plants in the 1950s was an example of the policy of autarchic industrialization which subsequently came to environmental grief. The plants were located as close as possible to the border with the Soviet Union from where the iron ore was imported. By the early 1990s, two (Eisenhütte in Eastern Germany and Nowa Huta/Sendzimira in Poland) faced serious commercial problems, and at least five – Nowa Huta, Košice in Slovakia, Dunaúj-város in Hungary, Galaţi in Romania, and Elbasan in Albania – were major polluters.

Even after the policy of self-sufficiency ended in the late 1950s, and Krushchev began the policy of national specialization and trade, the development of heavy industry continued to dominate. In Poland, for instance, the new enterprises were essentially mineral based – copper at Legnica and Glogów, and sulphur at Tarnobrzeg. They also proved to be an environmental catastrophe. In Eastern Germany, the development of the brown coal deposits in Cottbus made the district the largest source of dust and sulphur dioxide in the country.

Perhaps the main result of Krushchev's stress on specialization was in the energy field, with the USSR supplying oil and gas to Eastern Europe, in return for other raw materials and manufactured goods. From the

1970s onward, oil provided the basis for the refineries at Płock in Poland, Leuna and Schwedt in East Germany, Záluži and Bratislava in Czechoslovakia and Leninváros in Hungary. Soviet natural gas provided the feedstock for the chemical industry at Puławy in Poland. Though the reduced impact on the environment of burning fuels other than coal was beneficial, practically all these more modern plants also later became significant sources of pollution.

The political emphasis on heavy industry and energy (including electricity generation) required massive volumes of capital. For example, some three-quarters of industrial investment in Poland was for industries producing investment or capital goods in the Six Year Plan 1950–55. 'Total industrial investments were ten times higher than before the Second World War and accounted for a much higher share of the national income than in most capitalist countries ... Particularly rapid growth was to be achieved in the metallurgy, metal-processing and chemical industries', according to a recent book on Poland's economic history.[3]

THE CENTRAL PLANNING PROCESS

The perspectives from the West and East on central planning are different. In the West, the image of a planned economy was of an army of Kafkaesque bureaucrats wading through reams of paper and making crass decisions, such as reversing the flow of a river to provide water for irrigating cotton growing in inappropriate soils. Central planners were also typically blamed for providing the wrong type of railway wagons (or none at all) to move the harvest from the countryside to the town.

In reality, matters were usually different. Industrial enterprises were often able to run rings (or at least semi-circles) around the founding or parent ministry. The plan may have laid down a target output, but that was probably set after a round of negotiations between interested parties. Western text-books, in the view of two recent Czech authors, 'simplistically' used to describe East Europe's economic system as centrally planned. 'In fact', they say, it was 'influenced by a relationship between the economic centre and state firms based on negotiations and bidding, where the state was often actually a weak opponent to firms.'[4]

The uprisings in Czechoslovakia, Poland, Hungary and East Germany in the 1950s, Czechoslovakia again in the 1960s and Poland in 1970 showed the yearning for a less spartan and more democratic way of life. As the goal of the politicians became to catch up with the Western standard of living, they had to encourage a greater supply of consumer goods. Enterprise bosses thus had to meet increasingly high production targets at almost any cost. This meant disregard for the quality of output, whether goods or services, as well as for the environment. 'For at least three decades the acceptable level of pollution from a steel plant or copper mill was the amount it needed to discharge in order to meet its ever-increasing production quotas.'[5]

The political emphasis on unit output rather than quality also meant central planning was ill suited to meet the finicky demands of light industry and individual consumer preferences. Hence investment in the energy and heavy industrial sectors was not only supported by conventional wisdom. The planners preferred it, because of both the heroic achievement (of the completed dam or steel mill) and the bureaucratic difficulties of funding hundreds of small units all over a country.

The priority given to production obviously excluded allocations of zlotys, crowns or lei for environmental protection, cleaning up waste, maintenance and/or revamping. This often resulted in debilitated equipment, with serious consequences for dust emissions as well as air or water pollution. Professor Maciej Nowicki, Poland's Under Secretary of State for Environmental Protection in 1990, noted that equipment for reducing the discharge of pollutants to the environment was never treated as an integral part of the production process. '[It] often led', he said, 'to [the] relinquishment of construction and repairs of such appliances, in view of financial difficulties and the absolute priority given to production.'[6]

Moreover, central planning was conservative in allocating funds to new technology. In a planned economy with fixed five year growth targets, technical experiments were not welcome. In the '50s, the main technologies used in heavy industry caused air pollution for the simple reason that they were coal based. While we may now consider processes such as the open hearth furnace as primitive, then it was tried and tested. Later on, less polluting know-how may have been on offer by the West, but the cost was prohibitive. Also, as this was the cold war, licences for the transfer of the latest computer-based technology were often restricted for political or military reasons. Cocom, based in Paris, controlled all hi-tech exports to the region: Hungary was the first East European country to have all Cocom restrictions on its trade removed, but that was not till early 1992.

To find buyers for the high volume of output of coal, steel or power, prices had to be low and subsidized, with a number of serious consequences. These included waste and inefficiency. In the early 1980s, Czechoslovakia consumed about 30 per cent more metal per unit of industrial output than Western industrialized countries. Some 25 per cent of processed metal was then wasted.[7] Energy intensity per unit of GDP was to two to four times greater in the West. The low price of coal also removed any incentive for the planners and plant administrators to foster technical change. Thus in the steel industry in the late 1980s, some 55 to 60 per cent of steel was made with the open hearth process, compared with under 10 per cent in Western Europe and the USA.

Poland's Professor Jan Winiecki has said that rather than suffering from over-investment in some sectors and under-investment in others, Central and Eastern Europe suffered from 'misinvestment', during the communist times. This was because it was 'an economic system that squanders resources and eschews efficiency, resulting in chronic supply bottlenecks and unsatisfied demand'.[8] In other words, it misallocated resources, as the planners' proposals often did not take into account either the social and economic costs of a particular factory location or the relative scarcity/price of its raw materials and machinery.

The emphasis on production and not profit, with the corollary of low prices, meant more investment, particularly in energy-intensive heavy industry, than would have occurred in a free market. These inefficient mega-projects ate up scarce investment funds, forcing planners to slash other 'non-essential' expenditure. Combined with falling rates of economic growth during the 1960s, these trends reduced the overall availability of capital, bequeathing the region a debilitated economy and a polluted environment.

A MORE OPEN ECONOMIC SYSTEM

From the late 1960s, there was a growing realization among governments that many of the region's existing economic policies were not working well. The gap between West and East was growing, not diminishing. The command economy, which had been shut off from capitalist influence since the late 1940s, was henceforth open to a limited breath of free market fresh air. Governments began loosening the reins of central planning and taking an interest in Western technology and loans to pay for it. This led to developments such as 'goulash communism' in Hungary or the 'new economic system' in the GDR.

Though the new policies reduced the accent on energy and heavy industry, many of the Western transplants failed. It would seem this was because the root of the region's problems was not so much the lack of modern technology or a shortage of capital but the absence of incentives to improve efficiency. Economic restructuring was stymied by the ossified attitudes of a generation bred in the political and economic hot house of communism. Initiative was still frowned on. Consequently the loans from Western banks and governments were spent ineffectively and occasionally squandered. Certainly the quality of most manufactured goods produced by the revamped industry was too poor to be sold on the

Western market, so loan repayments slipped and debts mounted, particularly in Poland.

The failure of these efforts to revitalize the economy only served to reinforce old practices. Instead of allowing initiative to look for ways to cut costs or develop new sectors, the planners ploughed their past furrows. For example in Poland, to meet energy targets the mining of poorer quality coal at increasingly greater cost was given a higher priority than gas or water power. In the 1980s, the extraction of 1 tonne of coal in the Upper Silesian coal basin cost at least two to three times as much as in the 1950s.[9] And because it continued to be available at a low subsidized price, it remained the main fuel for domestic heating as well as industry. This was true for Poland, East Germany and Czechoslovakia and to a lesser extent Bulgaria and Hungary. Gas from the USSR was often used as a raw material feedstock for industry (for example in fertilizer manufacture) rather than as a fuel. In production terms, whether boilers were fuelled by hard or soft coal or by oil or gas was not important; pollution was not a valid yardstick for making judgments.

In Czechoslovakia and East Germany most of the coal was lignite – East Germany was the world's largest producer of lignite. The brown coal from both countries had a high ash and water content, a variable sulphur content, and a lower calorific value, which meant much more had to be burnt at power stations to generate a kilowatt hour of electricity. This meant high emissions of sulphur dioxide and nitrogen oxides. Poland was more fortunate, in that it had large deposits of better quality bituminous or hard coal. However, the best grades were either exported or converted into coke. Medium quality coal was used to generate power in the north of the country, while the lower quality, high ash and sulphurous coal as well as lignite was used near the mines. Bulgaria and Hungary had fewer coal deposits and were at least partially dependent on imports.

THE FAILURE OF THE LAW: 'POLLUTION PAYS'

A report for the German government prepared in 1991 said 'The socialist planning system finally led to a vicious circle', where 'the need for environmental protection measures was constantly growing on account of decades of negligence and because of continuing spending of infrastructure capital'. At the same time, it was becoming less and less possible to meet this need 'and on account of mismanagement and decreasing economic efficiency, to earn the funds needed for recovery and clean-up'.[10]

Environmental laws were passed – often with standards that were higher than in the OECD countries – but they were ineffective. The ostensible reasons included insufficient and poorly trained staff, excessive bureaucracy and the low level of user charges and fines. For instance in Czechoslovakia, other than in the electricity industry, payments typically represented less than 1 per cent of production costs. Air pollution fees set in 1967 remained unchanged.[11] There was obviously insufficient stimulus to keep the rules, when the cost of so doing was well above the cost of doing nothing.

The fundamental cause of this paradox was the political priority given to production, together with the informal and formal links inside the communist party between the planners, enterprise managers, environmental protection staff and judiciary. In the words of Istvan Jakab, the Deputy Director of Hungary's Borsod Chem, during those years management had 'a tight connection' with the state through the communist party. As a result, the regulatory authorities often set friendly 'individual' emission limits.[12]

Consequently it often benefitted the enterprise not to heed the law, or as Wojciech Beblo, the head of the ecology department in Katowice voivodeship, quipped 'pollution paid'. In Poland, if an enterprise did not have an official permit to discharge water into the local river, its fine was merely twice the unit cost of the user fee. However, if it had been 'stupid' enough to accept a permit from the local voivodeship, it paid ten times the cost. Hence enterprises used considerable ingenuity to avoid being served with an administrative order, or *decyzja*, officially permitting the discharge. Moreover as fines and fees were levied on an annual basis, in the year following the emissions, enterprises often found a range of excuses to postpone payment.

Even though the charges were low, the authorities failed to collect them. There was the belief that they were just another production cost and their payment gave a right to more or less 'limitless'[13] pollution. And to some extent this was true – the payments were simply a subsidized paper transfer from the state bank or parent ministry in the capital city to the ministry of environment. They were added to the enterprise's budget, so that in fact they became a subsidy to pollute. Furthermore, with production as the political priority, in any conflict between environmental protection and output, the latter had to take priority over the former.

Most CEE governments distinguished between 'organized' and 'disorganized' pollution. Charges were levied on the former as they could be calculated on the basis of throughput and the technology in use. They typically represented more than half the total pollution and included emissions from chimneys or water discharged into a river. As unmeasured fugitive emissions from broken windows, overspills, leaks or dumped waste could not be monitored, governments did not charge for it.

Obsolete technology, poor maintenance, and the failure to enforce the law all contributed to the concentration of pollution in the heavy industry and energy sectors during the late 1980s. Table 3.1 gives the broad brush results. Half to three-quarters of the air and water emissions came from a relatively small number of enterprises in these five industries. However a comparison made in 1988 (using 1984 figures) between the largest polluters in volume terms (for example in tonnes of sulphur dioxide) and the most dangerous to health revealed little overlap.[14] The former included the mines, power stations and the steel works; the latter were mostly chemical and non-ferrous metal works.

They included the Tarnobrzeg open cast and hot water based sulphur mines, which were second in the most dangerous list and 93rd on the largest polluter list. They polluted both surface and ground drinking waters as well as the air. The impact of disorganized emissions of 'hydrogen sulphide' (which is toxic) on air quality was 'of great importance', and was 'especially noxious' near their source. Other threats included 'sulphur self-ignition, leakage of sulphur, dusts from processing, storage, loading and transportation'.[15] The mines also contaminated the soil and produced a large volume of solid waste.

SUPPLYING RAW MATERIALS TO WESTERN EUROPE

Central and Eastern Europe was in general not poor, either absolutely or relatively. Over the years to 1989, the communist governments made impressive improvements in health, housing and education. Most people had sufficient to eat all the time. However, the explosion in the Lenin Shipyard in Gdańsk and the creation by intellectuals and workers of the Solidarity trade union in 1980, the persistence and imagination of Charter

Table 3.1   *The proportion of Poland's environmental pollution caused by the energy and heavy industrial fuel sectors, 1987*

Industry	Emission of dusts		Emission of gases		Liquid industrial wastes, discharged into ground waters mill m³/year		Solid industrial wastes prod per year mill tonnes	
	tonnes	%	tonnes	%		%		%
Coal	62.4	3.5	110.4	2.0	484.2	19.0	79.3	44.0
Fuel	22.9	1.3	268.2	5.0	49.5	1.9	0.2	0.1
Power	879.3	48.7	2592.0	48.0	288.2	11.3	42.9	23.8
Steel	192.2	10.7	913.5	16.9	174.8	6.9	10.9	6.0
NF metals	18.1	1.0	300.9	5.6	322.6	12.7	32.1	17.8
Total	1174.9	62.5	4185.2	77.5	1319.3	51.8	165.3	91.7

Note % refers to total emissions in each column; NF – non-ferrous

Source Maria Sierpinska, 'The necessity of introducing raw-material saving projects to Polish industry', *Environmental and Economic Aspects of the Industrial Development in Poland*, ed Kazimierz Gorka, Krakow Academy of Economics, Krakow, 1991

77 in Czechoslovakia and various opposition groups in Hungary and the GDR, all helped expose the contradictions in the way the communist governments operated. These included their abuse of the environment in the cause of production, and the ideological espousal of universal material prosperity, when there were insufficient means to meet it.

During the communist era, Western Europe relocated much of its heavy industry and other raw material processing industries into the third world. Or as the World Bank recently put it more delicately, 'Some of the potential problems facing developing countries – global warming and ozone depletion, in particular – stem from high consumption levels in rich countries.'[16] It was thus out of sight. In contrast industry in CEE countries was on everyone's doorstep and an object of disgruntlement.

In the 1970s and 1980s, it was not only the developing countries which supplied processed raw materials to the so-called industrialized countries; CEE had begun to join them, becoming a supplier particularly for Western Europe. As its own manufactures could not compete and it needed foreign exchange, basic commodity exports were increased. For instance, Western Europe's copper came from Poland's belching smelters as well as from the Zairean and Zambian copperbelts; its timber was imported from Czechoslovakia's fertilized forests as well as the tropical rain forests, and its tobacco was shipped from eroded Bulgarian state-owned farms as well as Zimbabwe's plantations. Oil bought cheaply from the USSR was re-exported for hard currency rather than being used domestically to reduce pollution from coal. Table 3.2 gives some of the region's major exports to the West.

By the late 1980s, the developed capitalist countries were really post-industrial. Most of their own natural resources had already been consumed or the costs of their exploitation were too high. Their economies were dominated by services; the industry which remained employed increasingly 'high tech' production methods or was relatively clean.

Table 3.2   *Major exports from Central and Eastern Europe to the West, 1987: major hard currency exports by country*

Albania*	Oil and oil products, chrome, iron ore, nickel, coal
Bulgaria	Oil and oil products, steel coil, tobacco, wine
Czechoslovakia	Timber, oil, cars, steel plate, shoes
East Germany	Oil and oil products, wooden furniture, steel plate
Hungary	Frozen chicken, oil, bird skins, shoes, preserved meat
Poland	Coal, refined copper, preserved meat, cars, frozen fish
Romania	Oil and oil products, wooden furniture
Yugoslavia	Cars, shoes, wooden furniture, timber, aluminium

Note * Top five export items irrespective of destination

Source *Comecon Yearbook,* 1989

Environmentally threatening industrial operations were banished to marginal areas or to outside the country altogether (where the rules were usually laxer and costs lower), while in other cases the goods were imported. USA markets sited these operations in Mexico or Central America, while Western Europe increasingly located them in Central or Eastern Europe.

4

A CAPITALIST JUMBLE SALE

SELLING THE FAMILY SILVER

In the early 1980s, Harold Macmillan described Britain's privatizations as selling the family silver. A decade later, at the end of the communist period, the countries of East and Central Europe had few such heirlooms. Instead they had inefficient state farms, run-down factories and ill-stocked shops, most of which understandably found few bidders. Poland's architect of the country's privatization programme, Leszek Balcerowicz, naturally took a more optimistic view. In mid-1991, he quipped: 'Privatization is not so much selling off the family silver, as taking it out of [the] mothballs of state ownership, in which it was not used to its full potential.'[1]

In 1990, Eastern European governments had a mammoth task in front of them, with state-owned enterprises (see Box 4.1) controlling some 70–95 per cent of economic activity. In Britain Margaret Thatcher was popularly credited with having privatized some 20 firms, representing around 5 per cent of the country's GDP over 10 years in a capitalist economy with a well-tuned capital market. With the passion of the newly converted, the new governments began immediately after they took power to reconstruct a legal basis for capitalism. The tasks facing them were enormous: out of the hulk of the planned economy, to develop a free market, to curb pollution and simultaneously to stimulate economic growth to meet the population's passion for consumer goods.

In achieving this, other than in Eastern Germany, governments were hindered by the low levels of foreign investment and international aid. In the former GDR, combined public and private investment (excluding financial transfers) was estimated to be equivalent to $2,500 a head. In the rest of the region it was $65 a head. In addition, the new Bundesländer were immediately incorporated into the EC, while the other ten or

Box 4.1 *Enterprises and companies*

Under central planning, where an economic entity (such as a farm or a factory) was engaged in production, and was owned by central or local government, it is described as an **enterprise**. This definition covers all state-owned concerns operating in the agricultural, industrial or service sectors. Strictly speaking, the term excludes cooperatives but, to avoid repetition, in many cases the word enterprise is assumed to take in all forms of socialized economic activity. Even after 1989/90, so long as the enterprise remained state owned, the term has continued to be used. For example, the **commercialization** of an enterprise removed it from under the wing of its founding ministry and was intended to make it a profit-seeking corporation; as it remained, however, owned by the state, for example the ministry of finance or the state treasury, it is still known as an enterprise.

In contrast, where the enterprise has been sold on or some other way privatized, the term **company** or **firm** has been used. The words **business** or **concern** are more general and simply refer to an economic entity, irrespective of ownership.

---

so countries were only given access for their less important exports. Overall, there was said to be a net outflow of resources from the region to the West.

This chapter focuses on the economic mutations in East and Central Europe in the early 1990s, and where and why they foundered. It has four sections. First it discusses the concepts and building blocks necessary for the construction of a free market; a discussion of privatization is followed by a review of the other preconditions necessary for a free market. The second and third sections examine the constraints and obstacles which governments faced in restructuring. The chapter concludes by examining some of the main repercussions for economic change of privatization and the removal of state controls.

THE FREE MARKET

While it has been argued that the introduction of a free market was the region's political priority when the communists were overthrown in 1989, it rarely had full popular support. The quiet revolutions of 1989 were essentially a popular rejection of Stakhanovite production for the sake of production, and empty shops. Society wanted to be able to enjoy mass consumption but without capitalism's trials and tears. In the Polish parliamentary elections of late 1991, the number of votes for parties supporting free market policies declined substantially from 1990; the electorates primarily voted for parties critical of market reform policies. Though the free market was supported as a general concept, it was roundly rejected when it put up prices and forced thousands out of work. Indeed in several countries, the ex-communists who generally favoured moderate reform became the major party in elections during the course of 1992.

By early 1991, one of the most obvious signs of the new free market to a regular visitor to Poland was the sudden increase in new retail outlets. Near the bus-stops on the housing estates, where there was once waste ground, one had started to see roadside stalls, small booths and kiosks set up to sell some 'forbidden fruit' of the communist era. Typically a wife and husband team was selling ground coffee, foreign cigarettes, fresh fruit and vegetables, fizzy drinks, sweets and basic groceries. In the town centres, the new stalls were more specialized – selling pirate tape recordings, flowers, cheap books, toys or newspapers. Existing purpose-built shops focused on imported consumer durables. Around the town, second-hand car lots sprang up. Other developments such as new petrol stations and district grocery chains were part of a second phase of development in late 1991 and 1992.

Yet the liberation of imports was only one of the structural reforms of the free marketeers, who were in government from 1989 onwards in Hungary, Poland and the Czech Republic. Their prime goal was to put the perceived ideas of Margaret Thatcher and Ronald Reagan and their reported mentor, Milton Friedman, into practice as soon as possible. In the 1980s, when right-wing economic policies were in vogue in the West, the East's so-called dissidents, who took power at the end of the decade, adopted *laissez-faire* capitalism as their central tenet. Their aim was to liberate the factories and people, on the grounds that Adam Smith's invisible hand would create a more rational industrial structure and stimulate economic growth.

Political dogma has muddied the expression 'free market economy': it is simply one where the supply and demand for a product is not subject to regulation. Generally the term is used synonymously with capitalism and as the converse of a planned economy. It is the word 'free' which is most loaded politically. All modern economies in reality lie on a continuum, with the non-existent extremes at either end: 'free' being generally defined relative to 'planned', rather than absolutely. Owing to ideological manipulation, both terms have lost any scientific purity. For in every free market some rules are in force and in every planned economy, there are areas not subject to regulation.

Nevertheless many of Eastern Europe's free marketeers were reluctant to divide industry according to which enterprises should be favoured and which should be left to die. The necessarily visible hand of government intervention in the modern market economy was often equated with the dead hand of communism.

The half-blind leading the blind

In 1990 in order to restructure, the invisible handers identified privatization and the removal of state supports and controls in the allocation of goods and services as their economic priorities. Foreign investment was their chosen instrument or catalyst. Restructuring is the process of economic, financial, organizational and technical adjustment – for both enterprises and whole economies; its aim at the micro-level is a competitive company and at the macro-level an efficient economy.

The difficulty was that in 1990 there was no accepted recipe on how to move from a planned economy to a free market, on what were the best ingredients and on how they should be sequenced and/or combined. There were no models, no textbooks, and only a few gurus, such as Harvard academic Jeffrey Sachs, the exponent of 'shock therapy'. In the absence of such models, governments' classical economic policies prevailed.

Western advisers had as little experience as the governments they were supposed to be advising. Their mission in 1990 was essentially ideological – to speed up the development of free market clones and encourage Western participation in the economic chaos that followed the quiet revolutions. Their task was like having to create a flourishing market garden out of the jungle closing in on a decaying farm: a challenge to an experienced horticulturist, but to an untried gardener with no seeds a near impossible task.

Privatization and the removal of state subsidies and controls were also the goals of the World Bank and IMF. Their inadequate models were the first and third worlds, as they had had little experience of working in centrally planned economies. On the one hand they would appear to have spiced their traditional ideological approach with practical garnish. 'Perhaps the clearest lesson from work on development during the past thirty years is that there is a premium on pragmatism and an open mind', said the World Bank's World Development Report for 1991. But, it added, conventional wisdom has to be replaced by 'New ideas [which] stress prices as signals; trade and competition as links to technological progress; and effective government as a scarce resource, to be employed sparingly and only where most needed.'[2]

Most economic consultants, for all their bravado in advising CEE governments, hardly understood the process of long-term growth. *The Economist* magazine in 1992 asked, 'How long will the ex-communist countries of Eastern Europe ... take to catch up with the West? To answer [this] question needs something that economics has so far been unable to provide – an understanding of the forces that drive long-term growth'. The article tentatively listed three factors that may positively affect the long-term trend in productive capacity – capital, skilled labour (which presumably included management skills) and technical progress or knowledge.[3] But, given the untested quality of the theory, it is hardly surprising that all the newly elected governments were, like newborn kittens, blind at birth.

For a few outside economists though, the tigers of South-east Asia provided the most apt model for Eastern Europe. Their transition from feudalism to capitalism in the 1960s was based on the rapid growth of low cost manufactures for export; this required rock-bottom wages, minimal social security and a never ending working week. People's expectations in East and Central Europe were more demanding, as well as more immediate. At times, it was almost as though the population desired German wages, Sweden's welfare state and the few hours a day of work they had been used to in the past. After 40 years of trying to make ends meet under communism, people were understandably reluctant to toil again through a 'transitional' phase.

On several occasions governments received violent warnings that the classical free market policies they were following did not have popular support. In Hungary in October 1990, taxi and lorry drivers brought the country to a standstill with their protests against higher petrol prices and declining living standards. In Romania, 40–50,000 Jiu valley coal miners swept down to Bucharest in September 1991 and forced out the government, delaying free market measures. In Poland, strikes against higher energy prices in January 1992 warned the government to slow down. In Germany in 1993 there were strikes by metal workers in favour of more equal wages East and West; implicitly, these were also against the way in which unification was proceeding and in particular the Western perception of Eastern workers as somehow second class.

Privatization

Privatization takes many different forms. It is typically used as a catch-all to include any reduction in the state's holding – from a majority to minority or zero stake, or even from a large majority to a lesser majority, so long as the ultimate aim is for private sector control. The sellers in Central and Eastern Europe included most ministries, but particularly the ministry of industry, and local municipalities. The governments' main goal was to create an economic revolution to parallel the political revolutions of 1989. Their intention was to close loss-making industrial dinosaurs and to encourage potentially successful enterprises. Said two leading Polish academics, 'Privatization here is more than selling state companies. It is a process of reconstruction of economy and society that were damaged by many years of communism.'[4]

Privatization of state-owned assets was essentially a Western import. The accountancy firm Price Waterhouse called it 'the economic phenomenon of the decade'.[5] Czechoslovakia's Minister of Finance and later the Prime Minister of the Czech Republic, Vaclav Klaus, described it as *the* priority for his country.[6] Poland's Ministry of Ownership Changes said its privatization programme had eight objectives, including the creation of a profitable private sector, more efficient use of labour, capital and management skills, reducing the 'burden on the public budget', generating funds from the sale of enterprises, and ensuring 'a wide diffusion of ownership of private shares'.[7] Hungary's State Property Agency listed the creation of a social market economy as well as 'a powerful stratum of entrepreneurs and a middle class' among its primary aims.[8] Germany's privatization agency, the Treuhandanstalt (usually abbreviated to Treuhand) also said it wished to develop the social market economy, ensure a speedy transition and make rapid gains in employment. Most governments were also looking forward to their own bureaucracies functioning more effectively, once the impossible burden of running a country's economic activities down to the last collective farm had been removed. Table 4.1 shows the trends in privatizing the economy.

A wide range of methods of privatization were and are being used. Though these have included the theatrical set-piece share issues beloved by the UK's Conservative party, the expense and time taken to sell shares through banks and post offices meant that other methods were generally preferred. Politically, mass privatization (which took several different

Table 4.1 *The state-owned sector as a proportion of value added/GDP in Central and Eastern Europe*

	Mid-1980s as % of value added	1992 as % of GDP
Ex-CSFR	97	na
Czech Republic	na	85
Slovakia	na	80
GDR	97	na
Hungary	86	60
Poland	82	58
Ex-Yugoslavia	87	na

Sources Mid-1980s value added figures: Branco Milanovic, 'Liberalisation and Entrepreneurship: Dynamics of Reforms in Socialism and Capitalism', New York, 1989 (taken from *The Economist*, 21 September 1991); 1992 GDP figures: national statistical offices

forms) was a useful tool for promoting a wide ownership of equity and countering those politicians who argued against the excessive sale of 'national' assets to foreigners. Other methods included spontaneous actions by enterprises, joint ventures, direct sales to foreign buyers (capital privatization), auctions, straightforward management or employee buy-outs, liquidation followed by restructuring, and free transfers (for example from the central to local government).

Structural reform

A smoothly operating free market also requires allowing the capitalist system's signals, such as prices, profit margins and currency exchange rates to function. To stimulate their operation, governments had to remove state controls and remould the legal framework. The emphasis was on the former. As a whole it was a process that was discussed less than privatization, possibly as it is both less glamorous and more complex. *The Economist* identified 'with hindsight' five major elements which were necessary for structural reform: besides privatization they were free prices, financial reform, industrial reform, dismantling trade barriers and allowing currency convertibility, and finally institution building.[9]

Freeing prices was not as straightforward as it sounded. Some countries, such as Poland, chose to liberalize most prices at the beginning of the reform process, while in others such as Romania a legal and regulatory framework for business was seen as a higher priority. By the end of 1991, Hungary, Czechoslovakia, Poland, Bulgaria and Romania had eliminated most subsidies on food, clothes and other consumer goods and were well down the road in scrapping them on energy, fuel and housing.

Financial reforms incorporated improved monetary control and the introduction of commercial banking. The sector had to be created practically out of nothing – the state-owned banks of the past were perhaps best described as glorified post offices. They needed to be taught modern methods of credit control. Moreover to prevent any loss of confidence, they had to be well regulated: an untoward bankruptcy would have discouraged personal saving and possibly led to a run on the currency.

Industrial reform meant encouraging domestic competition: this included anti-trust legislation to monitor, and if necessary break up, communism's all-powerful combines. In the case of the former, Poland's Anti-Monopoly Commission, created in April 1990, reviewed 1,500 cases of potential monopoly in its first year. Of these 200 were deemed monopolistic and a further 200 required substantial restructuring. Firm bankruptcy laws were necessary too.

Currency convertibility and lower trade barriers also encouraged competition by ensuring that domestic goods are not too expensive compared with the world market. Governments replaced the multiple and usually unrealistically high domestic currency quotations with devaluing 'crawling' rates broadly pegged to the dollar or other Western currencies. This killed the black market, though by late 1992 no country had made its currency completely convertible. In Czechoslovakia and Hungary at that time, the crown and the forint respectively were convertible for most businesses but not for individuals. In Poland, the zloty was internally convertible for both businesses and individuals. New institutions included foreign exchange markets and stock exchanges.

At the heart of the new system was the concept of profitability. The practice of maximizing profitability was alien to the administrators of the old enterprises who, with production geared to a plan target, did not weigh up the costs, revenues and profits of producing the extra widget required to meet their monthly or annual quota. While many believe they have mastered the new system (and for those who were active on the black market, the change was not so great), most local managers have yet to learn to think on their feet. There were no overnight solutions said Sir John Harvey Jones, former chairman of ICI, in September 1991, after visiting factories in Hungary and Poland. People 'can change, but it will take time. At best it will take three or four years for getting the businesses on track. Realistically, more like five to six years', he concluded.[10]

THE CONSTRAINTS ON RESTRUCTURING

Whichever factories Sir John visited in 1991, they were lucky to be making products people still wanted to buy. In the early 1990s, the region was faced with a deep recession, brought on principally by the moves to introduce a free market. Companies and countries often had little choice in making key decisions.

Underlying their debates were a range of internal and external constraints. Not only were there no agreed blueprints for the switch to capitalism, governments had to face the social and economic legacy of the past, the lack of local infrastructure and financial and human resources and heavy indebtedness, as well as their own lack of experience and ensuing indecisiveness. The constraints hindered not only the region's switch to a capitalist economy, but also its progress in curtailing pollution.

The social and economic legacy

A Polish sociologist writing about his country in the early '90s said, 'We are still a communist society, but we are not aware of it'.[11] By this he meant that though the country had lost its traditional communist party institutions and was in the process of acquiring new ones, the old perspectives remained. In particular, individuals still believed in the protective role of the state, though the state was relinquishing this role as quickly as it could. Personal passivity, an unwillingness to take or accept initiatives, and a something for nothing attitude were associated with this view.

The continuation of these attitudes and the lack of new intermediary institutions left many individuals at a social and psychological loss. Since 1989, most of the region's old institutions (other than the churches) have lost their standing, compromised by corruption and/or association with communism. However, at the same time the newer entities have still to develop the legitimacy they have acquired in the West. Some of the key social groups formed during the break up of communism, which attracted so much hope and trust in 1989 and 1990, have either fragmented or have become tainted with old methods. Though the new institutions of parliamentary democracy and the market economy (such as parliament itself, political parties, free trade unions, banks, companies, regulatory bodies) dominate the headlines of the mainstream media, in reality they have only been partially accepted.

The speed and violence of East Germany's absorption into the federal republic exacerbated its trauma. Germany's 'Ossies', from the Ost or east, who had been raised with a firm state safety net, felt acutely frightened of the Treuhand's restructuring strategies and its almost colonial arrogance. Opposition to privatization was another part of the legacy. Many in and out of government were unhappy politically with the process, some for their own economic reasons and others because it removed the cosy certainties of central planning. A public opinion survey in Poland at the end of 1991 showed that only 2 per cent of respondents thought that 'ordinary citizens' would benefit most from privatization. At the other end of the spectrum, 29 per cent thought 'the rich' would benefit and another 14 per cent that 'manipulators and cheaters' would gain the most.[12] There was also talk of a 'Bermuda Triangle' of management, workers' councils and trade unions who conspired to oppose change on the grounds that their positions would be much weaker or abolished after privatization.

The lack of local infrastructure and appropriate resources

A recent survey by Deloitte Touche Tohmatsu International[13] of managers of companies operating joint ventures in Central and Eastern Europe (including Russia) identified the banking system as one of the major constraints on business development. It said, 'In all countries, the banking system is . . . slow, unreliable, costly, understaffed and outdated'. Other particular difficulties cited included obtaining a telephone line, finding good suppliers and collecting accounts receivables from state owned customers in Czechoslovakia, Poland and Bulgaria. The survey noted that 'The fiscal environment [was] described in all countries as undefined, unstable and not properly regulated', while dealing with local government was problematic owing to 'bureaucratic attitudes, lack of knowledge of current laws', and an unwillingness to take responsibility.

Staffing issues were important, but less of an issue as imported managers could control them. 'Task management, which includes taking responsibility, making decisions within the job function, prioritizing tasks and solving problems, was cited by the survey respondents as the main problem encountered with local staff.' Others put personnel at the top. Henkel, the German chemical company, believed that the region's 'most pressing need [was] the training of managers and technicians'.[14]

Entrepreneurial attitudes had also been squashed by years of planning and nannying. The shortage of newly trained managers for both the public and private sectors allowed the old administrators to carry on their practices of the communist era. Their attitudes and habits were like glue rather than oil in the new system – they stopped it working flexibly. Freeing prices and removing subsidies were quite insufficient to give the economy the new suppleness it needed to restructure: for instance administrators of the state-owned monopoly producers simply passed on the freed higher prices to their customers, who after all were often their old friends from communist party days.

The management issue was one of quantity as well as quality. In 1991 Poland needed to train 100,000 managers to maintain its reforms, the World Bank was reported to have said.[15] Czechoslovakia and Hungary had similar difficulties. One of the Treuhand's major problems was finding good managers – by 1991 it had fired some 1,500 Ossies, but was still some 20,000 short of suitable new candidates, as few Western managers were willing to move eastward.[16] Elsewhere there was not even a similar agency to organize technical and managerial assistance, though dozens of management schools and training courses sprang up in the early 1990s, for aspiring 'biznesmen'.

Domestic levels of investment were low, due to the low level of retained earnings and restrictions on current public expenditure. Among Polish state-owned enterprises, the ratio of gross profits to total costs fell from 30 per cent to 6 per cent between the first eight months of 1990 and 1991.[17] However, the levels were not so low as to prevent a few local firms and individuals buying small state-owned enterprises. For instance, in late 1992, 70 per cent of the noted Polish china works Porcelana Walbrzych was bought by the Polish trade and transportation firm, S&K

Holding, for just over half a million dollars. It also promised to cover its debts totalling $1.2 million, to invest $0.8 million over three years and to keep employment at the same level for two years.

Governments made vague commitments to supporting reform but due to the IMF-imposed limits on the budget deficits, they were constrained from offering more than small amounts of money: Poland's Ministry of Industry in 1992 had only sufficient funds to wind up seven coal mines: the other 1,700 or so state-owned enterprises for which the ministry was responsible would have to look outside the budget, the Minister said in April 1992.[18] Ceilings on current government expenditure were not matched by an expansion of the tax base and improvements in tax collection. Eastern Germany was an exception in this, as the Treuhand had a clear responsibility for economic transformation as well as the finance to carry it out.

Bank loans were expensive (for example, 50–80 per cent a year interest in Poland in April 1992, though lower elsewhere) and hard to obtain. A high proportion of existing bank loans were classed as non-performing (a massive 40 per cent in Poland in early 1992[19]). Where stock exchanges had been established (Warsaw and Budapest), they lacked sufficient liquidity to assist more than a few companies. The low level of domestic household savings, due to inflation and spiralling poverty, aggravated the constraint.

Most reports or articles on the region failed to mention that success in restructuring was ultimately dependent upon improvements in the rate of savings by governments, businesses and individuals and that this was not happening. Indeed, the United Nations Economic Commission for Europe (ECE) has claimed that in the years 1990–2 there was a net outflow of financial resources from the region. The report for 1992 said, 'When debt servicing and other income payments are set in the balance against capital inflows, there was a net outflow of resources from most of the East European countries in 1992'.[20]

Heavy indebtedness

International debts were a constraint on the region because repayments absorbed precious foreign exchange (see Table 4.2) and they allowed the multilateral banks to influence policies. Romania was the main exception as in the 1980s Ceaucescu had eschewed foreign loans; Czechoslovakia also had a low level of indebtedness in 1989.

The most extreme example was Bulgaria. In March 1990, the Bulgarian Foreign Trade Bank suspended payments on the principal (but not the interest) of the country's $10.3 billion debt. As a result, further foreign credits were frozen by the international banks. In the spring of

Table 4.2   *Foreign debts in Central and Eastern Europe, 1990*

	$ bn	% GDP	% Exports
Bulgaria	10.4	42	497
CSFR	6.6	18	116
Hungary	19.4	59	328
Poland	40.8	72	408

Source Table 1.2, 'Indicators of external indebtedness for 1990', *Reforming the economies of Central and Eastern Europe*, OECD, Paris 1992, p65

1992, the IMF and World Bank said Bulgaria's parliament in Sofia had to pass controversial privatization and budget bills by mid-April before receiving further loans. Eventually it did and the way was open for new loans.

At around the same time, the IMF said Poland's budget deficit could not exceed 5 per cent of GDP, if it wanted access to $1.5 billion in Fund loans, the disbursement of which had been suspended in late 1991 when the country failed to meet set economic targets. Also dependent on parliamentary acceptance of the budget limit was a major cut in the country's official foreign debt, negotiated in 1991. Thus approval of an acceptable budget in early 1993 both released the IMF funds and reduced the country's official debt (some $30 billion) by at least 50 per cent, implying a cut in interest payments by 80 per cent over the period up to 1995.

Government muddle

Government inexperience also hampered change. Indeed, confronted by the gigantic task of transforming their economies, governments soon lost their early determination and confidence. Besides the constraints mentioned above, the civil service or executive often contained sympathizers with the certainties of the old system. This meant ministers, in the dark dawn of capitalism, were sometimes fumbling practically on their own to make the new rules. On top of all this, governments had to tussle with ethnic issues, referenda, coalition parties, parliamentary and presidential elections, and increasingly vociferous local authorities.

The result was indecision, decisions by default or repeated revisions of past decisions; it left governments responding to situations rather than anticipating them, and caused a lack of coordination between ministries. The economy was the principal focus of this Alice in Wonderland world. The complications of speeding up privatization and implementing the myriad other economic changes left ministers in a no man's land, under fire from all sides, and as a result industrial priorities were either not set, ignored or not seen as important. The formulation of industrial policies was also stifled by fears that they would mean a return to central planning.

In Hungary, Nynex (the US telephone company) decided after two years of negotiations that it was not interested in the region. It said its plans were stalled both by the lack of a legal structure and by indecision by the state-owned telephone company.[21] In Poland, with the regular change of governments, new ministers spent more time defending their own views on the scope and details of policy than on implementation. The paradoxical result of trying to speed up the process of privatization was its delay.[22]

With hindsight, it seems absurd to have expected inexperienced ministers in countries in social and economic (and sometimes political) turmoil to have been able to make decisions quickly and with certainty. For a variety of reasons, ministers made repeated changes to duties and tariffs, taxes, social security contributions and payments, investment incentives, environmental regulations and a host of other rules. Running a free market economy was never going to be easy, but the task was exacerbated by the sudden break-up of Comecon and the world recession.

OBSTACLES TO RESTRUCTURING

The obstacles to restructuring are distinguished from the constraints on the grounds that none related to the region's inherited conditions in 1989 and 1990. They were not inevitable, but were largely caused by the way the nascent free markets interacted with the rest of the world.

The early 1990s saw a quite specific confluence of circumstances, conterminous with the aftermath of the quiet revolutions. They in turn generated additional barriers to change in Central and Eastern Europe. The main elements were:

- The recession in the West; this was exacerbated by high German interest rates, brought on by the cost of redeveloping the new Bundesländer. It resulted in a lower level of retained earnings for investment.
- The contemporary belief that the invisible hand was stronger than the visible, so that the CEE governments were discouraged from taking measures to deal with some of the key failings of the free market, such as overcoming risk and building up trust.
- Parallel to this was the attitude of the US and UK governments that the West did not owe the East a living, and that trade and foreign investment rather than aid were the most appropriate instruments of change.

- The short-sightedness of the EC, which with the Maastricht Treaty was deepened rather than widened, thus withholding from the region the economic, trade and political umbrella it desperately needed.
- The priority being given by the IMF to price stabilization and associated monetary policies.

There were three principal obstacles. These were the shortage of foreign capital, the dearth of official assistance, and the recession in the East.

Foreign investment and official assistance

In 1990, foreign investment was seen by governments as the main method of promoting privatization and the removal of state controls. Foreign investors would bring skilled management and know-how too, for after the quiet revolutions the new governments accepted that they lacked the skills to run industry and that only companies had the nous to make commercial judgments.

Most companies, however, adopted a wait and see attitude. Japan's Mitsui was quoted in 1990 as saying, 'We have no plans to expand yet. Maybe in five or ten years, these countries will have sorted out their reforms.'[23] Some commentators believed that once the privatization process had run its course, foreign investors would step in. 'It seems the massive flow of foreign capital will come only after the privatization, because foreign partners prefer negotiations with private businessmen, rather than lengthy and ... not quite understandable dealings' with the state, said a recent report on Czechoslovakia's privatization.[24] The views of ABB, the massive Swedish/Swiss engineering company which has invested widely in the region, were similar but more positive. 'We don't expect a quick, easy payback,' said Percy Barnevik, ABB's president and chief executive.[25]

Foreign investment has both a quantitative and qualitative dimension. Estimates of the total required could only be approximate given the lack of data on the contemporary situation and the vagueness of the goals to be achieved. Besides environmental protection, the tasks in hand encompassed renewal of the physical infrastructure, industrial and agricultural reform and the development of a financial framework for doing business. The estimates had also to take into account the high cost of modern technology and the limited skills of the workers.

A study made in the early 1990s by the Institute for International Economics in the USA reached very high figures. It suggested that to raise the amount of productive capital per worker in Eastern Europe and the USSR (as it then was) to that of the West within ten years would require foreign capital imports of in excess of $1,000 billion a year for ten years.[26] Excluding the former Soviet Union would at least halve this estimate.

The contrast in the levels of investment between Eastern Germany and the other former socialist countries highlights the real cost of tackling the region's problems. Total public transfers to Eastern from Western Germany were expected to reach some $130 billion (DM220 billion) in 1992, out of which, capital investment was around $30 billion; most of the rest consisted of social security payments, training costs, and the like. According to unofficial figures from the Treuhand, total public and private capital investment in the new Bundesländer in 1991 was around $40 billion[27] and probably slightly more in 1992. Moreover, as the decade developed, it became clear that such sums were not just likely to be short-term aid but a regular commitment for at least a decade.

The East German figure for public and private investment was equivalent to around $2,500 per head per year. On the assumption that similar sums were required throughout East and Central Europe, the region as a whole should have received some $350 billion in investment in 1992 – approximately equivalent to the combined GDP of the region in 1990. Furthermore as the former East Germany was in some ways the most advanced of the eight countries in the region, the above figures are an underestimate of requirements.

It has to be remembered though that investment by Western Germany in the Eastern Bundesländer was a political rather than commercial act. Elsewhere this political will was missing. The rest of the region had no foreign sugar daddy. In 1990, there was a widely publicized suggestion that a new Marshall Plan was necessary to provide the governments and industry of Central and Eastern Europe with the investment capital they needed to modernize their economies and support environmental protection. The idea was soon rejected on both ideological and practical grounds. William Ryrie, Executive Vice-president of the International Finance Corporation (the private sector arm of the World Bank), noted in early 1990 that 'Throwing money at the problem may actually hinder the process of change everyone wants to see'.[28]

The consequence was a paltry level of capital inflow. Said *The Economist* magazine in the autumn of 1991, 'on the most optimistic of assumptions' Eastern Europe (other than Germany) will by 1995 be attracting only $7 billion a year in direct foreign investment. In addition, loans from international agencies, banks and the like could contribute between $10 and $20 billion a year.[29] Estimates by the Austrian Institute for Economic Research indicate that even these miserly totals were not met. Total capital inflows into the region (excluding Germany and Yugoslavia) were estimated at $8.9 and $8.6 billion in 1991 and 1992 respectively. Net capital inflows were $0.1 billion less. Poland took 'the lion's share' in

1991 with $2.5 billion, while in 1992 Hungary led with $2.1 billion. Of the total capital inflow, foreign direct investment was $2.2 and $2.5 billion, while official credits were $5.5 and $4.7 billion in 1991 and 1992, respectively. The balance was made up of commercial bank and other credits.[30]

Table 4.3 shows the reported aid allocations (excluding balance of payments and bilateral assistance) and estimates of foreign direct investment. The combined total for the early '90s was over $20 billion and appears broadly in line with the Austrian figures, but well below *The Economist*'s 'optimistic' forecasts. The figures in the table suggest that both official credits and foreign direct investment ran at around $4 billion a year, with ex-Czechoslovakia, Hungary and Poland taking four-fifths of the region's total.

The primary reasons for the low figures for direct investment were the reduced availability of funds from the recession-torn Western companies in the early 1990s, combined with the high commercial risks involved. In addition a few commentators claimed that the region's industrial base was virtually worthless,[31] and while this was something of an exaggeration most foreign companies had insufficient capital, managerial skills, and commitment to take on a state-owned enterprise, even at a knock-down price.

The reluctance to invest had implications also for the quality of the investment. Much of what was made available by foreign companies was used to build up stocks for the expanding wholesale and retail trade, where returns were high and the risk low. 'Most foreign investments are aimed at the sector of commerce and services (including hotels and restaurants), the sale of computer technology, software services, consulting

Table 4.3   *The inflow of public and private capital into Central and Eastern Europe, 1989–92 ($ million, approximate)*

	World Bank approved projects (7/89–6/92)	Phare,[1] EIB[2] and EBRD assistance[3] (1990–2)	Cumulative foreign direct investment (1991–2)	Totals
Albania	41	275	20	336
Bulgaria	267	375	500	1,142
Ex-CSFR	696	1,080	2,200	3,976
Hungary	1,116	1,625	4,200	6,941
Poland	2,611	1,290	1,500	5,401
Romania	830	850	500	2,180
Ex-Yugoslavia	992	na	na	992
Totals	**6,553**	**5,495**	**8,920**	**20,968**

Notes [1] See page 56; [2] European Investment Bank; [3] Excluding support for balance of payments

Sources World Bank, European Commission, OECD

and design', said the authors of a recent report on foreign investment in Czechoslovakia.[32] At the other end of the quality spectrum, an unknown proportion of investment was used for high-risk and/or short-term ventures (ranging from casinos to crime), which were in some way either marginal or even occasionally detrimental to the region's fundamental requirements.

The few investors in industry provided new or second-hand equipment, for greenfield sites or selected more modern state-owned enterprises, bypassing the heavy industrial sector and agriculture. The capital required for their modernization was generally too high, relative to the risks involved. By 1993, this had created a vicious circle, which left the antiquated steel mills, power stations, coal mines and bulk chemical concerns polluting and therefore even less attractive to foreign capital than they were in 1990. Moreover, the hope among employees and the government that foreign investors would somehow 'save' their heavy industry and agriculture was largely wishful thinking.

The problem was only marginally alleviated by the official credits that were earmarked for the region, for disbursements were well below allocations. One Polish report claimed that out of $7.6 billion total foreign credits granted to the country only $500 million (some 9 per cent) had actually been disbursed over the two years to the end of 1991.[33] The problems were at both ends – CEE governments found it hard to set their priorities, and to guarantee all loans made to state enterprises or local companies. In spring 1993, Bank Handlowy in Warsaw reportedly had a backlog of up to 300 loan applications waiting for a guarantee. In addition, the various multilateral institutions were sometimes understaffed and had bureaucratic procedures for obtaining a loan because, one suspects, there was a widespread desire to ensure good management of public funds.

The principal source of allocated intergovernmental aid was the World Bank, which in the fiscal 12 months to end June 1991 approved a total of 14 project loan agreements to the region to the value of $2.9 billion. In fiscal 1992, 10 project loans for $1.8 billion were made. Mostly these covered telecommunications, agriculture, and power; they also subsidized the process of structural reform.

The EBRD which began operations in early 1991 was a disappointment in its initial few years. It had a specific role of promoting entrepreneurship in Eastern Europe: 60 per cent of its business had to go into private sector transactions, according to its charter. In its first year to March 1992, the Bank committed approximately $570 million, 'a catalytic amount which may result in a total investment of more than Ecu1.5 billion with co-financiers and joint venture partners.'[34] It principally supported property, airlines, light industry and telecommunications.

'But', commented *The Economist* in spring 1992, 'the region's neediest ventures are too risky for a publicly owned bank with a [top notch] AAA rating',[35] and hence they go unfunded. It also had to be careful not to tread on the toes of the World Bank, and in sectors such as steel and agriculture insiders said it was actively discouraged from lending to Central and Eastern Europe by the EC, because of the threat to Community producers.[36]

The EC's own aid is through Phare, an acronym for 'Pologne, Hongrie: aide á la restructuration économique', though since its inception in mid-1989 it had grown to take on the former GDR, Czechoslovakia, Romania, Bulgaria and Yugoslavia as well as Poland and Hungary. In 1992, it granted around $1.1 billion in aid to the region, of which ex-Czechoslovakia, Hungary and Poland took nearly two-fifths. It was described by David Roche, chief European strategist with Morgan Stanley in London, as 'a little programme which hands out little bread crumbs. Nice crumbs, but only crumbs'.[37] It has a bigger technical assistance element than the other lending agencies – the largest fields were education and training (14 per cent), private sector development (9 per cent) and environment and nuclear safety (also 9 per cent).

The recession

The recession dominated the region's economic landscape in the early 1990s. It was far more serious than in the West, with cuts in industrial production of up to a third or more over several years. Its depth prevented many industrial enterprises from accumulating the surplus necessary to invest in modern plant and equipment, whether this was necessary to compete or to curb pollution. It also discouraged foreign investors: several Western companies which at one time had considered investing ended up withdrawing their offers – in late 1992 Dow Chemicals decided not to buy the Sokolov Chemical Works and around the same time Mercedes shelved its plans for a new truck factory outside Berlin and for a link with two Czech truck makers.

The downturn had actually begun in several countries prior to 1989, but became more widespread and serious during 1990, when the past links within Comecon were broken and trade barriers for Western exporters were removed in line with the new free market policies. The shock of both structural reforms (including privatization), and the IMF's stabilization policies greatly exacerbated the situation.

In more or less every country in the region, the IMF's policies were designed primarily to curb inflation. These were moderately successful, though the cost was high – cuts in government spending, monetary and fiscal austerity and towering interest rates, all of which contributed to the severity of the recession. Few voices were openly critical. One of the leading member's of Romania's Council of Reform said that the IMF's 'orthodox stabilisation package underestimate[d] – at least in the case of [the former] centrally planned economies – the importance of industrial and financial restructuring'.[38]

In mid-1990, Comecon agreed to drop the transferable rouble and barter arrangements in favour of dollar trading from January 1991. Once this decision was made, trade within Comecon collapsed (see Table 4.4), though there was a return to barter based on market values for some products to overcome the problems of hard currency liquidity. Russia's own political and economic revolution cut a further slice off aggregate demand. As 25–40 per cent of the region's exports had been sold to the USSR in the late 1980s, business was hit right in the solar plexus by the decline. At the same time, many local enterprises were threatened by the rising tide of imports from the West: they could neither compete with its low (and sometimes dumped) prices nor with the pent-up demand for Western goods. Many were forced to close.

Industrial production fell most steeply in those sectors where Western suppliers penetrated furthest and where concerns had been most dependent on shipments to the USSR. Table 4.5 shows the decline. Eastern Germany's manufacturing output in mid-1991 was, not surprisingly, only one-third of its 1989 level. In other countries, the fall was less steep. By 1992 in Albania and Bulgaria, industrial output had fallen by over 50 per cent, compared with 1989, while in Romania it had fallen by nearly a half. The smallest declines were in Hungary and Czechoslovakia which probably had the most competitive industry. Table 4.6 shows that employment had not fallen as steeply as industrial output, suggesting that the level of underemployment was high and rising and/or that many of those made redundant had found new jobs.

A World Bank report published in April 1991 reportedly forecast that Poland, Hungary and Czechoslovakia would not reach the income levels

Table 4.4   *Central and Eastern Europe's international trade, 1990 and 1991*

Trade by E Europe To/from (% change from previous year)	Exports		Imports	
	1990	1991	1990	1991
The world	−3.3	−11.0	+2.9	+11.4
Other E Europe/CIS	−18.6	−32.5	−18.2	−34.5
Industrial countries	+11.6	+9.2	+24.2	+27.5
Developing countries	−14.3	−24.6	na	−3.2

Source Economic Commission for Europe; taken from *Financial Times*, 20 March 1992

Table 4.5 *Industrial activity, 1988–92 (1989=100)*

	1988*	1989	1990	1991	1992*
Albania	na	100	na	50.0	40.0
Bulgaria	98.9	100	83.2	60.5	47.0
CSFR	99.0	100	98.3	75.2	62.0
GDR[1]	na	100	55.8	32.7	na
Hungary	101.0	100	90.8	74.5	65.0
Poland	102.5	100	75.8	67.7	70.0
Romania	102.1	100	85.7	70.5	54.0
Yugoslavia	na	100	89.3	73.3	na

Notes [1] Mid-year figure for 1990 and 1991; * approximate

Sources 1988: *The Economist,* 21 September 1991; 1989–91: *Rzeszpospolita,* 16 April 1992; and others

Table 4.6 *Unemployment, 1989–92 (as % of economically active population)*

	1989 Dec %	1990 Dec %	1991 Dec million	1991 Dec %	1992 June %
Albania	na	na	0.4	35.0	na
Bulgaria	na	2.3	0.4	11.0	na
CSFR	0.0	1.2	na	6.6	5.5
GDR[1]	na	7.0*	1.4*	23.0*	na
Hungary	0.3	2.1	na	8.5	10.1
Poland	0.3	6.1	2.2	11.8	12.6
Romania	0.0	na	0.3	2.6	na

Notes [1] Excludes short-time working and other forms of disguised unemployment, which at end 1990 would have been around 22% and end 1991 would have been around 40%; * approximate

Sources Various

they enjoyed in 1989 till 1996, and that Bulgaria, Romania and Yugoslavia would have to wait till the twenty-first century.[39] The ECE warned in late 1991 of a 'Thirties type depression'. It said that East and Central Europe was sliding into a depression comparable with that experienced by the West between 1929 and 1933.[40] The ECE's annual survey, published a few months later, commented that many in the region must now be wondering whether 'the invisible hand of the market is really an iron fist'.[41]

However by late 1992 there was some evidence that though the rate of decline was slowing, any turnaround would be insufficiently strong to match the World Bank forecasts of spring 1991. In Poland, while the decline in industrial production to 1991 was steep, in 1992 there was a small increase. A World Bank study of 75 of the country's 8,000 remaining state-owned enterprises in six product areas reportedly showed the sector was 'far from a write-off'.[42] Ian Hume, the World Bank's representative in Warsaw, was reported as saying, 'There was a lot of product switching. We were struck by the dynamism of the restructuring processes being designed or being implemented'.[43] There were also some signs of modest growth in industrial production in Hungary. In both countries the increase was insufficient to reverse a fall in GDP in 1992.

THE CONSEQUENCES OF PRIVATIZATION AND STRUCTURAL REFORM

Restructuring was intended by governments to switch the pattern of production from one which aimed at plan targets to one which met the demands of consumers. During the quiet revolutions, most economists and politicians believed that privatization, the removal of state controls and fostering foreign investment would quickly close down industrial dinosaurs, modernize the remaining industry, and open up new manufacturing and service companies. However the process was nowhere near as smooth as they had predicted. The express lane plans and timetables promulgated by governments in 1990 for restructuring their economies appeared far too optimistic several years later.

Central and Eastern Europe was tantamount to being a guinea pig. Rather than proceeding cautiously with the transition, governments were encouraged by the international banks, by shock therapists and by the media to restructure as quickly as possible. In the intoxicating atmosphere of the early 1990s, they underestimated the impact of the various constraints and obstacles, they ignored the innate deficiencies of the free market system and they disregarded the practical difficulties of implementing policies in a hybrid economy.

Below we identify the broad areas of success and failure of government measures, while in Chapter 5 we focus on those aspects of the transition which have had a significant impact on the physical environment.

A part of the world market

Since 1990, the region has been part of the world market for factors of production (capital, labour, and land) as well as for goods and services. This has changed the way in which the factors are or are not used and the pattern of distribution of goods and services. For instance, there has been increased demand for professional managers, a fall in demand for some types of unskilled labour, and practically no interest in purchasing state farms.

The impact of the market was strongest on the streets of the towns, where consumer goods were in demand. One indicator was the presence of Russian, Belorussian and Ukrainian tradespeople selling bric-à-brac, clothes, sports gear, and other odds and ends in the markets. They were in virtually every town and city in Poland, the Czech Republic and Slovakia, and in many towns further south – in the underpasses, on the street corners and at the stadia. The quality of their products was low, but so were the prices. Buyers included consumers and other traders. Another indicator was the race to find space for new bill board adverts for goods and services – cigarettes (Marlboro in particular), soft drinks, films and the like. Looking a little harder one noticed the smaller ads for allotments, and cars for sale, and for English and German lessons on the bus shelters. City shops were crowded both with window and real shoppers interested in local as well as imported (mostly German or Japanese) goods.

The wave of interest in branded Western consumer goods and services and to a lesser extent local produce contrasted with the lame moves to create a capital market – for state-owned enterprises, shares and credit. Tight land ownership regulations and the acute shortage of housing and mortgages also restricted the development of a property market.

That different concerns survived and grew in different ways may, for some, be a truism, but it was also a useful basis for examining why some businesses and individuals leapt at the opportunities offered by the free market and others failed to respond. The events of 1990 and 1991 can be compared to a rain storm falling on a desert. The region suddenly became ablaze with a range of small plants and flowers, all trying to find new commercial niches to survive, while most of the older larger plants, which had been adept at subsisting in the desert climate found it difficult to meet the new conditions.

Box 4.2 presents an intuitive classification of existing and new businesses, according to their perceived advantages and disadvantages in a free market. It highlights the difficulties faced by yesteryear's favourites, namely the capital-intensive industrial and agricultural combines, which formed the backbone of the socialist economy. On the industrial side these were the smelters, mines and bulk chemical operations run by unsophisticated administrators, who were more used to haggling over the instructions and state subsidies they used to receive, than in making innovative decisions.

The other categories represent the potentially more dynamic sectors of the economy. In industry they covered the lighter, less obsolete industrial sectors – food processing, ready made clothing, electrical engineering, and car and component manufacturing. Those existing enterprises which had strong management, with skilled and low wages, were especially fortunate.

New manufacturing however was shunned. In Poland, only 5–6 per

Box 4.2   *An intuitive classification of business concerns in Central and Eastern Europe in the early 1990s*

Existing, heavy industry/agriculture (eg steel, coal, power generation, basic chemicals, textiles, leather, pulp and paper, state farms): mostly old capital and labour intensive installations, many social subsidiaries, poor management, weak markets.

Other existing industry (eg chemical specialities, car and car components, electrical engineering, clothing, food processing, furniture): commonly more modern installations, labour intensive, many social subsidiaries, often weak management, potential to diversify into growing markets.

New industry (eg waste processing equipment, telecommunications): modern equipment, undercapitalized firms, product-driven management, growing markets.

Existing services (eg building, printing, general trading, market gardening): many small undercapitalized operations, old equipment, over-manned, fast-growing markets.

New services (eg car repairs, casinos, incinerators, specialized traders): many small undercapitalized operations, modern equipment, market-driven management, fast-growing markets.

New illegal services (eg smuggling, car theft, fraud): many small undercapitalized operations, modern equipment, uncertain but growing markets.

cent of the new firms set up since 1990 were in production. In the second half of 1991, the Poznan-based *Review of Commerce* surveyed the intentions of trading firms to invest in manufacturing. It concluded 'that there still exist many setbacks and hindrances, [such as] difficult access to credits', as well as high interest rates, and the view that production is not 'fashionable'.[44] With only limited supplies of capital available locally and high interest rates, many manufacturers could not invest in new equipment, cover their stock purchases or sometimes even supply credit to their buyers.

Most but not all services were in a relatively advantageous position. Exceptions included tailors who were being undercut by the import of cheap ready made clothing, and the state-owned television, which was bypassed by satellites. Retail and wholesale outlets opened and folded as quickly as in the West. New company registrations in Eastern Germany fell from 25,000 a month at the end of 1990 to around 20,000 in early

1992, while the number of company failures rose over the same period from 6,000 to 10,000. In the first two months of 1993 in the Czech Republic, 13 per cent of private businesses reportedly failed.[45]

Progress in privatization

Enterprise restructuring was part and parcel of economic restructuring: it involved closing social subsidiaries (such as holiday homes), laying off surplus workers, introducing more efficient management and methods of work, investing in more advanced machinery and rationalizing the number of products. The preferred methods of restructuring were privatization and foreign investment. While progress in privatizing shops, construction, restaurants and the like was fairly speedy, privatization of industry made much less progress.

This partly reflected what was being sold. According to Sanjay Dhar of the World Bank, restructuring was definitely worth while for about a third of the region's industrial activities. For the rest he noted that 'Studies by potential foreign investors suggest that about a third of the industrial sector is not likely to be viable' at all. For the remaining third, 'major restructuring would be required', though 'a positive return on the exercise could not necessarily be expected'.[46]

For example, in Eastern Germany, where the Treuhand had ready access to capital and top management skills, less than half the area's industrial enterprises were fully privatized in the two and a half years following unification in mid-1990. Of the 5,000 which were, some 2,000 were management buyouts. Proposed investment in these privatized firms amounted to just over $100 billion. Of the balance of 7,500 enterprises (many of which were subdivisions of former multifaceted combines), a third were being liquidated, a third had been disposed of in other ways, such as being returned to their original owners (reprivatization) or to the local authority, and a third were unsold. Of those that remained most were in forestry and agriculture, machine building, services/trading and heavy industry.

In Poland, moderate progress was made through liquidation, which allowed enterprises to write off debts and restructure. Some diversified into new areas, others just closed. Official figures said that a quarter of industry was in private or cooperative hands at the end of 1991. Of the 9,000 industrial enterprises in 1989, around 1,500 had been liquidated by end 1992; the pace of liquidation was however slowing down, with far fewer enterprises choosing this route in 1992 than in 1991. Over the same period, around 50 enterprises were privatized by the sale of stock, of which 12 were floated on the Warsaw stock exchange. However, the low level of trade sales to foreign investors and the repeated delays in launching the mass privatization programme meant that the future of many of the country's industrial concerns was threatened by their uncertain ownership.

Eventually, about two years after its first announcement, the mass privatization of up to 600 enterprises was agreed by the Sejm or parliament in Warsaw in late April 1993. It foresaw the establishment of 20 or more foreign-managed funds to run the enterprises competitively. Shares in the funds were to be issued to those Poles who paid a nominal fee.

Though Hungary succeeded in attracting a high proportion of the region's foreign investment, its progress in privatization was slow. In fact the sale of much of its most attractive industry to Western multinationals in 1990–2 created a political backlash, which towards the end of 1992 made the government turn to mass privatization, along Czech lines. In early 1993, the Budapest stock exchange, the region's first to reopen in June 1990, listed only 23 equities; trading was dominated by Austrian investors.

Even where privatization appeared to be succeeding, it was unclear to what extent the medicine would kill the patient. In Czechoslovakia, in the first wave of privatization, vouchers bought in May and June 1992 were used to bid for shares in 1,500 companies; in five computerized auctions, the shares were allocated to the participating individuals and 440 investment funds before the break-up of the country. The shares were due to be formally transferred during March and April 1993, to coincide with the opening of the Prague stock exchange. However the process was delayed by a dispute with Slovakia, with the Czech government threatening to seize the shares apportioned to Slovaks. A second wave of privatizations, covering a further 2,000 enterprises was planned by the Czech Republic for late 1993.

In 1992, the investment funds picked up three-quarters of the vouchers with the promise to redeem them at between 10 and 50 times their cost. While this move rescued the initial voucher purchase phase of the privatization programme, many commentators believed it would result in the collapse of both the funds and the companies they formally owned. Commenting on the voucher scheme in March 1992, Jan Vanous, the President of the PlanEcon business consultancy, wrote that its likely consequence would be the massive sale of assets to Western companies at knock-down prices. Moreover the Western investment would 'not involve prestigious projects by major multinationals involving tens or hundreds of millions of dollars. Rather, a large number of smaller, speculative investments in property and unlisted securities by Western bargain hunters is the likely result'.[47] Others believed that a new bankruptcy law passed in spring 1993 would kill many of those companies not bought by foreign investors.

Furthermore, governments specifically excluded strategic enterprises from their privatization programmes. The Czech Republic decided in 1991 not to privatize for at least five years some 600 industrial enterprises, for this reason. In late 1992, Hungary established a holding company to manage the 163 companies in which the state was to retain full or partial ownership; these reportedly produced about 50 per cent of Hungary's GDP. Unclear ownership of property was a further factor in delaying privatization. In Czechoslovakia, there were more than 30,000 requests for the return of property to the pre-communist owners and 20,000 requests for compensation for the loss of other assets in Czechoslovakia. In former East Germany, 1.5 million persons claimed 2.5 million titles to property expropriated by the communists. Of these only some 15 per cent had been resolved by end 1992.

Clearly privatization was much slower than the free market architects of 1990 had predicted. Even if it had progressed more smoothly, it was not certain to what extent it would have contributed to restructuring. In Germany, the Treuhand was strong enough to ensure a minimum level of new investment in the purchased asset, and the buyer's cooperation in cleaning up the site. But elsewhere, Western companies were allowed to remove potential competitors and/or to cream off profits from their cherry picked investments. In a paper presented in March 1992, Jouko Leskinen, vice-chairman of Neste Oy, the Finnish state-owned chemical company, distinguished four types of Western investor in the region: the institutional (such as pension funds), the state-owned company, the private company and the speculative. Leskinen noted that the speculative investors were 'likely to concentrate on taking advantage of legal and other loopholes'.[48]

Moreover, as reported above, most foreign investment was in the trading and small services sector. This may have helped restructure the economy, but it bypassed most of the enterprises which needed individual restructuring. In addition, governments had to offer incentives to attract investors. They included tariffs and quotas on imports, which had a negative impact on the economy as a whole. One such case was Hungary's steel industry: officials promised to curtail imports if Voest Alpine, the Austrian steel maker, bought a stake in Hungary's largest cold-rolling mill at Dunaújváros in early 1992. A few months later it introduced quotas on 15 steel products. Another case was Slovakia, which proposed tax holidays of up to seven years for foreign investors. Other privatization contracts allowed environmental escape clauses.

Progress in structural reform

The communist era was marked by a close working relationship between the government and state-owned enterprises, so that in 1990 little of the fiscal and legislative structure needed to manage a market economy was in place. These reforms were more diffuse than privatization but in some ways more important, as they provided the framework for restructuring. By 1993, much remained undone: the easiest tasks such as freeing prices had been almost completed, but the most necessary changes covering financial and industrial legislation and its implementation were mostly unrealized.

In a market economy, the key signal is price and the foremost gauge of success is profit. For such criteria to be useful, governments had to remove subsidies and allow prices to rise (or fall) to the market clearing level. According to the OECD, in 1989, subsidies in Central and Eastern Europe were typically 15–20 per cent of GDP, but by 1991 they averaged less than 5 per cent.[49] While the prices of most consumer goods with one or two minor exceptions had been freed, governments continued to intervene in energy and agriculture. By late 1991, it was claimed that some 90 per cent of Poland's prices were market determined. Hungary's subsidies as a proportion of GDP were down to 9 per cent in 1990 from 13 per cent in 1989 and were due to fall to around 4 per cent in 1993.

Financial reforms were the most pressing. The failure to reform the banks was a major problem and reflected the general difficulty governments had in establishing a capital market. Many of the older banks were technically insolvent due to their large number of non-performing loans, but they were not closed down. Governments' soft budget constraints in the early 1990s had allowed enterprises to build up credits from other enterprises as well as from the banks in order to survive. In Hungary, in late 1992, the banking system's classified (bad) debts were about 260 billion forints (over $3 billion), nearly 17 per cent of total loans, or about 10 per cent of GDP. Reform required an efficient payments system (in particular the use of cheques rather than cash), bank privatization (so risk was measured at arm's length) and cleansing the balance sheet of old credits. Banking operations were insufficiently regulated, increasing the possibility of fraud.

At a minimum, a successful industrial policy would have required the enforcement of hard budget constraints, bankruptcy rules and anti-monopoly laws. The actual results were mixed. Thus bankruptcy was always for the future and not the here and now. For managers of state-owned enterprises, survival in the free market was not a question of being commercially fit, but of defying insolvency for long enough either to obtain governmental subsidies or international aid, or to find a foreign joint venture partner. But as most enterprises failed to make a profit, inter-enterprise debt mounted significantly; unofficial estimates for the Czech Republic put it at over $7 billion. The Czechs moreover, perhaps because they had ostensibly made the most progress in privatization, were among the worst offenders. In late 1992 and again in 1993 they agreed to soften their law once they saw that many of their key state and soon to be privatized enterprises were likely to be wound up.

In 1991 and 1992 various estimates suggested that in Poland, Hungary, Czechoslovakia and Eastern Germany a third or more of industrial enterprises were actually insolvent and a further fifth were verging on bankruptcy. In Hungary in the second half of 1991, many big state companies were reportedly hanging on 'by selling assets and stocks, sending migrant workers home to Poland or Vietnam and simply not paying their bills'.[50] In spring 1992, Hungarian officials said that some 40–45 per cent of industrial companies under direct state authority were facing bankruptcy.[51]

Fiscal policies too were hard to enforce. Governmental tax receipts fell, due to the recession, late payments and the difficulty of taxing the burgeoning private sector. Expenditure remained stubbornly high – both Poland and Hungary ran budget deficits of about 8 per cent of GDP in 1992.

Opening up the economy to international competition required a free market exchange rate. In Hungary, this conflicted with the IMF's policy for a strong currency as part of its stabilization package. For instance, in March 1992 General Electric (GE), one of Hungary's first and largest foreign investors – in light bulb producer Tungsram – announced it was cutting the number of employees and its proposed investment in the company because of the subsidiary's 1991 losses. GE blamed these on rising costs and urged the devaluation of the forint to improve the country's export competitiveness. However, the Hungarian government's agreement with the IMF included a firm credit policy and a high exchange rate to maintain downward pressure on inflation. It was only after Tungsram's third year of losses in March 1993 that Hungary eventually agreed to devalue the forint by 2.9 per cent.

Though most trade barriers were reduced in 1990 and 1991, as the social costs of transformation rose governments started to reimpose restrictions. Poland, Hungary and Czechoslovakia have all reintroduced protection, particularly for agricultural inputs and processed foodstuffs during 1991 and 1992.

The hybrid economy

Since the late '80s, the region has been an economic maelstrom. In the new game, the players have all used different guidelines. The steel mills and coal mines have used the rules of communism – internal lobbying to ensure continued subsidies and perks, such as soft budget constraints.

Light industry and the burgeoning retail trade have used the rules of the unbridled free market. Multinationals have used the rules of the industrialized West, which require governments setting a (favourable) legal framework for their activities. Speculators have taken the Wild West as their model. The international banks have pushed the classical free market.

In the midst of this, governments have tried to make decisions, combining communism's stick and the free market carrot in whatever combination seemed most appropriate in the changing storm. So far they have not succeeded in transforming their countries. Eugenio Lari, Director of the World Bank for Europe and Central Asia, accurately pinpointed a key contradiction when describing the situation in 1992. He said that as a result of communism, 'There are numerous enterprises ... which have been producing goods, where the value of output has been less than the value of the sum of the inputs, even including labour'. He then added that 'Closing down or restructuring such value subtracting industries will, by itself, have a beneficial impact by increasing the efficiency of natural resource use, reducing pollution emissions and increasing economic efficiency'.[52]

The situation also created unemployment. McKinsey, the international management consultants, was reported in mid-1991 as saying that Eastern Germany could become a single large nature reserve unless the German government immediately took steps to reindustrialize the area.[53] Though not formally stated, it would seem that the multilateral banks, by default, actually favoured this policy. For they supported new investments in services and light industry in preference to restructuring existing heavy industries. Taken to its logical conclusion, this implied the latter's closure.

While market forces were indeed expected eventually to sweep most of the region's heavy industry away into Karl Marx's dustbin of history, this left unresolved such issues as timing and the social consequences. Tom Kolaja of Poland's Ministry of Privatization believed this 'economic Darwinism' would be over by the middle of the decade.[54] Others said it could take longer. Moreover the sudden shift to real rather than artificial prices had left governments without the tools they needed to deal with its ramifications. These included not only the threat of deindustrialization and unemployment at the macro-level, but fraud, car theft, and the increased smuggling of chemical wastes at the micro-level.

Though economic activity was formally market orientated, by 1993 neither the governments nor the individual players had had the time or the expertise to develop the response mechanisms the market needed to function efficiently and effectively. More large Western companies, which were regarded as the main potential agents of change, might have been

Box 4.3 *The association agreements between the EC and Czechoslovakia, Hungary and Poland*

Trade agreements between the European Community (EC) and Czechoslovakia, Hungary and Poland were signed in December 1991. They incorporated in their preamble a statement supporting eventual full membership. The transitional period, which came into force in March 1992, for the EC is two to five years, for Czechoslovakia and Poland seven years, and for Hungary ten years.

The agreements were intended to create a free flow of industrial goods between the EC and the three East European countries during the 1990s. They are based on an asymmetrical principle, with the EC reducing its barriers to trade faster than the three associated members. Over two to five years, the EC will remove most quotas and tariffs. Trade in agricultural goods, textiles, iron and steel and coal, which together accounted for a third to a half of these countries' exports and in the past faced substantial restrictions on being imported into the Community, will be liberalized under special protocols.

The Common Agricultural Policy (CAP) was a particular hindrance. Restrictions on EC imports of agricultural produce will remain for longest and will depend on how quickly CAP is reformed; it will be most advantageous for the three Central European countries if it is *not* reformed.

Restrictions on EC imports of textiles will be retained so long as it takes to dismantle the MultiFibre Agreement (MFA), under a separate agreement yet to be reached as part of the so-called Uruguay Round of tariff cuts. But the minimum period of transition will be five years. Irrespective of this, the outward processing of textiles (under which EC manufacturers typically send pre-cut fabrics for assembly into garments, which are then returned to the cutter) will be liberalized immediately.

Full Most Favoured Nation (ie the best available tariff and quota terms) treatment for coal and steel products entered into force in 1992. Yet difficulties remained. Czechoslovak, Hungarian and Polish goods have to conform with EC rules of origin, standards and other various rather bureaucratic rules. For example, East European manufactured goods will need to demonstrate at least 60 per cent local content to qualify for duty free entry into the Twelve. There is also the possibility of reintroducing trade barriers if there are 'serious' economic problems in an importing country.

Source Much of this is taken from 'EC protectionism threatens east European growth', *Financial Times*, 13 April 1992, and from *Global Economic Prospects and the Developing Countries*, World Bank, April 1992, p.27.

willing to invest if governments had provided a clear legal framework and an efficient commercial and physical infrastructure. In most instances however, the law was constantly being revised and the infrastructure was missing.

Instead Western firms often preferred to set up a sales office to test the waters before investing. There was thus an enormous increase in imports of consumer goods in the early 1990s. Consumers switched to a far larger extent than expected to Western products. 'Abandoning themselves' as producers, was how one German[55] described the behaviour of his fellow shoppers, but his words were just as relevant elsewhere in the region.

Most of the imports were from the EC. In spite of this boost for its exports, the Community was reluctant to open its doors to many of Central Europe's traditional exports. In the association agreements signed by Czechoslovakia, Hungary and Poland in December 1991 (see Box 4.3), easy access for basic products such as coal, steel, textiles, chemicals and agricultural produce was rejected by Brussels on the grounds of competition. There was the fear that higher imports from the East would put EC firms out of business. French farmers were particularly violent in their opposition to cheap Polish meat. Similar restrictions were included in the agreements with Romania and Bulgaria. In early 1993, several East European countries responded to the EC's rising protectionism by temporarily banning imports of EC meat.

Basing decision-making on price within a clear legal and financial framework rather than the fiat of the communist party was supposed to have made the process of economic distribution more rational. In global terms it actually meant Central and Eastern Europe having a marginal role on the fringes of Western Europe. In national macro-economic terms, it meant large scale unemployment and deindustrialization in some areas, while in terms of individual enterprises it meant success for some of those close to the end-consumer and failure for the rest.

5

HOW GREEN IS THE GRASS OF CAPITALISM? THE ENVIRONMENTAL CONSEQUENCES OF THE MARKET ECONOMY

COMPARING LIKE WITH LIKE

In the years following the quiet revolutions, it was sometimes implied that the transition from the centrally planned roundabouts to the free market swings would automatically bring environmental benefits. In autumn 1990, Bronisław Kaminski, Poland's Minister of Environment, said, 'The process of reversing [the] neglect of environmental protection in Western countries continued for many decades and has been crowned with success thanks to radical reform of the economic structure and investment in clean production technology. This same mode of thinking guides our intentions'.[1] The UK is also alleged to have made an analogous claim in June 1990 at a ministerial conference on Europe's environment, held near Prague.[2]

A discussion document prepared by World Bank staff in late 1992 took a broader view, noting that over the coming decade 'an important by-product of economic transformation will be large reductions in the amount of environmental damage associated with excessive energy use and with some forms of heavy industrial production'. To be effective, it said, this 'environmental free ride' would have to be supported by public investments and regulatory policies 'to address the failure of markets'.[3]

A superficial comparison between the developed industrialized countries of the late 20th century and the former socialist countries in the 1980s showed the latter as raw material and energy greedy, heavily polluting of air and water, and ridden with leaky nuclear power stations.

Some, including the World Bank's Director for Europe, Eugenio Lari, made the comparison between smog in London 40 years ago and in Katowice in 1992,[4] or Prague in February 1993.

Comparisons between Western Europe and CEE though politically appealing made less sense in economic terms. Central and Eastern Europe consisted of lower and upper middle income countries, similar in many respects to the so-called newly industrializing countries.[5] Rather than being compared to either the USA or the UK, a capitalist Poland or Slovakia should have been compared with Turkey or Iran, and a capitalist Czech Republic or Hungary with Greece, Portugal or Mexico. That these countries generally had a poor ecological record highlights the failure of the free market to achieve environmental progress outside the first world. Like CEE, their economic development was based on heavy industry and the exploitation of their natural resources. It was perhaps these similarities, combined with their environmental degradation, which politically made them unsuitable objects of comparison.

The purpose of this chapter is to analyse the environmental trends during the transition to a free market. It shows that the switch to capitalism has been found wanting. In spite of curbing some of the excesses of communism's pollution economy, the nascent market economy has so far failed to bring fundamental improvements and in the future is likely to reinforce old threats as well as create new ones.

Many of the points made are impressionistic, largely due to the absence of data, but where figures are available, they are presented. Table 5.1 outlines the main elements of the chapter.

Table 5.1 *The environmental consequences of the move to a free market in Central and Eastern Europe*

The environmental consequences	Supporting trends
Curbing some of the excesses of the pollution economy	1. Environmentally motivated closures 2. Reduced output 3. State regulations and expenditure 4. Foreign aid
The failure to bring fundamental improvement	1. The privatization process 2. Market prices for raw materials 3. Hard budget constraints 4. Limited investment for modernization 5. Economically targeted investments 6. Insufficient foreign aid 7. The narrowing and weakening of environmental legislation
Reinforcing old and creating new threats	1. A Western lifestyle 2. Environmental cost advantages; the waste trade

CURBING SOME OF THE WORST EXCESSES

In the early 1990s, environmental pollution in Central and Eastern Europe declined quite markedly. To some this may have suggested that the free market was curbing emissions automatically; however, most of the evidence points to the economic downturn. Additional reasons included political pressure from environmentalists for plant closures, and the environmental funds, direct budgetary allocations and foreign credits which supported technical change. While these were all targeted on individual plants, their impact compared with that of the recession was small.

Environmentally motivated closures

Throughout the region, opposition to rising environmental degradation was one of the main factors in the overthrow of the communist regimes. In Poland in early 1989 there were separate environmental round table discussions between Solidarity and the communist government, which agreed a list of plant closures. In East Germany during the late 1980s there was a growing number of environmental citizens' groups, often linked with the church. In the first half of 1990, before unification, the government began to heed their call to give priority to ecology over the economy.

As a result, the shut-down of the worst polluters was a top priority for the newly elected governments, particularly in Poland and Eastern Germany. In Poland, the government's short-term policy objectives, according to the National Environmental Policy, included 'the abandonment' or change in manufacturing process at 80 sites identified in 1989 by the central government as the worst national polluters, and at a further 800 identified by the voivodeship governments as the worst provincial polluters.

Of the 80, by February 1992 orders for the closure of 26 whole plants or individual units at them had been made. Of these it was said by the Ministry of Environment in Warsaw that 18 had closed, and one (Huta Bobrek – see Box 5.3) had refused.[6] It is not certain though whether all the first 18 had really closed, or had instead just taken steps to ensure their survival. For example, the first deadline for closure of one of the 18 – the sulphur crushing plant in Gdańsk – was end 1990; September 1993 was its third – by then it was supposed to install sufficient granulation capacity to stop sulphur dust being blown into the city, but there was no certainty it would.

A further seven sites had been given a year or more to close. The latter included the open hearth furnaces at Kraków's Huta Sendzimira, which had to close by end 1995. For the remaining 54 sites on the Polish national list, no definitive action had been proposed by February 1992. Ministry officials claimed steps towards closure or restructuring would be taken during the course of 1992, but a year later, as environmental interest waned, there had been little progress.

In Eastern Germany, the number of plants shut on environmental grounds was between 50 and 60. Most were closed prior to the union of the two Germanies, according to a report by the federal government. 'For prompt and substantial improvement of the state of the environment in the ecologically critical areas of the former GDR, reductions in production and discontinuation of production lines in plants having a particularly detrimental impact on the environment were introduced already in the first half of 1990. These include 39 production plants in the Bitterfeld/ Wolfen area and the Pirna plants producing viscose cord.'[7]

At the same time as monetary union in July 1990, the two states agreed an environmental union, which extended West German environmental law (with some small exceptions) into the new Bundesländer from October 1990. These steps accelerated some of the planned closures such as the carbonizing plants in Espenhain and Böhlen. Other announced closures for environmental reasons included the eight carbide furnaces, and the chlorine and calcium oxide plants at the Buna chemical works in Schkopau. Since unification the number of plants closed was probably less than a score, according to Dr Heiner Bonnenberg, the Treuhand director responsible for the environment.[8] It would seem greater priority was given by the agency to restructuring in line with the new standards.

From their 1989 levels, the 1990 closures in Eastern Germany were expected to contribute to cuts in sulphur dioxide and dust emissions by 10 and 13 per cent respectively. According to the federal government report, some 43 per cent of the reduction would be due to plant closures, 55 per cent to reduced output and 2 per cent to 'technical environmental protection measures'.[9]

Reduced output

Official and unofficial reports from the various ministries of environment suggested that due to the recession there was an across the board reduction in emissions of between a fifth and a quarter over the two years to end 1991 with a further substantial cut expected in 1992. Lower output had the largest impact on air and water emissions, and on the volume of solid waste dumped. For instance, falling food demand and lower food prices (as well as fewer subsidies) meant less use of fertilizer

Table 5.2   *The improvement in the quality of the Vistula river in Poland,*
1990–1

Measurement of contents		Class (%) I	II	III	Unclassed
Harmful chemicals	1990	–	8.3	50.0	41.7
	1991	–	41.7	37.5	20.8
Harmful bacteria	1990	–	37.5	50.0	12.5
	1991	–	41.7	54.2	4.1

Source Enterprise for Communal Hygiene, Warsaw (taken from *Gazeta Wyborcza*, 30 March 1992)

and pesticides. Fertilizer use on Polish farms (in kg/ha) in 1991/2 was only a third of the 1988/9 level. In late 1992, the Bulgarian Minister of Environment, Valentin Vasilev, was reported as saying that the main reason for the 30–40 per cent reduction in pollution in his country was 'economic decline',[10] though he admitted that closures were also a factor. In Saxony in the south of the ex-GDR, cleaner air came 'hand-in-hand with unemployment'.[11]

Statistically it is not easy to separate the environmental improvements arising from reduced output from those due to new laws or economic restructuring, though in a few situations it was possible. For instance, Polish researchers specifically identified the recession and the fall in industrial production and excluded 'pro-ecological measures', when they published the results of a survey into the quality of the water of the river Vistula in 1990 and 1991. Table 5.2 shows the results. In terms of both harmful chemicals and bacteria, the proportion of water that was too poor to be classified at least halved, while the share in class III (suitable for industrial use), measured by its content of harmful chemicals, fell by a third. While none of the water was yet seen fit to drink (class I), the proportion in class II (suitable for swimming and recreation) increased. The improvement was particularly noticeable in heavy metals, nitrogen compounds, iron, and chlorine and other dissolved substances, the researchers said.[12] The small improvement in the content of harmful bacteria reflected the lower volume of sewage treated.

Table 5.3 shows the reduction in airborne emissions generated by Poland's main air polluters between 1989 and 1991; emissions of dust and gas declined by around two-fifths and a third respectively. Comparing these emissions with output for specific industries would suggest that the decline in economic activity was the principal but not the only factor in curbing air emissions. Thus between 1989 and 1991, dust emissions from the cement industry fell by 55 per cent, and production by 30 per cent, while from the steel industry they declined by 33 per cent

Table 5.3 *The decrease in emissions from Polish enterprises 'particularly harmful for clean air', 1989–91 (000 tonnes/year)*

Type of emission	1989	1990	1991	Change 89/91 (%)
Dust, of which	1,513	1,163	923	–39
cinders/ash	1,193	933	754	–37
dust (from cement industry)	92	55	41	–55
dust (from metal industry)	85	66	44	–48
Gas, of which	5,113	4,115	3,552	–31
sulphur dioxide	2,790	2,210	2,035	–27
carbon monoxide	1,335	1,106	793	–41
nitrogen oxides	782	640	600	–23
hydrocarbons	114	110	85	–25

Sources Table 10, *Environmental Protection 1991*; Table 12, *Environmental Protection 1992*; Main Statistical Office, Warsaw

and raw steel production by 24 per cent. Other factors may have included the more efficient operation of filters at lower output levels, and closures for commercial reasons.

Though other statistical series show similar declines in the volume of air and water emissions, the recession's impact is likely to be merely temporary. Any increase in industrial production is expected to mean a reversal of the downward trend in emissions. Commenting on Eastern Germany, a semi-official government report published in December 1991 said, 'The detected reductions in pollution of receiving water do not imply a permanent change of the situation, as recent measures taken in the second half of 1991 prove. A lack of thorough technical reconstruction and renovation could mean that the resumption of production will cause a rapid increase of pollutant emissions'.[13]

State regulations and expenditure

In the past, the authorities used economic instruments to try to prevent environmental degradation. As they were abused in many ways (see Chapter 3), governments in 1990 raised charges and set about improving both the monitoring of air emissions and water discharges, and the collection of payments (see Chapter 6). Their success was ultimately conditional upon businesses accepting the responsibility of paying, and simultaneously making the necessary investments to reduce emissions.

In the early 1990s, economic instruments were important primarily because they nourished environmental funds, which were used as a lever to foster new investments. The incentive effect of higher environmental charges on the technology in use was modest though it was expected to grow. A large number of projects were financed through the funds with a small but calculable benefit to the environment. In 1991, the Polish National Fund for Environmental Protection (NFEP) claimed that its loans of $230 million resulted in a cut in dust emissions of just over 1 per cent, and that in 1992 this would rise to 2 per cent. The NFEP also funded the pilot plants set up to reduce the saline water discharges from several Polish coal mines. These were also supported by small grants from Phare and Japan. Two technologies were under investigation, with the anticipated reduction in salt outflows at 345,000 tonnes/year in 1992 and 1993.

The increase in fund disbursements was reflected in the figures for total state expenditure on the environment. In the Czech Republic expenditure was an estimated $260 million in 1991 and $360 million in 1992, according to Vaclav Klaus.[14] These figures represent an estimated 0.7 and 1.1 per cent of Czech GDP respectively. In Poland, in 1989 and 1990, reported expenditure was 0.6 and 0.8 per cent of GDP respectively, and in 1991 an estimated $840 million or 1.1 per cent of GDP. This total includes significant contributions from national and local state budgets, voivodeship funds for the environment, individual enterprises, the NFEP and foreign aid.

Foreign aid

Disbursed foreign aid was much less than locally financed expenditure. Total environmental allocations in the early 1990s in the region were estimated at $2–3 billion. While air and water pollution from the energy sector were correctly identified as the main areas of action, during this period only a few of the projects tackled head on the major threats. Most were soft, consisting, in other words, of research, studies, institution building and training, often involving foreign consultants.

There were of course some exceptions. Again Poland provides some interesting illustrations. One was the support from the Dutch Electricity Generating Board (SEP) to Poland's Clean Air Foundation. To offset the cost of its emissions in the Netherlands, SEP provided around $35 million for pollution control equipment at Belchatów lignite-fired power station, the country's largest and most polluting in terms of sulphur dioxide emissions. It contributed to the first two of the 12 planned wet flue gas desulphurization (FGD) scrubbers, and may contribute more in the future. SEP said that spending this sum in Poland rather than at home was more cost effective for Europe's environment.[15] Germany, through the Kreditanstalt für Wiederaufbau, was supporting the installation of FGD scrubbers at the Opole power station near the German border.

Another was the Finnish bilateral aid programme, which also part funded or funded four energy projects. These included cabling work for a district heating project in Kraków (this included training), the delivery of pressure filtration technology to control waste at a chemical plant and retrofitting a fluidized bed boiler at the Czeczott mine. The total amount of funding was thought to have been less than $15 million.

THE FAILURE TO BRING FUNDAMENTAL IMPROVEMENTS

Though some individual sources of pollution were closed and/or their emissions curtailed, the first three or four years of the 1990s did not witness any fundamental improvement in the environment of Central and Eastern Europe. For the Polish Ministry of Environment, fundamental change meant 'a reduction of energy, material and water demand by production processes, which will {in turn} slow down the use of natural resources and in most cases emission of pollutants'.[16] It also envisaged the greater use of cleaner technology, more waste recycling and the establishment of new businesses producing equipment for environmental protection.

Such improvements would have required deep-seated restructuring of the economies and individual businesses, new investment and the enforcement of effective environmental legislation. None of these occurred, essentially because of the failure of the reform programmes and the lack of resources. The region was trying to introduce capitalism without the capital and the environment lay well down on the list of both public and private priorities.

While restructuring was discussed from an economic point of view in Chapter 4, from the environmental point of view, the World Bank prefers to talk in terms of 'win-win' strategies. These it defined as policies in which market forces contribute to economic efficiency and simultaneously reduce environmental damage, 'at no net financial cost to governments'.[17] The main examples were privatization, allowing energy and natural resource prices to rise to market levels, and hard budget constraints. Restructuring, however, also required investment in existing and new businesses.

The environmental impact of these four elements of economic restructuring is analysed immediately below. It is followed by a review of the pattern of new investment in environmental products and services, and of the difficulties of expanding the remit of environmental legislation.

The privatization process

Privatization was seen as being at the heart of economic restructuring. This was particularly true for environmental economists, who rightly believed that in the absence of clear property rights, factories and farms would attempt to shift responsibility for the environment on to the state. To monitor pollution successfully, the relevant agencies had to be independent. However privatization on its own seems to have done little to make enterprises or firms more accountable.

Ruth Bell from the USA's Environmental Protection Agency in Washington said, 'Privatization is a natural transition point in which explicit responsibilities for pollution control can be recognized'. Privatization also gave 'an opportunity to address not only the form of ownership of these firms, but also the responsibilities that accompany private ownership'.[18] In practice though, most concerns, whether state or privately owned, were reluctant to accept any environmental responsibility. Greenpeace has prepared a number of contractual clauses (see Chapter 8) which could become part of a privatization agreement, in order to promote a more positive response from newly formed companies.

Responsible businesses by definition, accepted both the spirit and letter of national legislation and best Western practice. This included an obligation to keep their factory site clean and to consider the environmental consequences of their products and production processes. This approach though was taken only by a few companies. Foreign investors generally attempted to restrict their liability for past contamination (see Chapter 6), though most restructured enough to keep governments and shareholders off their backs.

The modern state-owned enterprise was similar. As most were hoping for privatization through a trade sale or flotation, it is not surprising that they mimicked the multinationals' attitudes. Said Andrzej Lipko, Poland's Minister of Industry and Trade in 1992, 'Western capital will not want to talk with us, unless enterprises present credible recovery programmes'.[19] For example managers at the modern state-owned Gdańsk oil refinery reduced their sulphur dioxide emissions by a third to 8,000 tonnes/year between 1988 and 1991, as they wanted potential buyers of the plant to know they were familiar with Western standards and practices.[20] Management attitudes at the Plovdiv metal smelter (see Box 5.1) were similar.

At the other extreme, some local investors and foreign companies, while aware of the law, looked for ways around it. One method was for the investor to lease the site from the state. Another was for it to buy the clean modern part and leave the dirty part state-owned. In one case – a zinc galvanizer – the polluting state-owned part was contracted to supply

Box 5.1   *The lead smelter, Plovdiv, Bulgaria*

The airborne emissions from the Plovdiv lead smelter include dust, zinc, sulphur dioxide, cadmium and lead. According to the World Bank[1] 'elevated blood lead levels' in children were widespread in the agricultural area around the smelter in the 1980s. In the village of Kuklen (3 km away) between 1986 and 1990 average lead level in the blood of children was said by the World Bank to be 335 micrograms (μg)/litre of blood, while in Assenovgrad (10 km away), they were around 225 μg/l. In the West, the median level among adults was approximately 100 μg/l,[2] but in Bulgaria it may be higher, due to the widespread use of lead in petrol.

During the late 1980s, before the overthrow of the communist government, both local residents and Ekoglasnost activists campaigned for the whole plant to be shut on health grounds. In early 1990, the new government gave the enterprise until 1994 to reduce emissions significantly or be closed down.

Consequently, locally developed jet filters were installed in the lead smelter, and production was cut by 40–50 per cent. In early 1992, more jet filters were installed in the refinery and the bag filters were revamped. By spring 1992, the combined effect of reduced lead production and the new filters was expected to be a cut in airborne heavy metal and dust emissions of about 75 per cent from their 1989 level.

With current technology, the volume of SO_2 emitted is proportional to lead output. Following the cut in production, the plant was reportedly able to meet the Bulgarian ambient SO_2 standard for old plants. There was little the enterprise could do to stop SO_2 emissions altogether, as it lacked the finance (up to $90 million) for appropriate new smelting technology.

For the plant, the advent of the free market in Bulgaria has been both a threat and a potential saviour. Though the enterprise was profitable in 1989 (under the communist accounting system then in force), its old technology meant that its costs were already above the level of its Western competitors. Rather than close, the managers used their new freedom to invest enterprise funds to forestall closure and to look for a foreign investor.

Sources [1]Environment Strategy Study, World Bank, November 1991; [2]WHO Air Quality guidelines for Europe (1987)

components to the clean privately owned part. In this case, the Western investor was neither responsible for the payment of user fees for water, nor for emission charges nor for fines.[21] These state-sanctioned ruses all meant the Western company did not have to take on the liability for past contamination. Indeed, with the investment famine, buyers were able to pick and choose which parts of factories they wanted, potentially leaving the state treasury or municipality with 'nothing but cleanup obligations'.[22] Governments would have preferred to ignore the issue of site contamination, but ultimately either by agreement or default they usually had to accept liability. (See Chapter 6 for a fuller analysis of this issue.)

In one of the few detailed research studies on the impact of privatization on the environment, Wojciech Stodulski of Warsaw's Institute for Sustainable Development interviewed ten (of Poland's 49) voivodeship environmental departments on the impact of privatization through liquidation. Up to early 1992, Poland had 550 such 'restructured' companies. His preliminary findings included their unwillingness to pay outstanding environmental charges and fines, their lack of interest in environmental restructuring ('many of them prepared unrealistic investment projects', he concluded), their attempts to keep secret their environmental licences or administrative *decyzja* and their refusal to take over the liabilities arising from past contamination of the site.[23]

Bankruptcy (one consequence of privatization) left the responsibility for clean-up unresolved. In Rzeszów in south-east Poland, to take one extreme case, the Polam lighting factory, which was on the list of 80, was liquidated in 1989. It is reported to have bequeathed the local population a dump of broken fluorescent tubes containing mercury, which was both being vaporized into the atmosphere and leached by acid rain into the ground, according to Piotr Rymanowicz of the polemic magazine *Green Brigades*. Neither the local authority nor the Ministry of Industry had the funds to decontaminate the site.

Market prices for raw materials

Charging market prices for raw materials was seen as another essential condition for environmental restructuring. As it was perceived as relatively straightforward, it was usually one of the new governments' first reforms. Its main impact was expected to be on air pollution. The World Bank estimated that energy subsidies in the late 1980s cost the governments of the USSR and East and Central Europe some \$180 billion a year. More than half the region's air pollution was 'attributable to these distortions'.[24]

Price increases 'provide incentives for energy conservation in all sectors of the economy, leading to substantial reductions in emissions of pollutants ... in addition to their general economic merits', said the World Bank's Eugenio Lari. He was then more specific: 'We have calculated that energy price reform could bring down particulate levels in air by almost 40 per cent in the next three to five years [and] almost 80 per cent by the end of the decade.'[25] This advice was followed. For example between the beginning of 1990 and late 1992, Polish lignite prices went up by about 400 per cent, compared with approximately double that for hard coal. Electricity supplied to industry also went up by nearly 800 per cent (see also Chapter 7).

In practice, the picture was significantly more complex than the World Bank models suggested. A tenth of electrical energy, a sixth of hard coal, a quarter of natural gas and a third of steam and hot water consumed in Poland was used by households where consumption was relatively inelastic. As most households were not able to switch off or regulate their supplies, or change their suppliers, higher prices were equivalent to a tax on energy use. Thus in Poland, while the move to market prices reduced industrial gas consumption (in line with production), it did not stop an increase in offtake by local authorities and households, according to the Central Planning Office.[26]

Though many other raw materials were also subsidized, the impact of market prices on water discharges and the accumulation of solid waste was not expected to be as large as on air pollution. Nevertheless, in certain specific cases, it was believed they could help improve efficiency. For instance, some three-quarters of Bulgaria's expenditure on water irrigation came from the budget of the Ministry of Agriculture and only a quarter from the agricultural complexes, which had direct contracts with the state irrigation enterprises. The latter payments underestimated the real cost, because the energy used by them was heavily subsidized. 'If Bulgaria used world energy prices as the basis to charge [for] its irrigation water, users would be asked to pay about 100 times what they pay now for water', commented the country's environmental strategy study.[27]

In 1991, as the government in Sofia could no longer afford to pay for its higher market priced coal imports, electrical power production was below requirement. The Varna thermal power station, the most modern in Bulgaria, consequently was only operating at 40 per cent capacity. Hence some two-thirds of heavy industry could run at only half capacity. This meant on the one hand lower pollution from industry and from energy generation. On the other hand, it meant that Kozloduy nuclear power station, one of the most dangerous in the region, could not be closed (see Box 5.2).

Hard budget constraints

The enforcement by governments of hard budget constraints was expected to close older less efficient operations, many of which were also substantial polluters. Though thousands of plants have been forced into bankruptcy, few were large polluters. The reasons paradoxically were either because they were so old they did not have to cover the cost of

Box 5.2   *Kozloduy nuclear power plant, Bulgaria*

Kozloduy, which is on the river Danube, consists of six pressurized water reactors with a total theoretical capacity of 3,760 MW. It began to generate electrical power in the mid-1970s. Since then, though it has had two serious accidents and a number of smaller mechanical failures, it could not be closed because it supplied Bulgaria with some 40 per cent of its electricity.

A further 10 per cent of Bulgaria's electricity was imported. The domestic coal mines have a high sulphur and ash content. More efficient methods of power production, distribution and use were the obvious answer but they required fresh capital and decisive government action.

Though Bulgaria joined the International Atomic Energy Authority (IAEA) in 1988, it was only in 1990 that it carried out its first survey. A second survey took place in spring 1991. The report of the inspectors is said to have indicated that it was 'imprudent to continue operations' unless 'severe safety deficiencies' were corrected in the first four units. Equipment was in need of repair and the local engineers needed training, as most of the power station's ex-Soviet advisers had returned home. There was, said the IAEA, 'a big danger that emergency systems would fail', if they were called upon.[1]

Ideally units 1–4, which were built between 1969 and 1974, should be decommissioned as soon as possible. Constructing containment and other facilities would be expensive (some estimates put the total figure at $1 billion). As a stopgap measure in July 1991, the EC committed $14 million for emergency repairs to switches and wiring to unit 2, and to the training of personnel. Germany also agreed to send spare parts (worth $11 million) and technicians from the idled Greifswald nuclear power station in former East Germany. Some $4 million in emergency aid from the EC followed under the Phare programme in 1992.

Source [1]'Nuclear perils in eastern Europe', *The Economist*, 27 July 1991

---

depreciation, or because they were major employers and could not be allowed to close for social reasons.

In the regional metals industry for instance, while several non-ferrous plants closed or switched to processing scrap, over 30 smelters kept operating as before. Of these over a dozen were listed as major regional sources of air pollution.[28] Most of the copper, lead or zinc units emitted sulphur dioxide and/or heavy metals, while the aluminium smelters, besides being heavy energy users, emitted fluorine. In addition, many were major sources of solid waste.

Eastern Germany's only alumina refinery at Lauta closed in September

1990: it had been built in 1916; much of the equipment was old, the price of electricity had reportedly tripled; and the supply of cheap raw materials dried up. The bauxite – the raw material for aluminium – could no longer be imported from Hungary for transferable roubles. The country's copper mines and the associated smelter at Helbra were in addition closed just after unification, and since then the other copper smelter at Mansfeld has processed only scrap. In Bulgaria, the Plovdiv lead smelter cut back production in the early 1990s. In Poland, parts of the country's lead and zinc industry was under risk because of the high costs: already in 1990 the older smelting furnace at Miasteczko Slaskie near Tarnowskie Góry in Upper Silesia was shut due to its low efficiency, high costs and air emissions.

A number of those that kept going were dangerous. In the words of *The Sunday Times*, the inhabitants of the villages around Glogów, the site of one of Poland's two obsolete copper smelters, suffered from 'chronic "metal fever", streaming eyes, assorted breathing complications, dizziness [and] fatigue. As well as airborne gas and coppery powder, they were living among slag hills of 30–50 per cent lead dust'.[29]

On the ferrous side, the situation was similar: only a few of the region's 100 iron and steel works had closed. If hard budget constraints had been ruthlessly applied, market forces would have probably shut down some two-thirds to three-quarters. The steel industry, having been at the centre of the command economy, found it particularly hard to adjust to market pricing (see Box 5.3); but in this respect, it was little different from steel industry in the European Community.

Limited investment for modernization

Just as hard budget constraints closed only a few of those plants it was expected to close, the lack of investment failed either to generate fundamental improvements in existing units or to replace them with new industrial activities. Other than in eastern Germany, the total supply of funds from governments, the enterprises themselves, domestic and foreign investors and aid agencies was quite insufficient to meet the environmental changes needed.

For instance in steel, to bring the region's 20–30 or so potentially viable steel mills up to world standards would have required at least $25 billion.[30] It was not available, so the plants were neither revamped nor closed. For instance in the spring of 1990 *The Economist* described Hungary's Ozd iron and steel company (Ostag) as 'a profit-making venture', with a product line 'to suit western tastes' and 'happy' workers and managers.[31] A year later, Germany's Metallgesellschaft and Korf which had invested in

Box 5.3 *Huta Bobrek, Poland*

The emissions from the Bobrek steel works, which was situated in a high population density urban area, included sulphur dioxide, nitrogen oxides, heavy metals, and suspended particulates. The works was on the list of the worst 80 polluters in the country.

Consequently it was told to close down the two principal offending sections – the coking and sintering units – by the end of 1990. As it refused, the voivodeship environmental office in Katowice in January 1991 imposed an administrative *decyzja* limiting its air emissions to zero. To stall the process of closure, the directors appealed to the country's highest court on two grounds – that industry was in general more important than the environment and that the works had not been proven guilty with detailed measurements of its emissions. The court's determination was a legal precedent. Bobrek was told to accept the *decyzja* on the grounds that everyone knew that Silesia was extremely polluted, and as such exact measurements of emissions were not necessary.

Soon after the judgment, the smelter began to see itself as a scapegoat. Its attitude hardened. To try to resolve the issue, the voivodeship called a meeting of all interested parties at which the factory was told to prepare a restructuring plan which included the closure of the coking and sintering plants. After two months, it came up with 14 possible restructuring plans, all depending on revenues from one or other or both the plants which had to be closed. Neither the smelter nor its founding agency, the Ministry of Industry, had any reserves to fund a restructuring plan.

In late summer 1991, Bobrek reversed its position. It discovered that as many of Poland's other iron and steel works were in a similar position, the first to liquidate might receive special assistance in restructuring. However, when a commission from Warsaw eventually examined its proposal in December, it was after the inconclusive parliamentary elections of that autumn.

While the old Liberal Democrat Minister of Industry had been willing to see Bobrek's immediate closure, the new incoming Christian Democrat Minister was not. His decision in early 1992 was for all the polluting sections of the plant to remain open to mid-1993, so as to earn a surplus to help pay off the plant's debts. Many suspected that as unemployment rose, a further lease of life would be given.

the plant withdrew, apparently for commercial reasons. The Hungarians still list it as one of their 14 major sources of air pollution.

The total restructuring costs for Poland's steel industry were estimated in 1992 at $4.5 billion over ten years. Of this $2 billion was expected to come from outside funding agencies such as the World Bank and the European Coal and Steel Community (ECSC), and the balance from the industry itself. Yet two-thirds of the country's mills were said to be in the red and the rest borderline. They included Huta Warszawa, which lost $25 million in the first six months of 1992. But, riding on the back of Fiat's investment in the Polish car industry and its need for steel, Italy's Lucchini bought it in 1992. Both the EBRD and European Coal and Steel Community (ECSC) helped finance the deal.

Where concerns were under pressure to curb emissions, few, if any, considered clean production; at best they were likely to install end-of-pipe technology. Whereas clean production technology involves restructuring the production process (so as to use sustainable resources, and avoid toxic waste and hazardous inputs and products), end-of-pipe technology reduces pollution without fundamentally altering the production process. It does this by using filters, scrubbers, high stacks and the like. This was true for both state and private concerns.

For an environmental conference in the USA in April 1991, Promasz, a Warsaw-based consulting firm, catalogued 100 industrial and municipal projects needing foreign investment to reduce environmental damage: 49 projects were for atmospheric protection, mainly flue gas desulphurization or fluid bed boilers, 30 for water protection; and 21 for incineration/ waste utilization. Most were end-of-pipe.[32] This was of course quite contrary to the government's stated policy. In late 1991, Tomasz Zylicz of the Ministry of Environment said, 'It will be the role of our [Poland's] policy instruments to ensure that the growing [environmental] expenditures are cost-effective and favour process integrated changes, while keeping end-of-pipe solutions to the necessary minimum. Emission charges and the funds they feed into, should help achieve this goal'.[33]

Even though the investment costs were limited (typically $5–50 million per project), after 12 months, the Ministry of Environment believed that only one or two of the projects had found favour with foreign investors.[34] A fuller report outlining myriad business opportunities for Western firms in the environmental arena published a year later met the same response.[35]

Allied Signal is a US multinational active in the chemicals industry. According to Jonathan Plaut, its Director of Environmental Compliance, the policy for investors in Central and Eastern Europe should be to do 'that which can be fixed over time', but 'that which is too expensive to fix, discard as soon as practicable'. But, he added in an aside at the meeting he was addressing, this may be 'very hard to do'.[36] This comment would seem to have implied that if it was too costly to fix using end-of-pipe methods, the pragmatic policy was to do nothing.

The problem of attracting investment, even for end-of-pipe investment, was highlighted by lack of growth in the number of filters in operation. Between 1989 and 1991, the number of plants in Poland equipped with air pollution control equipment did not change. The number with cyclones rose from 6,928 to 6,959, while those with wet units fell from 2,678 to 2,650.

There were one or two exceptions, where companies were interested in environmentally beneficial products. Denmark's Danfoss Gruppen opened a subsidiary for the manufacture of domestic radiator thermostats in Warsaw in late 1991. Legal changes in Poland in the middle of that year required all new and renovated properties to include individual thermostats on the radiators. As the production line was automated, the new company needed, however, only 40 workers including sales staff in Warsaw.[37] Also in Poland, during 1992, the Swiss–Swedish engineering multinational ABB tried to buy Rafako, the country's leading boiler maker. Its NFEP-supported development work on energy-efficient and clean boilers was said to have made it a market leader; in early 1993, it was 'thwarted by a worker and management buy out'.[38] In Bohemia, a Czech company Dobra Voda began in 1992 producing bottled drinking water at half the price of imported water. At first it wanted a foreign partner, but their conditions were too steep, according to Vaclav Benedikt, the company's director. They all wanted to own it. So the Czechs went their own way and took 70 per cent of the Czech bottled water market.[39]

Environmentally targeted investments

The sums needed for investment in environmental recovery were massive. Few estimates were made, because it was never clear exactly what needed to be done. The EBRD reportedly puts the figure at about $300 billion over the next 15–20 years.[40] However, on the basis of guesstimates from reliable sources within the region, it would seem the cost of bringing its industry and agriculture up to a reasonable environmental level could be as much as $600 billion, plus or minus $100 billion, over 20 or so years. This was approximately a fifth of the total investment needed (see Chapter 4).

Ball-park Polish estimates to establish and maintain a moderately clean physical environment ranged from $60 to $260 billion. One report from the Ministry of Environmental Protection said the country would have to spend annually some 4–5 per cent of its national income on environmental protection over 20 years 'in order to make up for lost time'.[41] This was equivalent to approximately $60 billion or $3 billion a year at current prices. In contrast, the country's national policy document said in 1990 that 'the implementation of the long term strategy of environmental protection requires inputs assessed at the level of $260 billion', but added that 'this figure also contains the cost of the desired change in the structure of the economy and the switch to environmentally safe technologies'.[42] Knowledgeable Poles said that the best estimate was $100–150 billion. An official estimate for Eastern Germany of DM220 billion[43] (equivalent to about $140 billion) was in the same range, as was the $50–100 billion World Bank estimate for the Czech Republic and Slovakia.[44] The rest was to be divided between Albania, Bulgaria, Hungary, Romania, and ex-Yugoslavia.

In terms of industries, half this sum ($250–350 billion) was estimated for restructuring the energy sector. This included building small district heating plants and renewing others, reducing the leakages of hot water and air emissions, installing safeguards at nuclear power stations where they could not be dismantled immediately, coal cleaning and flue gas desulphurization. Renewable energy and improved building insulation were barely ever mentioned, but were critical (see Chapter 7). Other important areas included water protection and cleansing, and providing for solid waste, each of which could require $100 billion or more. Table 5.4 intuitively breaks down the regional total into its major sectoral components.

The estimates are subject to a margin of error. The cost of revamping an enterprise is much higher than new build so that, depending on how much of an economy is actually retained and restructured, the figures could change. Some studies have shown that pollution control equipment retrofitted to a coal fired power station could add 45 per cent to the capital cost and 30 per cent to the operating cost. By integrating the changes into a design stage, the totals were only half this.[45]

In Germany, in late 1992, Bayer committed itself to investing $500 million in new projects in the Bitterfeld industrial park, which the

Table 5.4 *Intuitive breakdown of forecast requirements for environmental improvements in Central and Eastern Europe over the next 20 years*

	$ billion
Energy (mostly to combat air pollution), of which	250–350
Revamping district and local heating plants	50–100
Safeguards at nuclear power plants	5–15
Flue gas desulphurization	50–75
Building insulation	75–125
Developing renewable energy sources	1
Arresting and controlling water pollution	150–200
Providing for solid and municipal waste, of which	100–150
Land reclamation	25–50
Protection/use of natural resources	25–50
Total	500–700

Treuhand had prepared at a cost of $60 million, including $30 million in clean-up costs. The park was adjacent to the old Chemie Bitterfeld-Wolfen site, still owned by the Treuhand. In March 1993, the federal government agreed to spend $9 billion over five years in cleaning up this part of Germany. Such figures were in stark contrast with expenditure elsewhere in the region. For instance, total Polish environmental expenditure (again public and private) in 1991 was less than the billion dollars which government sources had claimed had been budgeted and well below the $3–5 billion or so which it said should have been spent.

Insufficient foreign aid

In the early 1990s, total external aid allocated for environmental recovery was approximately $3 billion. It was a rag-bag of dimes and cents, as Table 5.5 shows. To end 1992, actually approved credits and grants were around $1.5 billion, and those under negotiation $1.3 billion. In addition there were various regional programmes (around $100 million) and a nuclear safety fund, which also covered the former USSR. The target for the latter was $700 million, but less than 10 per cent of this had been raised by the second quarter of 1993.

By end 1992, disbursements were probably under $250 million. Moreover as most of the loans were not expected to be actually disbursed until the mid-1990s, the real contribution from the international community to the process of environmental recovery was probably less than $1 billion a year. Spread over a land area twice the size of France, with more than twice its population, but only a third of its GDP per head, the impact was not expected to be fundamental. It was also overshadowed by domestically generated finance, which in the early 1990s was the origin of 85–90 per cent of total environmental expenditure.

Conspicuous by its absence in the initial years was the EBRD. This was in spite of the importance it had originally said it would give environmental issues. To end 1992, it had granted funds for only two small energy projects – a $50 million loan for the rehabilitation of district heating in five Polish cities (with $340 million from the World Bank) and another of roughly the same size for the completion and FGD upgrading of the Maritza coal-fired power station in Bulgaria. By this date, none of the allocated finance had been disbursed. Further environmental loans totalling over $300 million were however scheduled to be approved in the first half of 1993. These also focused on energy, though around $20 million was due to be provided for waste water treatment in Gdańsk and $2 million for the Danube delta.

In addition, over this period the Bank financed around 25 small

Table 5.5 *Allocated and anticipated foreign environmental aid to Central and Eastern Europe, 1990–2 ($ million, approximate)*

Country/sector	EBRD	World Bank[1]	EC/EIB	Bilat/Other	Total
Albania					
Water		10.0*			
Energy		10.0*			
Other	+				
Total		20.0			20.0
Bulgaria					
Air/monitoring			3.5		
Water/sewage		100.0*	6.6		
Energy	50.0	93.0*	10.0[4]		
Other			2.0		
Total	50.0	193.0	22.1		265.1
Ex-Czechoslovakia					
Air/monitoring		na[2]		3.2	
Water/sewage		na[2]	7.2	3.0	
Energy		396.0*	10.0[4]	0.7	
Waste			7.0	49.5	
Other		150.0*	6.1	1.3	
Total		546.0	30.3	57.7	634.0
Hungary					
Air/monitoring			16.6		
Water/sewage			3.6	0.6	
Energy		150.0*	6.4[4]	0.3	
Transport			2.0	0.3	
Waste			3.0	1.2	
Other			13.4	2.2	
Total		150.0	45.0	4.6	199.6
Poland					
Air/monitoring		na[2]	12.4	28.0	
Water/sewage		80.0*	14.2	27.4	
Energy	50.0	590.0	31.3[4]	94.2	
Waste			11.4	6.4	
Forestry		154.5*		0.6	
Transport		153.0		0.3	
Other		18.0		1.8	
Total	50.0	995.5	89.7	158.7	1,293.9
Romania					
Water/sewage		100.0*		0.7	
Energy		320.0*	20.0[4]		
Other		na[3]	2.4	0.6	
Total		420.0	22.4	1.3	443.7
All countries					
Air/monitoring	–	–	32.5	31.2	63.7
Water/sewage	–	290.0	31.6	31.7	353.3
Energy	100.0	1,559.0	77.7	95.2	1,831.9
Other	–	475.5	67.7	64.2	607.4
Total	100.0	2,324.5	209.5	222.3	2,856.3

Notes +less than 0.1; *part or all not approved yet; [1]including GEF/Global Environmental Facility; [2]part of a World Bank structural adjustment loan – exact figures not available; [3]exact figure not available: part of a World Bank loan (June 1991) covering the cost of vital imports; [4]includes a nominal figure for the EIB

Sources EC, Phare programme, World Bank annual reports, EBRD annual report, Development Business, EIB, and report from Polish Ministry of Environmental Protection on foreign assistance technical cooperation projects with a significant environmental component. Examples included the assessment of the D5 motorway in Czechoslovakia (value $170,000), the Warsaw public transport study ($300,000) and a $185,000 study on Sofia's waste water.

The World Bank's contribution was more diffuse and potentially larger, though it too was said to be slow in making disbursements. One exception was an $18 million loan for environmental management in Katowice and Legnica, made in 1990 (see Chapter 6). In 1991, a Structural Adjustment Loan made to Czechoslovakia had an important $100 million-plus environmental component, requiring the governments to introduce a range of economic instruments and public participation in environmental decision-making.

The other important concern of the World Bank was energy. In 1992, it loaned $246 million to the Czech Republic for a $560 million project to improve efficiency and reduce emissions at the lignite-fuelled Prunerov II power station in northern Bohemia. Of the total credit, $140 was for FGD and $70 million for the reduction in particulate emissions in the region. In 1990, Prunerov II was the Czech Republic's largest emitter of sulphur dioxide and the second largest of nitrogen oxides.

The nuclear reactors in Bulgaria and Slovakia, which were in some ways more threatening than belching power stations, also received minimal help in the early 1990s. Eventually, after years of wrangling, an international fund for nuclear safety in the former USSR and Central and Eastern Europe was announced in early 1993. It was to be administered by the EBRD.

In contrast, the EC's Phare programme consciously selected a wide spread of mostly small technical projects in its first phase in Poland (1990): these included air and water protection, waste management and nature conservation. The second phase for Poland, Hungary and to a lesser extent Czechoslovakia (1990/1) was more focused, but again soft, reflecting contemporary government priorities. Bulgaria and Romania were also involved at this time. Phase 3 projects for Poland and Hungary were expected to supplement the national environmental funds. Total monies allocated for the environment between 1990 and 1992 were around $320 million, according to EC sources.

The main bilateral donors were Austria, Denmark, the Netherlands, Norway, Sweden and the USA. Their aid was the most varied, perhaps because it tended to reflect the needs of their locally headquartered multinationals and/or the countries' own priorities. In a rare instance of direct criticism of the way in which external demands sometimes dominated, a background paper prepared by World Bank staff noted that CEE governments within the region were 'being pressured to use scarce financial resources (and in some cases loans) to pay for *Western firms* to clean up pollution sources, which affect *Western countries*. This [was] particularly the case with regard to reductions of SO_2 emissions' (their italics).[46]

For instance in and around Krakow, the US Agency for International Development (USAID) funded a number of research projects, the results of which were then made available to US-based firms looking to invest in Poland. Sweden and Denmark tended to support Polish projects linked to the Baltic. The US delay in agreeing to the multilateral fund for nuclear safety was thought to reflect its desire to give direct support to US nuclear engineering companies.

Such criticisms could be extended to multilateral aid. It would seem that some of the latter was intended to support Western companies, in some cases directly, and in others indirectly by not funding projects which would enable the region to compete with or leapfrog the West. For example, only a small proportion of aid has gone on restructuring heavy industry, which would then compete with hard-pressed EC firms. Clean technologies have also been bypassed. For instance out of the $250 million in aid supplied to Poland bilaterally and from the EC, up to mid-1992 only five of the 140 or so projects, all funded by Denmark, with a total value of $1.6 million, were described as supporting renewable energy or clean or cleaner technology.

For similar reasons few Western credits or grants were made to support the development of indigenous technology or its transfer from the West. There were several exceptions. One was the Gravimelt process, which involved the chemical cleaning of brown coal to remove sulphur, ash and toxic heavy metals before combustion. Reportedly the feasibility study was partly funded by the Norwegian government. Fears have been raised though that the process was not as environmentally benign as the Norwegian backers and US developers claimed, at least partly because it involved highly corrosive chemicals. This may turn out to be one of the reasons why it was to be piloted in the Czech Republic and not in the West.

Another exception was the support given by Phare (and the NFEP) to Rafako in south-west Poland for the production of FGD equipment and fluidized bed boilers. Meanwhile in Eastern Germany, the Treuhand assisted Foron (formerly known as DKK Scharfenstein) to begin manufacturing fridges which do not use CFCs in early 1993. Initially the enterprise met opposition from the traditional German white goods industry, which apparently believed that the new model challenged its chosen technical path for the next generation of fridges. Yet a buyer for the factory was eventually found by the Treuhand and the fridge has since been shown to be efficient, safe and cost effective.

One small hope for the future was the Global Environmental Facility

(GEF). In December 1991 it made its first grant ever, to Poland for $4.5 million for preserving biodiversity in the forests of Bialowieza and the Sudety mountains. The former was described by the Ministry of Environment as a 'pearl of nature',[47] and the latter as 'a tragedy', due to the damage from acid rain. Some 18 months later, the reason for the grant surfaced. The World Bank negotiated, with the same ministry, a $150 million loan for 'a programme of environmentally sound forest management'.[48] Polish opposition to the latter centred on the increased lumber production from Bialowieza, which for some parts of the public was equivalent to a national shrine.

In addition in 1993 the GEF was expected to grant $25 million to Poland for the conversion of a district heating system from coal to gas and $6 million to Romania and Ukraine for the conservation and management of the Danube delta. The World Bank was also the executing agency for two GEF projects sponsored by the UN Development Programme (UNDP) – $10 million for the Black Sea and $8.5 million for the sustainable management of the Danube river basin.

The narrowing and weakening of environmental legislation

Basic improvements in the physical environment also require tough and consistent legislation. Laws and rules needed to be drafted to take into account economic reality (but not to bow to it), and to focus on those sectors of economic activity which threatened the natural environment. In fact the opposite happened – at least in Poland: the ambit of official environmental involvement was slowly pushed back from addressing the failures of the market system to its traditional flora and fauna corner.

This was in line with Polish public opinion. 'According to the Public Opinion Research Centre, two thirds of the population living in areas that have experienced severe environmental degradation are against the closure of polluting plants or directing investment toward clean-up.' The official report on environmental business opportunities which mentioned this then added, paradoxically, that people 'prefer being poisoned slowly to losing their jobs and thus experiencing an immediate reduction in their income'.[49]

Such opinions were mirrored by government, which in the early 1990s downgraded the importance of the environment in its foreign investment policy. The 1988 law on economic activity involving foreign companies both disallowed foreign investment on certain environmental grounds, and gave investors who took special measures to protect the environment an extended tax holiday. Neither measure was included in the joint venture law which was passed in 1991, replacing that of the late '80s.

In 1991, Tom Kolaja from Poland's Ministry of Privatization, claimed that environmental issues were just not perceived as a priority for the strong ministries. By this he meant ministries such as finance, industry and privatization which are managing the process of economic change. Thus when the Polish Ministry of Environment tried to introduce an average 4 per cent *ad valorem* fuel charge, earmarked for environmental protection, the proposal met with almost unanimous opposition. The official opinion of Solidarity was typical: it read 'while the Union is for environmental protection, it will not approve any such burden laid on the impoverished society'.[50]

A Polish report for Global 2000, the Austrian NGO active in Central and Eastern Europe, noted that cross-sectoral economic issues were slowly removed from successive drafts of environmental policy in the early 1990s. In 1990, environmental guidelines on energy, industry and transport, water management and mining provoked such strong criticism from the other departments that they were either watered down or eliminated. The report commented that the process of developing environmental policy plans 'reflects the key problem with ... environmental policy: it is generally incompatible with the sectoral polices of other departments'.[51]

The growing hiatus between economic and environmental policy was also acknowledged by ministry officials of the Ministry of Environment. In the ten voivodeships in north and mid-east Poland, maintaining bio-diversity was part of the ministry's policy; the provinces represent 25 per cent of the land area of the country, but only 13 per cent of the population and 10 per cent of industrial output. In this part of the country 'There is a great risk that in the course of [the] desperate process of seeking development opportunities, many of the [area's] precious natural assets ... will be lost or irreversibly damaged', one official said in 1991.[52]

Nor was the law consistent. Table 5.6 shows the fluctuations in emission charges in Poland for four substances in the early 1990s. The charges were set by the Council of Ministers, and as its political composition changed so did its priorities. To force enterprises to install new technology, emission charges have to be maintained for a long period. For if there are any signs of weakness, businesses are likely to lobby hard for reductions to avoid investing. Indeed, in such a situation, most other firms will postpone investing until they are sure that the rules of the game are permanent. Those that have invested are put at a competitive disadvantage. In October 1992, it is known that at least one power station (Jaworzno III) publicly protested against the government's decision to reduce charges, apparently on the grounds that the investments it had already made were now worthless.

Whether economic instruments replaced or supplemented command and control methods was less of an issue than the need for tough

Table 5.6 *Polish charges for air emissions of lead, sulphur dioxide, benzene and fluorine, 1991–3 (zlotys and approximate $ values)*

Period	Application	Lead/kg	SO$_2$/kg	Benzene/kg	Fluorine/kg
1 Jan 1991– 31 Dec 1991	Full year	36,000	680	1,800	3,600
		($3.79)	($0.07)	($0.19)	($0.38)
1 Jan 1992– 31 Dec 1992	Announced end 1991; cancelled 14 Oct 1992	500,000 ($38.46)	1,100 ($0.08)	1,000,000 ($76.92)	3,000 ($0.23)
1 Jan 1992– 31 Dec 1992	New rates applied retroactively from Jan 92	50,000 ($3.85)	770 ($0.05)	100,000 ($7.69)	2,100 ($0.16)
1 Jan 1993– 31 Dec 1993	Not known	500,000 ($31.25)	1,100 ($0.07)	1,000,000 ($62.5)	3,000 ($0.19)

Sources *Ustaw Dziennik* (The Polish official journal) 21 December 1991 and 14 October 1992, and others

enforcement by a competent local ecological 'police'. The essence of its activity should have been effective inspection and monitoring, but it lacked competence and resources, while the businesses being policed were reluctant to acknowledge their responsibilities (see above and Chapter 6). The local authorities were not helped by the slothfulness of governments in revising environmental legislation, including the introduction of credible standards.

The retreat of environmental policy, and the excessively high standards inherited from communist days combined with lax implementation, increasingly left the region open to unscrupulous investors. For while the old ambient standards were generally stricter than in the EC, for a number of the pollutants monitoring was difficult if not impossible. This made an ass of the law. Moreover, in a political climate where the economy took priority over environmental health, the strict enforcement of the law was sometimes impossible. Stanislaw Sitnicki, a senior official in Poland's Ministry of Environment, maintained in late 1991 that 'enforcement was the weakest link in voivodeship management'.[53] He might have added that it was generally expected to remain so for many years.

REINFORCING OLD AND CREATING NEW THREATS

From a global point of view, the region is increasingly functioning as a market and low cost production centre for West European businesses. This section discusses the environmental implications of this. In the early 1990s, Western companies were able to entice governments with the carrot of additional jobs, or threaten them with alternative locations to establish economic and environmental privileges.

The difficulties of enforcing strict environmental legislation were recognized by everyone from the local business to the multinational. In a northern suburb of Warsaw, in the second half of 1991, local businesses made an informal agreement not to complain to the authorities about the environmental impact of the new trades being started by one another. The principle was to give everyone a commercial chance. But this meant that the first few firms to establish themselves benefited most. As a result, the ex-teacher who wanted to start a small organic farm in his garden and a vegetable stall to sell the produce was not able to do so because of the spray and fumes from the nearby car repair shop.

In November 1991, East European governments and multinational companies at a conference in Budapest discussed a set of Guiding Principles on the Environment, Industry and Investment Decisions in Central and Eastern Europe. The draft preamble to the principles put the burden of responsibility on the foreign investor, because of the weakness of the governments. 'Industry and investors have therefore a special duty to act in an environmentally responsible way in their dealings with Central and Eastern Europe. Precisely because the necessary legislative and societal framework is not yet in place to achieve effective environmental protection and improvements, businessmen must seek to pursue standards no less protective of public health and the environment than they would expect to see applied in their own countries.'

A Western lifestyle

For those with money, the quiet revolutions meant a more acquisitive lifestyle. Economic reform whetted their appetite for consumer goods and services, either Western in origin or in apparent style. The situation was put more philosophically by Stefan Kozlowski, Poland's Minister of Environment in early 1992. He said 'Mindless fascination with the western way of life and economic model may lead to an artificial and unwarranted rise in the consumption of goods that are of little worth and use. Consumption is by nature hostile to the environment and in the long run poses a threat to human civilization as a whole'.[54]

The rise in consumption resulted in more waste packaging, a decline in the proportion of waste recycled, and rising pressure on landfill sites. While figures from Poland's Ministry of Environment claimed that the volume of municipal solid waste declined in 1990 to 43 million cubic metres, from 46 million in 1989, other reports say it increased significantly over the period since 1989. For example, one Polish press report in late 1991, apparently quoting a Ministry of Health official, said that the volume of rubbish generated in the country had increased by 40 per cent since 1989 due to the import of foreign goods.[55] This has led to growing pressures for incineration and a rise in fly tipping (of old cars, television sets and other household waste) in peripheral urban areas.

A decline in recycling was due partly to the change in the materials used as containers. Western techniques of food processing and storage pushed out some of the more environmentally acceptable materials used in the past. For example, beer was increasingly canned, while milk was increasingly packaged in plastic bags and cartons, in contrast to the heavy (but reuseable) glass bottles or small milk churns of the past. Tetra Pak, the Swedish company specializing in the manufacture of non-returnable beverage packagings was 'one company taking advantage of the new Polish conditions'.[56] For the future, investment analysts Credit Suisse First Boston (CSFB) forecast an increase in packaging production in Central and Eastern Europe by 50 per cent over the decade to the year 2000. For example, it noted 'as competition is introduced and consumer choice becomes a reality, manufacturers will require more packaging and better packaging to increase the appeal of their products in the market place'.[57]

The waste collection systems of the past, which were motivated as much by national shortages of raw materials as by the prices paid, became much weaker under the free market. With trade barriers falling, the rise in supplies of paper from Germany undercut Polish prices. In Poland in early 1992, the price of scrap newspaper imported from Germany was zloty (zl) 700/tonne, while the price paid for old Polish newspaper was zl1,000/tonne.

Meanwhile escalating sales of consumer durables posed other threats. For example the rising number of washing machines in rural areas was not matched by waste water treatment capacity. This state of affairs, combined with the continuing production of phosphate-containing detergents by both indigenous enterprises and Western acquisitions, meant more nutrient-rich sewage flowing into the surrounding seas, none of which was tidal.

Vehicle ownership was an even greater problem. In the late 1980s, some three-quarters of freight travelled by rail; in the early 1990s, the pattern began to shift as private businesses sought the increased flexibility offered by private transport. In 1991, some 300,000 new and second-hand cars were imported into Poland. In Eastern Germany, the number of registered cars increased by nearly a million (some 23 per cent) in the first six months of union. In Hungary in 1992, the number of cars brought into the country increased by a factor of five to 75,000; some 80 per cent were over four years old. With the liberalization of imports, consumers strapped for cash in the deep recession, bought old second-hand diesel cars from Western Europe.

Table 5.7   *Air emissions from car engines in Poland, 1985–90*

Emissions (000 tonnes)	1985	1989	1990	1991
Carbon monoxide	1192	1380	1418	1470
Hydrocarbons	337	390	401	410
Nitrogen oxides	460	509	469	460
Dust etc	23	23	na	20
Lead	1.01	1.35	1.16	na

Source Table 92, 'Environmental Protection 1991'; Table 110, 'Environmental Protection 1992', Main Statistical Office, Warsaw

The consequence was a rise in some emission levels (see Table 5.7). Over the next ten years, one forecast has indicated that Polish emissions of nitrogen oxides from vehicles could rise by 100 per cent and those of carbon monoxide by 70 per cent.[58] It remains to be seen to what extent the introduction of stringent regulations on car testing (including exhausts) in Hungary and Czechoslovakia will reverse this trend. They clearly had not begun to work by February 1993, when Prague and parts of northern Bohemia were hit by one of the worst smogs in a decade.

Western car companies were the largest investors in Eastern Germany, Czechoslovakia, Hungary and Poland: their initial goal was to gain market access for their brands. But with rising imports, sales were low. For example, General Motors sold only 2,200 cars in Hungary in 1991. Nevertheless, the companies seemed likely to maintain their presence in the region, for with car ownership at a half to a third of Western levels (see Table 5.8), they expected a major increase in sales in the medium term. The impact was likely to be felt, as in the West, in both the declining usefulness of the region's generally good public transport sys-

Table 5.8   *Car ownership per 1,000 population in 1980, 1989 and 1990 in selected countries*

	1980	1989	1990
Ex-Czechoslovakia	149	199	na
Ex-East Germany	160	234	na
Hungary	94	164	184
Poland	67	127	138
West Germany	388	480	384*
Great Britain	277	366	383
Ex-Yugoslavia	108	140	147
USA	598	643	na

Notes *including former GDR

Sources *Polish Statistical Yearbooks*, 1991 and 1992, using figures from the Annual Bulletin of Transport Statistics for Europe, UN

tem and increased environmental degradation, especially in towns.

The vehicle manufacturers were followed by the oil companies. The comment of one of Esso's senior executives summarizes the view of many Western companies: 'The density and quality [of the retail petrol networks] are totally inadequate even for today's demand. To use this one-time opportunity to enter a new market and offer to customers the services which they deserve for their good money is a temptation no major oil company can resist.'[59]

Environmental cost advantages

The environmental advantages, in cost terms, of an East or Central European location for a business were sometimes considerable. They included unspoilt landscapes, and relatively cheap electricity (see Box 5.4 on the Ziar nad Hronom aluminium smelter), weak monitoring of environmental rules and easy waste disposal. Of course these points often supplemented the advantage of labour costs which were only 10 per cent of those in Germany.

How valuable these were for a business depended on its sphere of activities and specific requirements. For most, there were few gains because of their need for a specific mix of machinery and skills to produce the appropriate quality product. For a few existing concerns and foreign investors, however, the increased margins were potentially substantial.

In 1990, the US-financed Tatra Development Corporation announced it wanted to develop a large tourist complex in the unspoilt Tatra mountains in the north of Slovakia. Planned investment was over $100 million. Negotiations between the company and the government were led by a Slovak emigrant to the USA, who was also an adviser to the Prime Minister. After a delegation had visited the States, an initial agreement was signed by senior Slovak officials. However, opposition from SZOPK (the Slovak Union of Nature and Landscape Protectors) led to a parliamentary commission investigating the affair and eventually deciding that the initial agreement was invalid.

In late 1992, a US consortium led by Atlantic Partners, and apparently involving consultants PlanEcon and Waste Management International, attempted to buy and demolish the Czech village of Chabarovice in northern Bohemia. In its place, they proposed a new village nearby, a 'model non-polluting brown coal mine', and a processing plant to produce clean-burning briquettes from the estimated 100 million tonnes of brown coal under the village. The consortium also offered to clean up a nearby toxic dump. The 400 villagers rejected the offer in late 1992.[60]

A few smaller and medium-sized foreign companies, less scrupulous than the multinationals, set up joint ventures in country towns, for the

Box 5.4   *Ziar nad Hronom aluminium smelter, Slovakia*

The Ziar nad Hronom smelter, together with its main electricity supplier, the Novaky power station, were among the top five air polluters in Slovakia. The smelter emitted fluorine while the power plant, which burns brown coal, emitted sulphur dioxide, suspended particulates and heavy metals. The fluorine is reported to have increased the incidence of allergies, bronchitis, immunity disorders and cancer among local children.

Smelter modernization and increased production capacity at a cost of around $200 million were agreed by the Slovak government in May 1991. The reasons advanced include a reduction in fluorine emissions and an improvement in profitability. The revamping was due to start in 1993 and finish by 1995.

Financing the project was difficult. The government agreed to pay interest on a loan from a Bratislava bank, as the result of a strike in 1991 demanding government support. Potential investors reportedly included Norsk Hydro, Norway's state-owned aluminium company and Marc Rich, one of the world's largest trading conglomerates. Their agreement was said to be dependent on a guarantee from the Slovak government that the cost of electricity would not rise above 3.5 US cents/kwh for ten years. Higher power costs would cancel out the advantage of low labour costs. The Western world average was about 2 US cents/kwh.

The Slovak Green Party said the modernization would not solve the environmental problem, but rather limit it. The Slovak Union of Nature and Landscape Protectors mounted an inconclusive campaign against the investment, writing to Gro Harlem Bruntland, then Norway's prime minister. It argued against the investment on economic grounds. It said that any agreement with Norsk Hydro would 'present both an economic and ecological nightmare for Slovakia ... Other than a temporary cheap labour force, Slovakia offers no competitive advantage for producing aluminium. Czechoslovakia imports all its bauxite from abroad. More importantly, aluminium manufacturing is one of the most electricity-intensive industries'.

In early 1992, the enterprise, in response to these criticisms, said (in a letter to the author) that talks with foreign investors were continuing and that when the modernization and expansion were complete, the 'new smelter will be the cleanest in the world'.

production of food, furniture, timber or chemicals. According to Wojciech Stodulski, they chose such locations because the enforcement of environmental legislation was much weaker there than in the cities. One example he cited was a Dutch company which imported shrimps into Poland, where they were cleansed and then either frozen or canned before being re-exported. The company chose the north-east of Poland, as unemployment there was high and the environmental controls on dumping the process waste in the sea were low.[61]

In the long term inefficient polluters were expected to close, but in the short term the situation was less clear cut. While the steel mills in Hungary and chemical plants in Bulgaria might be inefficient by Western standards, they had 'a significant comparative advantage',[62] over those in the other countries of Central and Eastern Europe, according to the staff of the World Bank. (The same was true too for the Košiče steel works, which was one of the main sources of the 400 per cent increase in exports of Czechoslovak steel tubes to Germany in the first half of 1992 and which was high on the list of Slovakia's main polluters).

In other words, such operations were expected to contract less than others in the region, 'so that the fall in total emissions may be less than might be expected from the decline in total industrial output'.[63] In some cases the emissions from those plants might even increase. Commenting on the steel and machinery industries at around this time, Eugenio Lari of the World Bank spoke of 'an increase in potentially harmful dust emissions until such time as better environmental controls become economically worthwhile'.[64] In addition, food processing, wood products, and paper, 'all significant sources of water pollution',[65] were expected to expand.

Tomasz Zylicz, at one time an adviser to Poland's Minister of Environment, noted: 'This paradox can be explained in terms of lack of abatement equipment in the existing industries, whose output is most likely to expand in response to market stimuli, before [the] environmental authorities have even an opportunity to react.'[66]

The waste trade

In economic terms, the waste trade was another illustration of foreign firms taking advantage of the region's lower costs, in this case the lax implementation of environmental regulations. This was true whether the waste was processed (recycled), burnt or dumped. In the late 1980s, as Poland opened up to the West, low-penalty environmental rules almost made the country into the dustbin of Europe. This was documented in the Greenpeace report *Poland, the Waste Invasion*, which said 'Complete plants for incinerating waste and "recycling" used oil have been offered free, on condition that the plants accept imports, and [the] residues from these processes necessarily remain in Poland'.[67] Greenpeace was against waste incineration on the grounds that it removed the most powerful incentive for clean production, and sometimes produced compounds more toxic and persistent in the environment than the original waste.

The absolute ban on waste imports, which was introduced in Poland in mid-1989 was not initially effective. It took the Greenpeace report to make the Poles aware of the way in which their environment was being used. However, it created particular problems for the copper industry, which as an extractive industry had close links with the Ministry of Environment and Natural Resources. Sulphite lye, a waste product from the pulp and paper industry, was an 'essential' raw material for the copper industry. Without it, short-term refined copper production would have fallen by as much as 40 per cent and, as refined copper was one of Poland's major foreign currency earners, the industry made a strong economic case for its import. The minister at the time, Maciej Nowicki, eventually had to deny the lye was waste, for it to be allowed in. Some 96,000 tonnes were imported in 1990 and 80,000 tonnes in 1991. The lye however played a role in the country's continuing environmental degradation, for the two smelters which needed it employed obsolete technology and were on the list of 80. If they had been modernized, the lye would not have been needed.

The ban also played havoc with the paper industry. In spring 1992, the new minister, Stefan Kozlowski, gave once-off permission for 50,000 tonnes of waste paper to be imported. The reason was said to be economic – without the waste paper it was claimed that several of Poland's paper mills would have to close. As further imports would have made the 1989 law irrelevant, a new less rigid law was introduced into the Sejm or Polish parliament in spring 1992 and passed in early 1993.

This provided for the import of secondary raw materials if there was insufficient in Poland and if the factory was able to process it safely without aggravating environmental problems. The beneficiaries were expected to be not only the paper industry, but also Huta Warszawa, which was a major processor of steel scrap and the only steel mill in Poland to attract a foreign investor.

Toxic and hazardous waste imports were to remain officially banned, though Greenpeace's Iza Kruszewska believed this would be impossible to enforce. Polish customs officers have no powers to sample incoming goods and have been told just to go by the freight docket, she said. Moreover, whilst the absolute ban was in force, the Polish border services department believes it only managed to stop some 80 per cent of waste that could have been imported. In 1991 nearly 50 transporters of harmful materials were turned back at the border, according to Tadeusz Hadys, chemicals specialist at the department's headquarters. In 1992, an estimated 200 waste import shipments were thwarted.

After the 1989 law was passed, foreign companies began to offer incinerators for domestic municipal waste only. The Promasz catalogue mentioned earlier (page 85), produced for the government in April 1991, listed ten. In spring 1993, Greenpeace recorded 30 proposals and, though not all were expected to go ahead, if a glut of incineration capacity developed, pressures to remove the ban completely and allow in all imports were expected.

Poland's geographical position was particularly weak. The new German laws on waste and recycling (known as Dual System Deutschland or DSD) brought in at the end of 1991 required that by 1995 German industry collects and recycles 80 per cent of all plastic waste: other targets were set for board and paper packages and higher standards for glass, tin plate and aluminium. Because of the high labour and stringent environmental laws within Germany, recycling in Poland would have substantial cost advantages. Thus it was not surprising that once the new law was announced, the Polish government received a number of requests for setting up treatment plants for imported cardboard and plastic boxes.

IMPROVEMENTS, WHAT IMPROVEMENTS?

There have been improvements. The recession has reduced emissions. Some enterprises have begun to modernize helped by the environmental funds and their own accumulated earnings. A few foreign companies have started to produce environmentally benign products, but the process has been agonizingly slow and has to be set alongside the continuing pollution bequeathed by the insolvent and obsolete heavy industrial and energy sectors. Moreover in the near and medium term, the slow realignment of household and corporate activity to the new economic framework poses substantial new environmental threats.

The new governments gave top priority to economic recovery. Domestic and international political pressures forced them to introduce privatization, remove trade barriers and foster foreign investment. The lesson of Lancashire, Ohio and the Ruhr, however, was that these policies in themselves were unlikely to bring radical change. The environmental situation in the West progressed essentially because cost pressures closed down dirty basic industries such as coal mining and steel making. Buyers substituted other products (such as gas), cleaner technologies (such as mini-mills for steel) or cheaper imports from the developing countries, where the environmental standards were lower.

Though some economic restructuring has gone ahead, for fear of jeopardizing this, governments became reluctant to push for the environmental changes which were needed. These included substantial new public investments and the enforcement of stringent ecological laws.

For the future, there is no straightforward answer to the question of whether the free market in East and Central Europe will benefit the environment. Depending on how exactly the words are defined, the answers to this question could be 'yes, maybe' or 'yes, but' or 'no'. It would be 'yes, maybe' if all the terms were defined loosely. Hence if a strong free market does develop in the region, it is ultimately likely to have a similar economic structure to other middle income countries, such as Turkey, Mexico or South Korea. In environmental terms, it is questionable whether this would be a real improvement compared with 1980s communism.

The answer 'yes, but' is conditional. For example one reply might be 'yes, but' only if the recession ends quickly. Another might be dependent on sufficient public support for both higher environmental expenditure and the introduction and enforcement of stronger laws.

The answer would be 'no' if the terms free market and environmental benefit were strictly defined. For instance if the term free market excluded all or most governmental involvement, it seems highly unlikely that the environment would ever recover. If government participation was allowed, but the gain to the environment had to be sustainable, the answer again would be 'no'. Indeed, it would require quite a long list of additional qualifications to give a positive answer to this precisely defined question.

6

EXPERIMENTING WITH ENVIRONMENTAL CHANGE

THE POLLUTER PAYS PRINCIPLE

'Any environmental action programme must ... be based on a clear understanding [of] what will be achieved through price adjustments, industrial restructuring, privatization, on one hand, and explicit environmental policies and investments on the other.'[1] This chapter focuses on these issues – namely the development of economically based environmental policies. It covers the liability of foreign investors for past contamination, the use of economic instruments, environmental funds and their use in environmental investments, a market in pollution permits, debt for nature swaps, and codes of environmental conduct.

While governments have had to follow barren Western recipes in economic restructuring, in environmental issues there have been attempts at innovation. This has largely consisted of proposals to introduce economic criteria into environmental policy. However, their impact has been slight so far due in part to the recession, to vested interest and to the slow speed with which the free market took hold.

The key to the new departures was the polluter pays principle (PPP) as a replacement for the operative tenet under communism that pollution paid. As defined by the OECD, PPP meant that 'the polluter should bear the cost of measures to reduce pollution decided upon by public authorities to ensure that the environment is in an acceptable state'.[2] PPP was adopted as the basis for environmental control in the West in the first half of the 1970s; academic economists saw it as a means of forcing business to take commercial account of the pollution costs it imposes on the community. Since then, Western governments have increasingly used economic instruments (such as effluent charges and deposit-refund systems) as an adjunct to environmental regulations. This was on the grounds that their direct impact on prices and costs was both a more efficient and effective way of changing behaviour than traditional command and control techniques.

ENVIRONMENTAL LIABILITY

The liability for past site contamination by a state-owned enterprise was a major worry for most foreign and some domestic investors. According to the law throughout the region, such liabilities were normally transferred to the new owner, if and when there was one. This, however, has not always happened, as many foreign buyers have negotiated some sort of deal with the government in order either to remove or to reduce their liability.

Others, however, have been put off by the perceived size and uncertainty of the environmental obligation. A study made in 1992 by the OECD and World Bank of the attitudes of the largest companies in North America and Western Europe highlighted the importance they attached to environmental risks in the region. The survey's preliminary results suggested that some two-thirds of companies thought that environmental and non-environmental threats (such as unstable economic reforms and exchange rate risks) were of equal importance in impeding investment. Environmental concerns included liability for past contamination, uncertainty about standards and the unpredictable cost of clean-up.[3]

The survey results reflect genuinely held attitudes, mostly arising from the costly consequences of US Superfund legislation on cleaning up hazardous chemical dump sites. Yet no definitive estimates are readily available to support their views. Speaking in May 1991, Heiner Bonnenberg, the Treuhand's Director of Environmental Protection, said: 'There is no doubt that the climate for investment is influenced considerably by the repeated debates on the very bad soil contamination at East German industrial sites, in fact the problem is not as extensive as mentioned in these discussions.'[4] For the ex-GRD, the Treuhand's estimate of clean-up (to a 'safe' level) was around $15 billion.

In contrast, Greenpeace's estimate was reportedly $125 billion.[5] Its views were echoed by a semi-official German report. It said that in areas where the chemical industry was strong, such as the Leipzig/Bitterfeld/Halle district, 'unsolved questions regarding clean-up of existing waste have been one of the largest hindrances to investment'. The area had over 5,000 abandoned waste sites, of which some 500 plus were seen as highly hazardous.[6]

To overcome these qualms and encourage foreign investment, the region's privatization agencies were forced to consider ways of limiting the potential cost of the clean-up to be borne by the investor. Such measures were also important for the banks and insurers. In the early 1990s, the Polish and German governments were furthest ahead.

The Polish response to liability

In Poland, the issue of environmental liability was raised first by Philips Lighting of the Netherlands, in its negotiations for the purchase of light bulb manufacturer Polam Pila. This was in spring 1991. At the last minute, the Dutch company wanted a full environmental indemnity as a condition of purchase. This the government could not give, essentially because it lacked the finance; but also because neither the Ministry of Finance (nor the Ministry of Privatization acting on its behalf) was allowed legally to make an open-ended financial commitment on the state budget. The solution was to raise Philips' stake from 51 to 66 per cent, the additional 15 per cent covering the estimated cost ($5 million) of restoring the site to a reasonable condition.

This experience resulted in most Polish state-owned enterprises auditing their sites for environmental liability at an early stage. The required asset valuation was extended to include an environmental review. As Western consultants carried more weight with Western investors, they, rather than local firms, carried out most of the initial work. Since then as some local auditors have trained, domestic firms have increasingly been used.

In the first phase of the audit, the consultants typically spent one to three days at the site, talking to company officials and visually surveying it. The cost was $8,000–15,000, which the firm being privatized could usually afford, according to Tom Kolaja, who was responsible for environmental issues at the Ministry of Privatization in 1991. The consultant's brief was to identify the environmental costs that the government would legally have to bear if the plant was closed tomorrow. Its main focus thus was the pollutants present in the soil, and ground water, asbestos in the buildings, PCBs in transformers and the like.

This mini-audit formed the basis of detailed negotiations between the Ministry and the potential buyer over liability. In a few cases a fixed-sum indemnity (no greater than the value of the sale) was agreed. In others, such as Unilever's purchase of the Pollena detergent plant at Bydgoszcz, adjustments were made to the purchase price. More often than not, both parties settled for placing some 90 per cent of the estimated clean-up sum in an escrow bank account. Ten per cent came from the investor, which was also obliged to take on managerial responsibility for the clean-up operation, using local firms. Usually under the terms of the sales contract, clean-up had to begin within a year and to be completed within four or five years.

Most of the early sales did not require an expensive clean-up; one ministry source said that the highest estimated cost in the first year was $50 million. This may have been because investors only bought the clean slice of the site and/or they were not interested at all in heavily contaminated properties. Potentially high costs may also have been a reason for the exclusion of 'environmentally troublesome enterprises' from phase one of the country's mass privatization.[7]

Speaking at the conference on foreign investment and environmental liability, in Warsaw in May 1992, Kolaja instanced three typical variants dealt with by his ministry (see Figure 6.1). In A, a vegetable processing plant, the risks were identifiable and the audited contamination minimal. Hence the government was willing to give a fixed and time limited indemnity. In light manufacturing facility B, which was sold for $15 million, a small escrow account was established to cover liabilities estimated at $5 million. In C, a battery plant, the cost of site remediation was estimated to be greater than the value of the assets. Hence the ministry would have had to consider not only an escrow account, but also the possibility of tax breaks and/or low-interest development loans.

The process developed in Poland had a number of loopholes. Perhaps the principal one was that it excluded most enterprises being privatized through the two main routes – liquidation and joint ventures. According to Kolaja, 'If an investor does not raise the issue of environmental liability, it is not addressed'.[8] In general, investors from East and Central Europe were less concerned than those from the West and they may, he added, 'as a result, be purchasing unquantified environmental liabilities'.

In 1991, the lack of clear policy guidelines and negotiating experience meant officials had to think on their feet, giving ad hoc answers to investors. 'Inexperienced regulators must negotiate with and impose requirements on foreign investors who have considerable negotiating and litigating experience [from] dealing with the environmental agencies in the West',[9] commented Ruth Bell. Greenpeace's contractual clauses (see Chapter 8) would have provided governments with a clear starting point.

The regulators' task was made more complex by the range of standards used by the auditors. Generally, the consultants based their review on 'good environmental practice'. Poland's own strict standards were one basis, West European standards another. For example, one large UK firm used the Dutch standards for water and soil contamination, and the German TA Luft for air pollution. If the investor was from the USA, it used US standards.

A third loophole was the exclusion from the audit of process-related

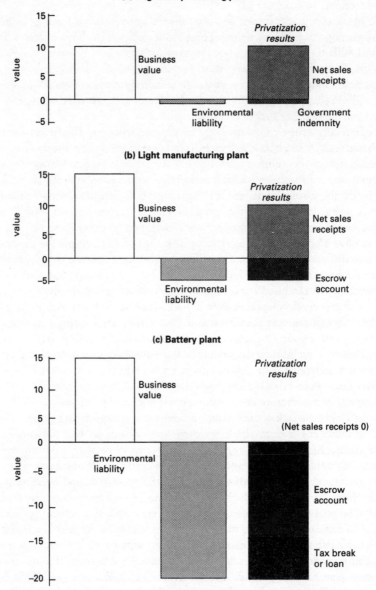

Figure 6.1 *Dealing with environmental liability in the trade sales of Polish enterprises*

technology; the investor was simply expected to bear the full costs of restructuring the factory to bring it into compliance with local laws. According to Bell, the danger in excluding this element from the negotiations was that 'Current pollution may pose more risk to health or the environment and may be more capable of being controlled'. She justifiably commented that it might be preferable not to clean up all past contamination immediately: if necessary some 'could be isolated or capped relatively cheaply in a way that would effectively reduce any real risks'.[10] The threat to health should be the priority for action.

Fourthly, for cost reasons the initial audits excluded soil and ground water sampling. If they were essential, relevant consultancy time was bought later. In at least a few cases, the potential buyer was said to have helped defray this cost, particularly if it was keen on the property and if its own corporate rules required an audit, in advance of purchase.

The public was excluded from the process. As the audits were paid for by the enterprise, the results were its property. There was no system for publicizing the results or the subsequent negotiations, usually leaving the workers and the community in the dark as to how far the buyer was committed to cleaning up the site. This sometimes created the suspicion that the government had sold the property below its perceived worth. Information on the true value of the various assets being sold would have been part of the government's defence, particularly if a key reason for the low price of the sale was soil contamination and/or the existence of toxic waste.

Finally, the Ministry of Privatization was ill equipped to deal with environmental issues on its own. It only became the key ministry in order to speed up the process of selling off enterprises. 'There is no evidence that the ministry of environment was involved in writing the privatization law or anticipated its environmental importance',[11] says Bell. In the spring of 1992, officials at Privatization proposed that a liaison unit of the Ministry of Environment should be set up within the Privatization Ministry to advise on the scope of the audit, to participate in the negotiations with the investor, and to assist in monitoring the implementation of clean-up agreements.

The process of establishing a joint group, comprising officials of both ministries, brought to the surface the difficulties each had in understanding the other: Privatization was reluctant to sanction any brake on selling, while Environment wanted all sales, and particularly the country's mass privatization programme, to be brought within the group's competence. It also wanted more detailed audits of the sites, something that was resisted by the Privatization officials on the grounds of expense and time; if enterprises could not afford a more detailed audit, who, if anyone, was going to pay? A cursory audit was better than no audit, they believed.

These arguments pointed to a major gap in the country's privatization strategy. Formulating integrated policies (for example on how to involve the public, or what standards to use) was not easy. From the environmental point of view, without a shared approach to liability, cleaning up the dirt of the '70s and '80s (and before) might not have progressed beyond the signed sales contract. Nevertheless they were sufficiently resolved by February 1993, when an interministerial environmental unit was set up in the Ministry of Privatization.

The German response to liability

Though some areas of Eastern Germany were as contaminated as parts of Poland, environmental liability and indemnification there was less of an issue. This was partly because the state had (or thought it had) sufficient funds to tackle the issue itself. In addition, as the economic and environmental strategies for the worst polluted areas were integrated, the costs of clean-up were considered within the plans for economic restructuring.

As in Poland, it was the privatization agency (in other words the Treuhand), which took the initiative, but in contrast to Poland, it had from an early stage a special department for environmental issues. Moreover, a new owner could be released from a liability arising from before 1 July, 1990, if the Land agreed. Based on health risk, it had to decide how clean the site had to be. Given the pace of privatization and the lack of personnel, however, none of the Länder was able to keep pace with the large number of applications: some 30,000 were pending in May 1992. A decision that rehabilitation would be necessary obliged the Land to pay a substantial part of the cost of clean-up.

As the Länder lacked the resources to bear this unknown risk, the Treuhand stepped in at an early stage, on the instructions of the federal Ministry of Finance. It had to promise the investor to underwrite a large part of the cost of the treatment which could be required by the Land. As in Poland, the buyer had to bear a certain proportion of the costs itself; in theory, the investor should have paid half this so-called basic sum, and the Land/Treuhand the other half. In practice, most investors paid 10 per cent, and the Treuhand the balance.[12] During 1992, there were proposals to divide this 90 per cent into two, with the Land taking its 45 per cent share directly from Bonn.

The Treuhand's payment of 90 per cent was conditional upon the decontaminated land being used for similar purposes to that in the past (in other words not for 'luxury developments'). Once the Treuhand had made a preliminary agreement to sell a site, a firm of environmental consultants agreed by both sides was asked to state what needed to be done and estimate the cost. The actual work was then carried out by an environmental engineering company and monitored by a third concern, acting on behalf of the Land. The priority in decontamination was danger to health, such as toxic waste leaking into drinking water.

The Treuhand was also directly involved in several ways. First it began inspecting 'hot spots', where immediate remediation was necessary. Such sites were being examined at the rate of around 70 a month in mid-1992 and an anticipated 100 a month by the end of 1992. Second, it had responsibility for the demolition of old buildings, and recycling land. This was mainly paid for by the federal job creation programme (Arbeits Beschäftigungs Massnahmen or ABM), which in mid-1992 was employing some 80,000 people.

Environmental liability in Hungary and Czechoslovakia

In Hungary, liability was dealt with on an ad hoc basis. As it had fewer contaminated sites than either Poland or Eastern Germany, such a method was politically acceptable in the early 1990s. Indeed, in 1991 the parliament in Budapest turned down a resolution to set up a revolving fund to cover clean-up costs. While it was able to attract the bulk of Western investment, it was not so successful at privatizing individual concerns.

Some potential foreign investors dropped out altogether; others were able to force the government to reduce the purchase price, perhaps excessively. In several cases, 'as no environmental audits were conducted, the government reduced the purchase price without knowing the extent of the environmental problems and with no specifications regarding the extent of clean-up'.[13] Istvan Jakab, Deputy Director of Hungary's Borsod Chem, which sought joint venture partners for its various operations, did not believe in this approach. He said his concern's experience in 1991 of offering to reduce the price in return for buyers taking on environmental liabilities was 'not positive', and that 'such a kind of "noble act" cannot be expected'.[14]

Furthermore, where the enterprise managers were 'not interested in revealing all environmental damages', the State Privatization Agency (SPA) had to step in to carry out the audit. In these cases, it usually made sense for the agency itself to take on 'the risk and burden of undiscoverable damage', in the form of an indemnity.[15] The absence of clear legislation would also appear to be the reason why there have been conflicting accounts on how the Hungarian government tackled the environmental liabilities of Lehel Refrigerators, when it was sold to Electrolux in 1991. One report, noting that only a part of the enterprise's liabilities was transferred to the buyer, said that 'this particular type of financial restructuring was necessary mainly because of the undisclosed and undiscoverable environmental damages'.[16] Another said the government refunded one-sixth of the purchase price (estimated at $10 million) 'for auditing and restoration of the original state of the environment'.[17]

Czechoslovakian practice would appear to have lain in between that of Poland and Hungary. Most of the first foreign investors were said to have passed the liability back to the state on an ad hoc basis.[18] This reportedly led to a number of disputes. In 1991, the government was apparently surprised at being presented with a $30 million clean-up bill from a large German investor. The lack of clear legislation is also believed to have discouraged one oil major from investing[19] and in late 1992 to have led to Germany's Continental threatening to withdraw from a deal to take over Barum-Holding.[20]

While the first wave of Czech privatization was also largely unencumbered with environmental issues, in February 1992 the federal parliament agreed a law requiring all large-scale privatizations in the second wave to be audited.[21] But this law did not say where liability should lie. The implication was that though the state agreed to take on responsibility, the clean-up costs would be split between the government and the newly formed private company. It is uncertain whether this law would work in practice.

It is also unclear whether the two successor states have kept this law on their statute books. The governmental Slovak Commission on the Environment (SCE) certainly believed six months before the break-up that few of the enterprises privatized in either the first or second wave would have either sufficient funding or interest to meet their legal requirements. Maria Klimekova, who is responsible for economic questions in the SCE, believed that the practical effect of the law would be small.[22] Shareholders, she felt, would not be willing to see their dividends invested in cleaning up old factories. The only exception she saw was where pressure from the founding ministry required it: 38 enterprises belonging to the Slovak Ministry of Tourism in the second wave had reportedly been instructed to consider environmental issues before their privatization.

ECONOMIC INSTRUMENTS

In the immediate aftermath of the revolutions, governments looked primarily to economic instruments to meet their obligations under PPP. These included taxes (for example reduced taxes on lead-free petrol or higher taxes on sulphur-rich coal), tax allowances, user charges (for example for clean water), fines and differential pricing, tradeable emission permits as well as environmental funds. Their effectiveness in influencing the process of production (or consumption) was dependent on the extent to which they pushed costs up or down, and the responsiveness of the buyer.

Poland in 1990 and 1991 raised its emission fees (for sulphur dioxide etc) and user charges (ie for air and water) by a factor of 40 in money terms and 10 in real terms, compared with 1989. Plans to introduce a whole new set of instruments covering lead-free petrol, deposits on packages and batteries as well as tradeable permits were stalled by changes in government and waning public interest.

The Czech Republic had even more grandiose plans. In the early 1990s, they covered waste, air pollution, the use of underground water, mining, noise and environmentally benign and undesirable goods. Higher charges were one priority. The charge for extracting ground water was set at 2 crowns per cubic metre in 1989; in 1991 when this was equivalent to about 6 US cents, the ministry's proposals centred on increasing it, cancelling exemptions, and differentiating between plants according to the quality of water used and the supply–demand balance for water in the area'.[23]

Proposals to give a lower VAT rating to a long list of goods perceived as environmentally favourable was also under consideration; the goods included catalysts, mechanical sprays, naturally degradable packaging materials, instruments for emission control, electric cars, insulation, and products made from recycled paper. Goods threatened with higher consumption taxes included products containing freon, batteries containing mercury and cadmium, selected mineral fertilizers and pesticides, and some chemical cleaning agents. Other ideas focused on differential customs duties, charges for mining (related to the extent of rehabilitation undertaken) and for using agricultural or forested land for another purpose, such as building.

Most of these ideas were blocked by the Czech Ministry of Finance. Exceptions were mainly where Western practice could be pinpointed. For example a new system of paying for industrial discharges into running water was introduced in February 1992. Previously, the system had set fairly rigid limits for ambient water quality following the discharge. Under the new law charges and emission permits were set by the local river boards. They took into account the type of industry, the BOD (Biological Oxygen Demand) of the discharge, the weight of suspended solids, and its acidity. The receipts were earmarked for the Republic-based environmental funds.[24]

In Hungary, the Ministry of Environment was more successful in gaining the cooperation of the Ministry of Finance. According to the former Deputy State Secretary for the Environment, Dr G Szabo, new tax allowances included zero purchase tax on environmental services. They also included a profit tax allowance for the neutralization of hazardous wastes (though incineration was often a cause of environmental degradation rather than a solution). In addition, the ministry agreed to reduce the purchase tax on the price of lead-free petrol; this made it 'possible to put an end to the odd situation where environmentally more desirable fuel was more expensive than the more polluting petrol with the same use-value'. There was also a tax allowance for cars with a catalyst.

Monitoring and inspection

Monitoring and inspection were the weakest link of the chain from policy formulation to implementation. Without them, the new economic instruments were expected to be as much a failure as those in communist days. This issue was glossed over in most environmental reports, because there were no easy answers.

Setting aside corruption, there were three major related difficulties. The first was that though compliance with the law had been (rightly) decentralized, the local offices lacked the staff and skills to enforce the legislation. In Poland in 1990 moreover, less than half the country's 14,000 significant waste water dischargers had permits;[25] thus the majority were not under a legal obligation to accept national emission standards. According to Wojciech Beblo, director of Katowice voivodeship ecology department, only a quarter of the province's industrial units, including most but not all the large ones, had permits in 1991.[26]

In Katowice voivodeship, in order to improve monitoring procedures, the provincial authorities began working with the local district authorities in late 1992. As a result of their monitoring of small and medium-sized enterprises, and the voivodeship concentrating on the large enterprises, the total number of units regulated was due to rise to 20,000 from 4,000. In addition, the voivodeship set up a number of automatic ambient air monitoring stations with its World Bank credit (see Box 6.1). Elsewhere in the region, such help was not available so that progress in strengthening local management was slower or non-existent.

The second constraint was that many plants lacked control equipment. According to Polish figures, out of the 1,623 major air polluters in 1991, 1,405 had some sort of equipment to curtail dust emissions but only 165 had equipment to curb gaseous emissions such as sulphur dioxide. Since 1989, the numbers in both categories had increased, though there were no figures on how efficiently the equipment worked.

Third, owing to the recession and the low priority given to the environment, the government allowed enterprises to sidestep payment of charges and fines. In 1990, Polish enterprises paid just over 100 per cent

Box 6.1   *The World Bank Polish Environmental Management Project*

Because Katowice had such high levels of pollution, it (and the Legnica district) were the focus of an $18 million World Bank loan for developing a decentralized institutional and regulatory framework. Its action programme highlighted the gaps in the Polish structure of local environmental management. It included the following components.

Industrial and environmental efficiency

- Local training in industrial efficiency and environmental reviews.
- Diagnostic reviews in about 10 enterprises – to form case studies/models for use throughout Poland.
- Detailed reviews in 12 enterprises – to gain support from the international community.
- Foreign training in industrial pollution management and control.

Air quality management

- Ambient air quality monitoring in the Katowice–Kraków areas.
- Equipment for mobile monitoring of point source pollution.
- Plant specific emission control surveys.
- Local and foreign training in air quality management.
- Preparation of a least-cost policy and investment analysis for air pollution control in the district.

Water resource management

- Strengthening of the water management council for the Upper Vistula river.
- Establishment of a network of water monitoring stations, and development of a water demand reduction programme.
- Establishment of environmental laboratories.
- Preparation of a least-cost policy and investment analysis for region water pollution control.

---

of the environmental charges due to the voivodeships and some 68 per cent of the fines. This was the time of rapid inflation, and rising charges, so that payment for the previous year or years was relatively easy. In 1991, the rate for payment of charges fell to 75 per cent and of fines to 42 per cent. It was hard to convince Polish enterprises to honour their debts, when the Polish Ministry of Finance agreed to pay or annul the accumulated environmental fines of concerns being sold to foreign investors. This reportedly happened when Thomson bought television manufacturer Polkolor and when Fiat bought FSM, the state-owned car producer.

Environmental funds

Motivating laggard enterprises to invest in new technologies required both a carrot and stick. If pollution charges were the stick, environmental funds provided the nourishment. They are a form of economic instrument, in fact nominally more consistent with PPP than some of the direct budget subsidies used by Western governments to support environmental projects. Where the money raised from charges is primarily used to support environmental improvements, economists have dubbed this mechanism the 'polluters pay principle'.

Funds were first used in communist times in Czechoslovakia, Hungary and Poland. In Poland during the 1980s there were at least nine separate environmental funds, according to Bogusław Fiedor of the Wrocław Academy of Economics. Three or four still operate today. For example the revenue for the fund for restoring land damaged by mining was and is taken from a surcharge on extraction costs and is managed by the enterprises themselves. The Forest Fund's aims include reforestation, reducing harmful industrial emissions and financing 'the intensification of forest production'.[27] Revenues come principally from a surcharge on the local administrations' operations, but also from fees for converting forest to non-forest, fines for premature cutting of timber, and compensation payments by industrial polluters. The Funds' income in 1991 was said to have been $340 million.

The only fund in the '80s having a universal character, in the sense of receiving fees and fines from, and allocating money to, all sectors of the economy, was the Environmental Protection Fund. The fund for water economy, established in 1976, also had a fairly wide remit. Both received over 90 per cent of their income from fees and fines and were split into regional and centrally administered parts. Taking their combined expenditures, sewage treatment plants dominated. In 1989, in order to improve cooperation, these two funds were merged to create the National Fund for Environmental Protection and Water Resources or NFEP.

Controversially, the revenues raised have been divided, as before, into one central and 49 regional mini-funds. The NFEP justifies its existence by supporting those projects that are either of national or international significance. It reports to a board of trustees, with a chairperson appointed by the minister, and sets its own expenditure criteria. Each mini-fund is managed by the voivodeship ecological department and used for local projects.

Table 6.1 *Expenditure of Poland's voivodeship funds for environmental protection and water economy, 1991 ($ million approx)*

Function	Expenditure	Per cent of total
Air protection	51	22.4
Water protection, of which	115	50.4
sewage works	105	46.0
recycling works	1	0.6
new reservoirs	6	2.8
flood control	2	1.0
Rural water supply	16	7.1
Waste treatment, of which	15	6.6
waste dumps	15	6.4
recycling wastes	+	0.2
Green and open space	4	1.6
Monitoring and research	7	2.9
Land recultivation	1	0.3
Recreation	16	1.7
Not listed	16	6.8
Total	**228**	**100.0**

Notes Totals may not add due to rounding; + less than $1 million

Source Table 12 (259), 'Environmental Protection 1992', Ministry of Environment and Water Protection, Warsaw, 1992

Estimated combined revenue for the voivodeship funds and the NFEP was some $30 million in 1990 and $400 million in 1991. The growth principally reflects the higher level of environmental payments. Nevertheless, the amounts collected in 1991 were below expectation, as many enterprises 'have been trying their best to put off payment of dues or to cancel them'[28] The voivodeships collect all the revenue; fees for using the environment constituted about 95 per cent of total income in 1991 and fines 5 per cent. The voivodeships then pass to the NFEP all payments relating to sulphur dioxide, nitrogen oxide and saline water discharges and a proportion of other receipts.

Expenditure by the voivodeship funds amounted to around $230 million in 1991. Of this (see Table 6.1), expenditure on water cleansing and supply took just over half. Air protection was less than a quarter. Meanwhile, the NFEP in the same year agreed to 219 loans (with a total value of $247 million) and 129 subsidies or grants (with a total value of about $15 million). Actual payments in 1991 were however much less – on credit only $112.5 million and as grants or subsidies only $10.5 million (see Table 6.2).

Most of the NFEP's loans were to municipalities or state-owned enterprises for the construction or upgrading of sewage works, desulphurization equipment and boiler modernization; the subsidies were also

Table 6.2 *Expenditure of Poland's National Fund for Environmental Protection and Water Economy, 1991 ($ million approx)*

Function	Total Expenditure	Per cent as loans	Per cent of total expenditure
Air protection	60	97.8	49.2
Water protection	49	89.0	40.1
Soil protection	9	99.4	7.4
Environmental monitoring	2	14.4	1.6
Nature protection	1	3.4	1.0
Ecological education	1	0.0	0.6
Total	**123**		**100.0**

Source Report of the National Fund for Environmental Protection and Water Economy, 1991

for sewage works, but in addition covered publications, monitoring, and educational work, for example by the national parks.

Expenditure on air protection (just under half) was much higher than by the voivodeships, reflecting both the structure of its revenue and the international pressures for the reduction of sulphur dioxide emissions. One of the fund's first projects was to invest in a production line at Rafako, a joint venture at Raciborz, in Upper Silesia, for manufacturing fluidized bed boilers. These burn coal economically in a way which reduces both sulphur dioxide and nitrogen oxide emissions. In addition, some 40 per cent of the NFEP's expenditure went on water protection: in 1989, only 45 per cent of Poland's urban population was linked to sewage plants (see Box 6.2).

As the credits are a lever for inducing additional expenditure from an individual polluter's own resources, they normally covered 50 per cent or less of the cost of the investment. The interest charged in 1991 was between 11 and 35 per cent, compared with upwards of 50 per cent on the commercial market. Municipal investments had the highest subsidies, while enterprises manufacturing equipment for environmental protection or monitoring were subsidized by between 40 and 60 per cent. Other projects only carried a small subsidy.

The NFEP was the main shareholder in the Bank for Environmental Protection, which was established in 1990. At the end of 1992, its capital value was $14 million. Besides normal banking activities, it grants preferential loans to ecological projects, though these amounted to a mere $33,000 for ten investors in 1992. They included the Zawiercie glass works (for modernization and heat management), and three sewage treatment plants.

In Czechoslovakia, the funds were much smaller but worked in a similar way. In the 1980s, separate funds covered water, air and cropland

Box 6.2 *Clean water – a scarce and expensive resource*

Though clean water is a scarce resource throughout the region, water shortages do not often make the headlines. Its short supply has been caused by urbanization which reduced the level of the water table, industrial pollution and the lack of municipal sewage works. In Bulgaria, Poland, Hungary and the Czech Republic around two-thirds of the water supply is used by industry, essentially the energy sector. Consumption per head is particularly high in Bulgaria due to irrigation. In Poland, in 1991, annual consumption was $67m^3$ per urban dweller and $19m^3$ per rural dweller. Some experts say up to a third of Polish water is wasted.

Economic instruments, including price, can induce industry to curb water use and discharges. However the cost of treating water is high: Saxony in the former GDR estimates it will need to spend DM20–30 billion ($13–20 billion) over the next ten years for its water to meet West German standards.

In 1991, some two-thirds of Polish waste water that needed treatment was processed – either partially or fully – mechanically, chemically or biologically. Yet to reach reasonable standards, Poland still needed to build 1,900 large municipal or industrial waste water treatment plants, and 8,000 rural treatment plants, and extend its sewage system by thousands of kilometres. The astronomical cost is being largely met from local resources. The Polish government's improvement priorities include the coastal areas of the Baltic (to keep the international community happy), and domestic drinking water. Due to the foul taste of piped water in most of the large towns, taking water from a well was still part of daily life.

Others say that the priority should be improved management. Both Poland and the Czech Republic have recently restructured their water supply management structures according to catchment area. These bodies are responsible for issuing permits to take and discharge water, and for collecting payments for use by the environmental funds.

In spite of the existing low quality of water, there is opposition to private companies modernizing the networks. In Gdańsk in 1992, petitions urged the town council to reject a proposal from the French company SAUR. The company responded with an advert in the local press saying that Gdańsk could go 'with SAUR into the EEC'. In the end it won, but at a cost to the local residents – in early 1993 the domestic price of water was increased by over a half.

protection. Their revenues included state budget subsidies as well as fees for sewage and waste disposal, fees for underground water and charges for converting farmland away from agricultural purposes. In the early 1990s, the funds were merged into two, one for each Republic.

The Czech State Fund for the Formation and Protection of the Environment was headed by a council which included representatives of the Czech parliament, various departments, regional authorities, and banks. As before, its revenues include a subvention from the state. In 1991, its budget is thought to have been around $50 million, down from $80 million in 1990. In Slovakia, the Fund for Environment was also centrally managed by the SCE and largely funded by the state, but a proposal to allow lower tier authorities to manage a fifth of the revenues was under consideration.

Trading emission permits

An emission permit is an allowance to emit a specified weight/volume of pollutant, such as a tonne of sulphur dioxide. Trading consists of buying and selling permits, thus redistributing them within a maximum level of monitored emissions laid down for a country or area. In theory, the firm with the lowest anti-pollution investment costs will reduce its emissions most, and then sell its permits to others which have higher investment costs. In this way, national pollution control becomes more cost effective as not all firms need to invest to the same extent to meet government targets. Initially, permits are either allocated, auctioned or sold at par, according to a predetermined ratio.

In 1991, in the south of Poland, in cooperation with the Ministry of Environment, the New York-based Environmental Defence Fund (EDF) began a pilot trading project in Chorzow, one of the most polluted towns in Upper Silesia. The EDF noted that 'Because of the complexity of the economic situation, especially if we take into account its social aspects, there is no simple solution to environmental problems in Polish cities like Chorzow. Tradeable rights are recommended as one option of environmental improvement policy.'

The district was selected because some industrial restructuring was already underway, the heads of both the Katowice voivodeship and the town ecological departments were supportive and the air pollution from the town's heavy industry was affecting the health of a significant proportion of the residents. Its coal mines, steel mills and chemical plants developed in the late 19th century and early 20th century and are grouped around the town centre (see Map 6.1). The environmental problems were aggravated by the widespread use of coal-fired domestic water heating systems: only a fifth of the flats in the city were connected to a district heating system. Others took heat from the power station. Vehicle emissions compounded the town centre's air pollution.

The experiment set out to cover six large enterprises and a number of small district heating plants. Out of the six, three were on the list of 80:

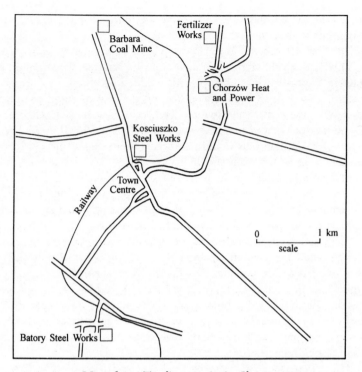

Map 6.1   *Trading permits in Chorzow*

Huta Kosciuszko steel works, the Hajduki chemical works and the P Findera fertilizer works. The Chorzow heat and power station was a major emitter of particulates, while the other two – the Barbara coal mine and the Batory steel mill appeared on the voivodeship pollution list.

Negotiations with the potential participants started in mid-1991 and by November they had formed a municipal consortium to manage the trading. As one of the main objectives was to reduce pollution and encourage firms to be in compliance with the regulations on emissions of particulates, sulphur dioxide and nitrogen oxides, the initial experimental stage was limited to two key enterprises – the Huta Kosciuszko steel works and the heat and power station. The former was willing to close its blast furnace and coking plant and to switch to natural gas for reheating steel for the production of semi-fabricated products. Closure of the coking plant would mean a substantial reduction in the emissions of hydrocarbons. In contrast, the power station had operated without a permit since 1985 and, due to old age, the pollution abatement equipment on its steam boilers was ineffective. Particulate emission levels were exceeded by more than three times, but it had no money either to pay the fines or to rebuild its boilers.

The first alternative was to close down the power station as it was not complying with the norms laid down for its operation. This would have made 600-plus workers unemployed, required additional investment to bring in power from elsewhere and cut off the heating supplied to large sections of the community (winter temperatures were well below zero). The second alternative was new investment. To install FGD scrubbers at a cost of $5 million-plus would take several years and would not be cost efficient if the boilers really should have been closed. To rebuild the power station would take at least six years and cost an estimated $170 million. If either of the latter two options were followed, pollution levels over the intervening years would remain high. There was also no guarantee that sufficient funds for rebuilding would be forthcoming.

The third solution was to trade permissions to pollute. If the power station bought particulate emission permits from the steel mill, the former could begin to comply with the emission regulations (as its total emission limit would be larger) and the latter would have extra finance to install a natural gas distribution and depressurizing station for its own and the town's use. To help gain support for the approach, the voivodeship environmental fund set up a revolving fund, of which the steel mill was the first recipient.

The actual trade between the steel mill and the power station was however delayed for a number of reasons. It was first due to be contracted in late 1991 and then again in early January 1992; other deadlines also came and went. It would seem that though the steel mill was willing to sell its permits, the power station was not willing to buy. According to Zbigniew Kulczynski of the Warsaw School of Economics, which is monitoring the project, the power utility initially used every trick in the bureaucrat's book to delay the purchase.[30] Dan Dudek of the EDF has added that it was prevaricating because it knew the level of environmental charges would be reduced (see Table 5.6) so that any monetary pressure to buy the permit would not be there.[31]

DEBT FOR NATURE SWAPS

The high level of international indebtedness was one of the constraints facing most governments in the region. In April 1991, the Paris Club which monitors official government to government debt agreed to 'exceptional debt relief' for Poland (see page 50). In addition it agreed that individual creditor governments could cancel a further 10 per cent through debt swaps on a voluntary basis.

Under the Polish programme, a creditor government would agree to buy back 10 per cent of its debt in exchange for the Polish government's commitment to spend the corresponding amount in zlotys on environmental protection. Prior to the 1991 agreement, only very small quantities of international debt had been bought by NGOs, mostly for action in the rain forests of Latin America. If all Paris Club members accepted the Polish offer, the funds available would be about $3.1 billion in net present value terms, or some $120 million a year in the early 1990s, rising to about $400 million a year at the end of the decade.

Poland used the 10 per cent clause to set up a debt for environment swap programme and a special environmental Eco-Fund. Its objectives included financing investments specifically aimed at alleviating Poland's contributions to regional and global environmental problems. The four priorities were transboundary sulphur dioxide and nitrogen oxide emissions; pollution of the Baltic Sea; greenhouse gas emissions; and biodiversity and nature conservation. The projects were also meant to be 'additional in the sense that, without the assistance of the fund, they would either have not proceeded at all or only proceeded at a substantially later date, despite their international importance'.[32]

In fact initially only the US government acceded to the programme, to the full 10 per cent, and France, to the tune of 1 per cent. However, the chairman of the fund, former minister Maciej Nowicki, believed that other countries such as Switzerland, the Netherlands, Norway and Sweden would eventually come in. In early 1993, France said it would put in the other 9 per cent, once the fund came up with specific projects.

The USA did not specify where its contribution, which amounted to $6 million in the first year, should be spent. The fund therefore focused on small projects, which could be completed with only a little investment. For 1992, these were infrastructure for the Bialowieza national park (apparently for nature conservation/biodiversity), the protection of the rare white eagle (Poland's national emblem) and completing waste water treatment plants at Gdynia and Gdańsk on the Baltic.

GUIDELINES AND CODES OF CONDUCT

In Budapest in November 1991, a number of governmental and corporate representatives agreed a set of guiding principles on the environment, industry and investment. As the conclusions to the conference state, the proposal for this so-called corporate 'code of conduct' was initially made by European environment ministers, meeting in Dublin in June 1990. At that time, the ministers said that European 'Community-based industries locating in the countries of Central and Eastern Europe should be encouraged to develop and abide by codes of conduct taking into account EC environmental protection standards or similar standards'.[33]

The reason for the code was the fear that EC companies would take advantage of the weaker compliance mechanisms of CEE to gain a competitive advantage and further degrade its environment. This happened but not to the extent originally envisaged. The main reason would appear to be the low level of corporate investment, rather than any code of conduct. If the economies start to grow, strict regulations could become necessary.

Indeed the guidelines agreed in Budapest were a charade. They had no legal force and said little that was new. At the time and subsequently, some commentators claimed that the code was counter-productive, in that it would allow investors to claim they were abiding by a set of environmental principles when they were not. For example, principle four noted that investors should design and construct installations to the pollution norms and standards found in the EC and EFTA, 'taking into account best available technology, energy efficiency and the availability of local resources'.[34] Using Western Europe as the reference point covered both strict and lax regulatory regimes, and excluded Japan or the USA, where standards in some cases were higher. Moreover by making pollution curbs conditional upon the availability of local resources the core principle was directly negated. By implication, if there were no local resources, it would be acceptable to have no controls.

Other investment codes were more rigorous. For example, the Business Charter for Sustainable Development prepared by the International Chamber of Commerce (ICC) provides a basic framework of action by individual businesses throughout the world. Principle eight says that signatories should 'develop, design and operate facilities and conduct activities taking into consideration the efficient use of energy and materials, the sustainable use of renewable resources, the minimisation of adverse environmental impact and waste generation and responsible disposal of residual wastes'.[35]

Though the Budapest guidelines were not formally adopted or signed by the participants, as they were relatively weak they in fact sanctioned lower environmental standards than in say Germany, Sweden or the Netherlands. To have been effective, they would have needed to have fully reflected best Western practice, to have had the force of law and to have had strong supportive mechanisms to ensure compliance. Such moves have long been rejected by Western companies pleading the advantages of self-regulation.

Greenpeace prepared a dossier for the meeting – *Avoiding Western Mistakes: a guide to clean investment in Eastern and Central Europe*. It aimed to make businesses replace the concept of assimilative capacity by the precautionary principle and of end-of-pipe technology by clean production. Neither however was taken seriously. In the absence of multilateral treaties, Greenpeace suggested, the governments of Central and Eastern Europe must take the lead themselves and introduce more stringent legislation ensuring clean investment in the manufacturing. This was a reason why the organization prepared the contractual clauses outlined in Chapter 8. The experience of the energy sector, discussed in Chapter 7, showed how necessary they were.

THE ENERGY SWITCH-ON

A MISSED OPPORTUNITY

The production and use of energy in different forms by industry, transport, agriculture and domestic households was the most fundamental of the environmental concerns facing Central and Eastern Europe in the early 1990s. Energy's key role meant it should have been at the core of moves to restructure the economy. Instead the lack of resources and government dithering created a void which by 1993 had been filled by conventional wisdom, vested interests and the search for profits.

In the early 1990s, the economic transition gave the region the chance to begin to save energy. Due to the recession and higher prices, energy demand declined, presenting governments with a breathing space during which they could have introduced a range of innovative measures both to improve the efficiency with which energy was used and to develop new, less conventional sources.

This did not happen. The former top officials in the power industry used the policy void as an occasion to entrench their position and where possible expand conventional energy sources. New fossil-fuelled or nuclear power stations were portrayed as an essential requirement of the anticipated higher economic growth that all believed would accompany the market economy. Energy saving was relegated to backroom NGOs.

Energy problems in Central and Eastern Europe, in no order of priority, included:

- energy-intensive economic structures from communism's pollution economy;
- inherited subsidized prices;
- air emissions, water discharges and solid waste from mining and power generation;
- nuclear radiation;

- minimal energy conservation;
- an excessive reliance on a narrow range of energy sources including locally mined brown (low calorific) coal in some cases, and nuclear power in others; dependence on oil and gas imports largely from the former USSR;
- centralized control of electricity generation;
- the lax implementation of regulations at nuclear plants; and
- insignificant awareness and use of renewable energy.

The region's problems lay not only with coal-fired power stations, but with practically all major energy sources and users. They included coking plants, steel mills, small and large district heating systems, coal mines, aluminium smelters, bulk chemical works and in some countries dams and oil wells.

A short report on any one of these issues could fill many pages: one short section of a book such as this cannot do justice to the scale and complexity of the problems. This chapter therefore focuses on three questions: first, the inefficient production and use of energy; second, the various sources of energy; and third the control of the energy industry.

THE EFFICIENCY OF ENERGY PRODUCTION AND CONSUMPTION

Under communism, cheap Soviet oil and gas exports, combined with less than market prices for domestic fuels, meant that energy was almost a free good. One commentator has even talked in terms of a $100 billion oil and gas subsidy by the USSR to the region during the 1980s.[1] Energy consumption increased in line with economic growth as industry and households alike ignored its cost. As a result it was often in short supply.

Table 7.1 provides three sets of comparative figures on energy use in the late 1980s, contrasting the countries of Central and Eastern Europe with several of those in the West. The table measures energy consumption in joules. One gigajoule or GJ (10^9 joules) is the amount of energy consumed by a 1 kilowatt electric fire switched on permanently for around 11½ days. The same fire would consume one megajoule or MJ (10^6 joules) in about 16 minutes, or in other words a thousandth of the time.

Apart from Turkey and Albania at one extreme and the GDR and the USA at the top end, the countries listed in the table were fairly equal in terms of commercial consumption measured in gigajoules per head. The Albanian annual per capita commercial energy consumption was equivalent to burning the 1 kilowatt fire for a year and a bit, while the equivalent period for the GDR was nearly 7 years.

Table 7.1   *Commercial energy consumption, by country, 1989*

	GJ per head	MJ per $ total GDP[1]	MJ per $ industrial GDP[2]
Albania	37	na	na
Bulgaria	144	47	26
CSFR	175	51	40
GDR	219	na	na
Hungary	107	46	34
Poland	134	79	43*
Romania	132	56	na
Yugoslavia	75	27	15
Mexico	51	30	23
Turkey	28	22	21
UK	147	11	7
USA	295	15	12
West Germany	156	8	6

Notes [1]Measured using 1987 GDP/GNP; [2]Use by industry, per unit of industrial GDP; GJ gigajoules (10⁹); MJ megajoules (10⁶); *author's calculation

Source World Resources 1992–3, *World Resources Institute*, OUP, New York, 1992

However when measured in terms of unit value of output, East and Central Europe was several times less efficient than the West; this is shown in the second column. There were several reasons for this difference. The third column of Table 7.1 shows the principal one. Other than in Yugoslavia, industry (broadly defined) in CEE was four or more times less energy efficient than the UK. This reflected the region's relatively high proportion of energy-intensive extractive industries, its greater use of raw materials and energy in manufacturing, and the lower added value of raw materials processing than manufacturing.

Moreover within the industrial sector, CEE's own energy industry (power generating, district heating plants etc) was even less efficient than those in the West. Figures for coal-intensive Poland illustrate the conundrum, though the situation was not as bad as in Czechoslovakia. Poland's coal mines consumed approximately 10 per cent of the electricity generated and one-fifth of all the country's steel. In other words, mining coal was very energy intensive, and in recent years it has become even more so, as the easy to work seams were exhausted. The efficiency of coal-based power generation was low, and some 11 per cent of power generated was subsequently lost during distribution in the 110kV and lower tension lines. In Spain the figure for such losses was half this.[3]

The EBRD energy operations policy published in March 1992 said, 'Western experts estimate that countries of Central and Eastern Europe and the former Soviet Union lose approximately one third of their total primary energy supplies through conversion losses, losses in distribution,

Table 7.2   *Selected heating prices in Czechoslovakia, 1989–91*

Type of unit/installation	Cost of fuel		Cost of heat		Cost per flat[1]	
	1989 price	1991 price	1989 price K/GJ	1991 price K/GJ	1989 price K/yr	1991 price K/yr
District heating						
Boiler < 5.8 MW	21 K/GJ	89 K/GJ	21	89	1,540	6,074
District heating: boiler > 5.8 MW						
Coke blend	48 K/100 kg	210 K/100 kg	27.4	199.8	2,249	8,019
Small brown coal	26 K/100 kg	62 K/100 kg	22.3	54.2	1,832	3,857
Large brown coal	18 K/100 kg	55 K/100 kg	17.4	53.2	1,430	3,722
Natural gas	0.8 K/m³	1.9 K/m³	29.8	70.9	2,261	4,851
Light oil	90 K/100 kg	250 K/100 kg	28.0	77.8	2,298	5,442
Individual heating						
Natural gas	0.9 K/m³	2.2 K/m³	33.6	82.8	2,019	4,966
Electricity[2]	0.26 K/KWh	0.41 K/KWh	72.7	113.9	4,333	6,833
Electricity[3]	0.19 K/KWh	0.32 K/KWh	52.0	88.9	3,117	5,333
Large brown coal	18 K/100 kg	55 K/100 kg	17.4	46.6	1,045	2,794
Briquettes	28 K/100 kg	88 K/100 kg	20.6	64.7	1,235	3,882

Notes [1]Assumes average flat of 50m³, needing approx 60GJ/yr to heat; [2]Direct heating; [3]Indirect heating, for example with a brick radiator; K: the Czechoslovakian crown (K) was worth $29.50 on average in 1989.

Source SEVEn, Prague

and inefficient end-use utilisation'.[4] More specifically, according to Lulin Radulov, President of Bulgaria's Energy Committee, 'We waste about 30 per cent of electricity because of the inefficient way we produce it. Another 10 per cent is wasted as it runs through the grid system'.[5]

To improve the efficiency of energy use required virtually the same strategies as to reduce air and water pollution, namely the restructuring of the economy and individual enterprises, investment in energy production, distribution and consumption, and new legislation. Of the three main policies undertaken to foster restructuring, privatization was very slow to start, market prices were brought in quickly but failed to make a significant impact, while hard budget constraints were resisted by managers and workers who were used to being the pampered elite.

Table 7.2 gives figures for the increase in household heating costs in Czechoslovakia between 1989 and 1991, and Table 7.3 the increases in Polish energy prices from 1990 to 1992. Czech prices increased by a multiple of two to four between 1989 and 1991. Polish price increases were generally greater due to inflation; they were also higher in the household sector than the industrial, reflecting the low prices paid by the former in the later 1980s.

For most people and for many enterprises, the price increases were seen as excessive and therefore they were not paid. In Hungary in 1992, non-payment reportedly became fairly general and payments owed to the electricity board doubled. Throughout the region, households paid a monthly heating charge based not on actual energy consumption but on their flat's floor area. Most housing blocks, whether old or new were

Table 7.3 *Increases in selected energy prices in Poland (1989 to November 1992)*

Item	Multiple by which price increased
Goods and services	17
Hard coal	
for industry	16
for households	42
Lignite	4*
Natural gas	
for industry	9
for households	90
Electric energy	
for industry	8
for households	33

Note *to mid-1992

Source *Preliminary report on the social and economic situation in 1992*, Central Planning Office, Warsaw, February 1993; *Economic Survey Poland 1992*, OECD, Paris

poorly insulated and the windows, though double glazed, often did not close properly. There were few moisture barriers, and radiator valves often did not work. This suggested that even where hot water charges reflected the market levels, their impact on the household sector's energy use was unlikely to be large.

Nevertheless it was anticipated that in appropriate circumstances households would ultimately reduce their energy use in response to higher prices. Besides higher prices, the conditions included the installation and use of meters, better insulation and improved controls on consumption. In Czechoslovakia, the government reportedly planned to meter all blocks of flats by end 1995 but it was unclear whether there would be sufficient resources to do this.

Governments typically set up national agencies to support energy conservation; their approach, however, often appeared piecemeal and limited. Bulgaria's energy efficiency centre, established in late 1992, put forward suggestions for a survey of power consumption, and energy management training. The Polish Foundation for Energy Efficiency focused on projects that were backed by an international sponsor, seemingly irrespective of their effectiveness. SEVEn (Stredisko pro Efektivni Vyuzivani Energie), the Czech and Slovak NGO, which was supported by the US Agency for International Development (USAID), organized seminars and studies and developed a database of local companies offering energy efficient products and services.

The UN Economic Commission for Europe took a bolder approach with the support of several CEE governments. By late 1992, it was making preparations to implement 15 energy efficiency demonstration projects in the ex-socialist countries. One of these was in Ceska Lipa in northern Bohemia, an area seriously affected by air pollution and additionally contaminated by radioactive waste from the nearby uranium mines. The $600 million-plus project incorporated new housing, an airport, a hospital, a trade centre and industrial enterprises. Its aim over the next decade was to pioneer new energy-saving technologies (including local micro-hydroenergy units, and biogas), new fiscal instruments, and new methods for combating the worst environmental effects of uranium mining. However, there were no hints as to where the funds would come from, though the governments of the region were collectively applying for a $6 million GEF grant (see pages 91 and 92).

The private sector was not especially active in promoting energy efficiency, partly because most facilities were still in state hands and making a loss. One exception was Thion, a French company, which in late 1992 said it hoped to recoup the $6 million expenditure on modernizing the heating system on a housing estate in Szczecin on Poland's Baltic coast within two years. Improved operations would, it forecast, reduce the estate's coal consumption by 10,000 tonnes/year and the amount of heat generated by a fifth. This and other similar projects in the region were part financed by the French government. Subsequent schemes were dependent on new finance from the EBRD and/or the World Bank.

In contrast to most expectations, the early 1990s saw the efficiency of energy use deteriorate. By way of illustration, between 1989 and 1991, Polish industrial energy consumption declined by a quarter, while the value of industrial output (in constant prices) declined by a third. Hungary's industrial energy consumption in 1991 reportedly declined by 17 per cent, while industrial production declined by 18 per cent. In agriculture, consumption fell by 12 per cent, while in the domestic sector consumption rose by nearly 9 per cent, in spite of higher prices.[6]

Looking at the region as a whole, two OPEC researchers drawing on information provided by the US consultancy PlanEcon claimed that in Poland, Czechoslovakia and Hungary, 'energy consumption levels . . . fell at a much slower rate than the fall in aggregate output, which led to a considerable deterioration of aggregate efficiency'. They added that in Bulgaria efficiency did not change, while 'Romania was the only country [in the region] to experience an improvement in energy efficiency because the decrease in [total] energy consumption was of much greater magnitude than that of GDP'.[7]

Charles Movit of PlanEcon, noted that 'there are large fixed energy requirements in any economy'.[8] In Central and Eastern Europe, these in particular reflected heavy industry's survival strategies. In Poland, though less than a third of the 70 coal mines were said to be profitable, only six of the major loss makers were scheduled for closure in 1993. In Slovakia, the government's plan to expand the production of Ziar nad Hronom aluminium smelter by half (see Box 5.4) was expected to lead to an increase in energy consumption by a quarter. SEVEn commented that 'The continuous production of aluminium [was] looked upon as a stabilizing factor by the utilities, in this case the Gabčikovo hydro plant'.[9]

Though demand was down and energy efficiency, if pursued, could have reduced consumption further, governments led by the power utilities and in some cases Western electrical engineering companies were unable to switch off their past passion for new power stations. The next section looks at the various energy sources and their environmental implications.

EXISTING AND NEW SOURCES OF ENERGY

Coal was and is expected to remain one of the main sources of energy for the region. Table 7.4 gives the pattern of primary energy demand and Table 7.5 final energy demand in the late 1980s. Table 7.4 highlights the importance of coal in Poland and its neighbours, and shows that in Hungary and Romania, oil and gas were just as or more important than coal as primary sources of energy. In addition, it indicates that other than in Romania, where water was used to generate 15 per cent of the country's power, renewable sources of energy were insignificant.

Table 7.5 gives the pattern of final energy consumption in 1988. It shows hot water's high overall share, which reflected the widespread use of district heating. In addition, oil was less important than in the West, due to the lower number of cars on the road. The table also implies, and other figures (from 1988) confirm, the importance of coal as the main fuel for power generation in Czechoslovakia (53 per cent), East Germany (82

Table 7.4 *Structure of primary energy demand, by country, 1988 (%)*

	Bulgaria	Czechoslovakia	East Germany	Hungary	Poland	Romania
Coal	42	60	70	27	78	24
Oil	37	21	18	31	13	24
Gas	12	11	8	29	8	47
Nuclear	7	6	3	8	–	–
Renewable	2	2	1	1	1	5
Imports	1	–	–	3	–	–
Total	100	100	100	100	100	100

Note Totals may not sum due to rounding

Source *Environmental Protection 1992*, Ministry of Environment, Warsaw

Table 7.5 *Structure of final energy demand, by country, 1988 (%)*

	Czechoslovakia	East Germany	Hungary	Poland
Coal	45	32	16	41
Oil	21	25	34	21
Gas	10	9	18	10
Electricity	12	13	12	12
Hot Water	13	22	20	13
Total	100	100	100	100

Sources Statistical Yearbook of the IEA; 'World Energy Statistics and Balances', in *Energie für die Slowakei*, Worldwide Fund for Nature, Vienna, March 1992

per cent) and Poland (90 per cent – hard coal 55 per cent and lignite 35 per cent). Nuclear power provided Hungary with 34 per cent of its electricity, but by 1992 this figure is said to have reached half. In Bulgaria, nuclear power and coal were of equal importance at around 40 per cent each.[10]

Coal and pollution

Inefficient and polluting solid fuels dominated the power, steam and heat generating energy sectors in the three northern countries, and to a lesser extent in Bulgaria, Hungary and Romania. The environmental consequences were worst in Czechoslovakia and Eastern Germany. Polish coal was generally of higher quality, but this was offset by its greater use of coal as a primary source of energy.

Burning coal and lignite was the principal cause of the 'black triangle'. In the GDR in 1989, energy installations produced some 94 per cent of sulphur dioxide, 73 per cent of dust and 81 per cent of nitrogen oxides. In Poland in 1987 (see Table 3.1), energy installations generated just over half the sulphur dioxide and nitrogen oxides and a similar proportion of the dust. Comparable figures for Czechoslovakia are not so easily obtainable: but of the top 20 sources of dust and sulphur dioxide in the federal republic around 15 were energy installations of one sort or another.

It would be wrong to imagine that these figures refer only to monster power stations. A quarter or more of Poland's sulphur dioxide emissions and particulates came from local coal-fired boilers and domestic heating systems. The Kraków and Katowice areas in the south of the country were particularly bad. In the mid-1980s in Kraków, 1,300 boiler houses and 200,000 home stoves, most of them more than 25 years old, contributed some 35 per cent of the city's sulphur dioxide, in contrast to 18 per cent from local power stations.[11] The boilers had no controls for sulphur dioxide and the chimneys were coated with unburnt carbon. Winter temperature inversions compounded the problem. In the late 1980s, in the former GDR, just under a fifth of boiler capacity was installed in similar decentralized small energy supply operations.

Progress in reducing emissions within the triangle has so far been slight. German emissions are however likely to be reduced by 1996 as a result of EC regulations and the environmental agreement signed alongside the unification treaty. In the Czech Republic and Poland, the lack of finance has delayed improvements. World Bank finance has been used to fund FGD at Prúneřov, but that leaves several other large power plants such as Počerady and Tušimice in the Czech Republic and Turów in Poland.

Furthermore, the introduction of market prices has in some ways exacerbated the situation by stimulating the use of coal. The OPEC researchers mentioned above noted that currency convertibility and open borders resulted in 'a noticeable switch to cheaper domestic energy sources away from the relatively expensive imported fuels such as refined products and natural gas'.[12] In a similar vein, by increasing the price of lignite by less than the price of hard coal, some industrial buyers in Poland were said to have switched to the lower quality/dirtier product. The International Energy Agency (IEA), whilst predicting increases in oil and gas consumption, also forecast a regional increase in coal consumption in the coming decade from 270 to 308 million toe (tonnes oil equivalent).[13]

Higher prices had a relatively limited impact on emissions in the early 1990s. In one of the few independent reports to examine the energy situation, Jeremy Russell, who was seconded from Shell to the UK-based Royal Institute of International Affairs, wrote in 1991 that 'degradation of the environment as a result of coal combustion will ... continue, but at a reduced level'. He maintained that 'Even if massive capital availability were, somehow, forthcoming and applied immediately, it is likely that there would be numerous instances of "water being poured onto the sand". The existing management, economic and maintenance systems, let alone the physical and human infrastructures, simply are not ready to absorb and operate ... new technology, in unfamiliar management conditions, in such a way as to produce optimum environmental enhancement'.[14]

The cheapest technology for reducing air emissions was coal cleaning/enrichment, which reduced the ash and sulphur content of coal before it was burnt. The cost was just under $700 per tonne of sulphur dioxide removed according to Poland's NFEP. The World Bank put the cost of cleaning at $15/kW, compared with $1,000/kW for the construction cost of a 1,000 MW power station.[15]

In spite of its higher cost and the large volumes of gypsum generated, most governments and multilateral banks opted for the more expensive FGD. It was 3 to 12 times as costly as coal cleaning per tonne of sulphur dioxide removed, according to Poland's NFEP. A report prepared by Westinghouse for the Warsaw government showed just how expensive. It reportedly said that to make major improvements to six of the country's largest power stations, burning 20 million tonnes per year of hard coal, would cost over $1 billion.[16] This was equivalent to over 1 per cent of the country's GDP. Adding FGD to the lignite-burning power stations at Belchatów, Konin and Turów would have at least doubled this percentage. It is tempting to say that FGD was proposed because Western companies were the most likely beneficiaries. The Dutch Electricity Board put in Hoogovens units at Belchatow in central Poland, while at Opole to the west, where the $230 million revamp programme was German funded, the contract went to Klöckner and Lurgi, two German companies.

Fluidized bed combustion was 'the most expensive technology'.[17] According to the NFEP, it was 40 times more costly than coal cleaning per tonne of sulphur dioxide removed. Yet, the Nordic Investment Bank and the Swedish Export Credit Guarantee Board agreed in mid-1992 to finance a $134 million pressurized fluidized bed combined cycle plant in Ostrava in Moravia. It was to be constructed by ABB Carbon, one of the engineering multinational's many subsidiaries. In contrast to these large sums, only small amounts were spent on coal cleaning and other more cost-effective emission-reducing technologies, which could have directly helped boost the local economy.

Nuclear power

Western public opinion's ambivalence to nuclear power was matched in Eastern and Central Europe. Outside the former USSR, Poland was the country most affected by the radioactive fallout from Chernobyl, and as a result public opinion in the late 1980s halted construction of the country's first nuclear power plant at Zarnowiec near Gdańsk. The disaster also encouraged protests in the Czech Republic, Bulgaria and Yugoslavia, where there were already strong anti-nuclear lobbies. In contrast, in Hungary and Slovakia in particular, nuclear power was seen, perhaps as in France in the 1970s, as an element in the country's economic independence. It reflected 'a bit of healthy nationalism', according to one member of the Hungarian National Atomic Energy Committee.[18]

It is possible the media exaggerated the dangers of Russian nuclear technology, as with air and water emissions, in order to castigate communism, but this seems unlikely. While West European anxieties about safety in general helped support multilateral funding for modifications to the reactors, and thus provided sorely needed contracts for Western engineering companies, if such worries had become too powerful, moves to revamp the plants would have been rejected by public opinion. An uneasy compromise thus emerged with the engineering companies claiming that the reactors both could be made safe, at least temporarily, and had to be made safe to provide the energy the countries needed to maintain their economies. Both these points were debatable.

None of the nuclear power stations in the region had a Chernobyl-type RBMK reactor, since these were designed to produce plutonium for the Soviet military and were not exported. The main risk was from the first generation pressurized water VVER 440–230 reactors, which dated from the 1970s. In the words of the EC Phare programme, these 'are reputed to be the world's most dangerous'.[19] Two reactors of this type are sited at Jaslovske Bohunice plant in western Slovakia and four at Kozloduy on the Danube in north-west Bulgaria (see Table 7.6). The Greifswald complex on the Baltic Sea, which had this type of reactor, closed down in 1990.

Hungary's generating complex at Paks and the Czech Republic's site at Dukovany have a later type of pressurized water (VVER 440-213) reactor. The construction of two type VVER 440-1000 reactors at Temelin in the Czech Republic was stopped after Chernobyl. Yugoslavia adopted Westinghouse technology at Krsko, which is now in Slovenia,

Table 7.6 *Nuclear power plants, by country, 1992*

Country	Site	Number	Unit MW	Type
Bulgaria	Kozluduy	4	408	VVER-440 type 230
		2	953	VVER-1000 type 320
	Belene*	2	953	VVER-1000
Czech Republic	Dukovany	4	408	VVER-440 type 213
	Temelin*	2	890	VVER-1000 type 320
East Germany	Greifswald+	4	408	VVER-440 type 230
	Greifswald+	1	408	VVER-440 type 213
	Rheinsberg+	1	70	
	Hamm-Uentrop+	1	296	High temp gas-cooled
Hungary	Paks	4	410	VVER-440 type 213
			430	
Romania	Cernavoda*	5	620	Candu-6
Slovakia	Bohunice	2	408	VVER-440 type 230
		2	408	VVER-440 type 213
	Mochovce*	4	390	VVER-440 type 213
Slovenia	Krsko	1	620	PWR-664 (Westinghouse)

Notes *units under construction; +closed

and Romania was building five Canadian Candu reactors at Cernavoda. Though one or two dangerous units were closed during the communist era, since the revolutions, on the one hand, governments have found it harder to ignore the threat of another Chernobyl-type explosion. On the other hand, as the local resource constraints on incorporating safeguards became tighter, Western companies stepped up their pressure to secure business. The influential *Petroleum Economist* magazine noted in mid-1992 that 'The emerging regional strategy of improving safety in stages ... may well revive the flagging fortunes of the western nuclear power industries'.[20]

Estimates of the costs involved in bringing all the ex-socialist countries' plants up to a reasonable safety standard ranged from $5 billion to over $30 billion. There were two monetary issues involved in this. First, such sums were not on offer and were never likely to be. Second, who was to provide the little that was available? The leading Western industrial nations spent several years haggling over the fund in order to ensure their own engineering companies each had a slice. In the end there was a range of funds. The Germans, French and British committed $50–70 million to a multilateral fund, which it was hoped would reach $700 million. Set up in early 1993, it was to be administered by the EBRD. Westinghouse, to help make sure it secured the contract to complete Temelin, raised credits of $400 million or more, mostly from the US Import-Export Bank. Canada provided over $300 million to AECI of Canada and Renel of Romania to complete the country's reactors. Japan too favoured bilateral aid.

The third issue, given the dearth of funds, was deciding priorities. This had several dimensions. The nuclear industry, West and East, by keeping a tight hold on decision-making, ensured that alternatives to revamping the plants were not considered. Their views were narrowly supply orientated. The EBRD's nuclear power advisory group, which is made up of ex-officials from different national nuclear regulatory authorities, inconsistently argued the nuclear case on the basis of forecast rises in electricity use and the risk of becoming too reliant on imports of gas or other fuels. Yet demand was not increasing and these alternatives were less expensive, less risky and less polluting. Moreover, the group's contribution to the EBRD's published Energy Operations Policy only once touched on decommissioning.

It said 'The energy deficiency constraint facing Bulgaria makes it very difficult to advance the needed decommissioning of Bulgaria's nuclear capacity in the near future', though it recognized that Kozloduy's 'infrastructure and quality of software is very poor'.[21] Events showed that the 'constraint' was less than real. In the autumn of 1992, the fifth and sixth reactors at Kozloduy were hit by fires and closed for repairs for several months. During part of this period, the nominally 3,760 MW complex supplied, from reactor 4, only 400 MW to the Bulgarian national grid. The country survived, reportedly without serious power cuts. The situation became even more absurd when the country offered to export surplus power for the duration of spring and summer 1993.

Instead of closure, the Western policy was one of patching, though officially only for those plants deemed 'safe' enough to be worth upgrading. It was unclear how independent the nuclear industry would be in making such decisions – the experience of the early 1990s was not reassuring. For instance in 1993, Phare was expected to agree to repair Kozloduy reactor 1, which should have been closed. In 1991/2, it funded the World Association of Nuclear Operators (Wano) and several of its associated companies including Electricité de France to repair unit number 2 at Kozloduy (see Box 5.2), which should also have been closed. It did however provide $12 million for the Bulgarian Committee for the Peaceful Use of Atomic Energy to determine energy policy, new sources of energy, and 'alternative methods of disposing of nuclear waste previously shipped back to the ex-USSR'.[22] Though non-conventional energy sources were available and could have been followed up with this aid, the Sofia government in early 1993 formally decided to reconsider completing the nuclear plant at Belene, where construction was halted in the early 1990s due to public opposition.

In 1991, Austria was so concerned about the risk posed by the two ageing reactors at Jaslovske Bohunice in Slovakia, that it offered to subsidize the building of a new conventional power station if they were closed. The EBRD nuclear advisory group made the same recommendation, but they continued to operate, virtually unmodified. Slovakia was also expected to start the first of four slightly more advanced reactors at Mochovce in late 1993.

In the Czech Republic, Temelin's completion was ordered in March 1993 in spite of Austrian opposition and a damning report by the US firm Power International for the Czech government. This report had supposedly concluded that the full cost of completion would result in electricity some three to five times more expensive than from a modern coal-fired plant and that the electricity was not needed.[23]

Elsewhere Siemens talked with the Croatian electricity utility about its first nuclear power plant, while in Slovenia some $40 million was spent on employing Western contractors for maintenance and safety installations at Krsko. Hungary was said to have been considering the purchase of a new $3.5 billion plant, probably from PreussenElektra and Electricité de France. There were even rumours that Poland was planning a new nuclear plant near Szczecin.

The Chernobyl disaster occurred in May 1986. Seven years later public anxieties had sufficiently diminished for the Slovak government to plan to commission Mochovce, the Czech government to give the go-ahead for Temelin and the Bulgarian government to reconsider Belene. These projects were no longer just for local needs. While official funding was made available from abroad for some of the work, the balance needed bankable commercial credits, supported by energy exports. Power companies in Germany, Italy, Switzerland and Austria apparently obliged with small purchasing contracts, with the nuclear engineering companies among the beneficiaries. These contracts were expected to expand as soon as high tension East–West power links were complete.

Gas lights the path

Jeremy Russell said in his energy report that 'many hopes for eventually reducing power generation related environmental degradation in Europe rest with the [ex-] Soviet gas industry'.[24] The advantages of gas included the lower levels of sulphur dioxide emissions, particulates and carbon dioxide; while exploitation absorbed less energy than coal mining, this was partially offset by the very high infrastructure costs and the time taken to increase supply.

There was indigenous gas production in Romania and in small quantities in Poland and Hungary. Other than in Romania, Russia supplied more than half the gas used in the region in 1991. Both Slovakia and the Czech Republic took gas from the Transgas pipeline which was the main gas artery from Russia to the West, while Poland received gas from a spur through Belarus. Hungary's link was the Soyuz pipeline via Ukraine.

'On the basis of increased imports, gas consumption could well double in Poland, Bulgaria and former East Germany, and increase significantly in Czechoslovakia and Hungary', Russell noted.[25] In Romania, Russell added, consumption was scheduled to fall, partly because gas was being used to compensate for the shortfall in coal and partly because local supplies were dwindling.

While Russia was expected to remain the main source of gas in the short and medium term, most of Central and Eastern Europe was keen to diversify the source of their imports as soon as possible. Thus Bulgaria was said to be considering imports through a new pipeline from Iraq via Turkey, while Poland had initially looked to Norway. However, with Russia's Gazprom proposing a new $10 billion pipeline to Germany through Poland, it seemed likely that this was one customer it would keep. Hungary and the Czech Republic were said to have considered imports from Algeria and also Norway, but due to the high costs had not concluded an agreement with either supplier.

To offset reduced coal production/consumption and meet a forecast increase in energy demand, the Polish government expects gas use to double at least and nuclear power to supply 5 per cent of primary energy demand by 2010. Gas is used for cooking and as an industrial raw material; it is not used widely for heating. Moreover, given its high cost, this is unlikely to change: most households will continue to use coal-fired boilers on the grounds of price.

Poland allowed its gas production to decline in the late 1970s, but in 1990 the World Bank granted Polish Oil and Gas a $250 million credit to develop new production facilities. One result was that in late 1992 Amoco won a tender to explore for hydrocarbons in two locations – south-west of Warsaw and on the Ukrainian border south-east of Lublin.[26] There were also plans to produce and enrich the low-quality coal bed methane found in Upper Silesia as well as further south.

Because of its existing and new domestic supplies and the proposed Russian pipeline, Poland was probably in a better position to look to gas than its neighbours. The gas is primarily intended to fuel combined-cycle gas-turbine generators, which are much more efficient at producing electrical power than coal-fired power stations. The low grade methane, for instance, was expected to be used in this way. Irrespective of location, new supplies of gas were unlikely to be cheap. Nevertheless, in Hungary there has been at least one proposal for a 200 MW private gas-fired combined-cycle power station – a joint venture between Belgium's Tractebel and two Hungarian companies, including the state oil and gas combine, and gas-fuelled power stations have been talked about in other countries.

Renewables and the Danube dams

Most of the plans and forecasts ignored renewables. Their development would have been expensive, but not impossible. In the early 1990s, one or two experimental Danish windmills were erected near Gdańsk, and wind power could have become quite important with some commitment. In Poland and elsewhere, a case was made for biomass. Professor P J Kowalik of the Technical University of Gdańsk said that biomass (particularly straw and hay) could supply the Polish energy market with around 11 per cent of its energy needs.[27] Ex-Czechoslovakia, the former GDR, Hungary and Romania all have biomass potential.

Elsewhere, for example in Bulgaria, Hungary, Poland and Romania, geothermal energy could be, and in places was, exploited, while in Romania there is an embryonic solar power programme.[28] There was also a potential for hydroelectricity, mainly using small turbines throughout the region. Large hydroelectric power projects nonetheless were out of favour, following the controversy over the Gabčikovo–Nagymaros dam system on the Danube. As with several of the other energy schemes in the region, conventional wisdom was the dominant influence in this sad saga, the tail end of which recently began to destroy one of Europe's last riverine wildernesses. The conventional wisdom in this case was that damming made sense.

In 1977, the Hungarian and Czechoslovak governments agreed to build two dams on the river Danube – one at Gabčikovo in Slovakia, and another over 120 km downstream at Nagymaros in Hungary, some 30 kilometres north of Budapest (see Map 7.1). The water to power Gabčikovo was to have been diverted into a 17-kilometre canal on the northern Slovak side by a weir at Dunakiliti, just after the river became the international frontier between Hungary and ex-Czechoslovakia. The dimensions of this canal 'are greater than those of the Suez Canal', said its opponents.[29] It is 700 metres wide in places and up to 18 metres above

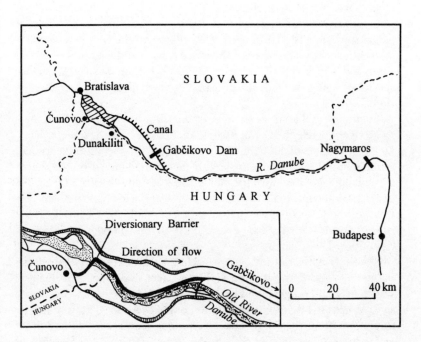

Map 7.1   *The Gabčikovo dam*

the surrounding land. Originally the project was intended to generate 800 MW of electricity, protect the area against flooding, improve navigation and protect ground water levels.

In the later 1980s, Hungary's communist government withdrew unilaterally from the project. The environmentalists in the Danube Circle linked the river's emotional significance and ecological arguments. However, the 1977 treaty was an unstoppable steam roller, and the Slovak government continued to build its part. In addition, to ensure the viability of its contribution, it extended the project's scope, with a new diversionary barrier, activated in October 1992, at Čunovo, some 10 kilometres upstream from Dunakiliti. This placed the Gabčikovo element of the project entirely within Slovakia.

This was just prior to Slovakia's independence in January 1993 and led to an EC-brokered compromise, which ruled out using the Gabčikovo dam for power generation. Yet a month or so later, the Slovaks were talking of its privatization. Hydro Quebec and Germany's Bayernwerk were said to be interested in putting up the $230 million needed to complete the project, but this has never been confirmed. As the cost of the project to the Czechoslovak state budget over the 15 years to 1992 was estimated at $500–1,000 million, private investment at this late stage could have been fairly profitable.

Opposition to the project has come from various angles. This part of Slovakia is ethnically Hungarian. The villagers in the area were virtually stranded on the island between the raised canal and the natural river bed. From the Slovak capital Bratislava, local opposition was categorized as special pleading, while from Budapest it was viewed as 'indirect eviction'.[30]

Environmental accusations were dismissed as irrelevant in Bratislava. In Hungary, while the Danube Circle's actions against the project were a factor in the downfall of the communists, by 1993 their influence had diminished. The environmental arguments focused on the destruction of this inland delta area, with its unique landscape and flora and fauna, the degradation of the quality of the ground water, and the loss of land for farming and forestry. If the precautionary principle means anything, the project should be stopped, at least until all the allegations have been thoroughly investigated.

Slovakia's privatization plans include the electricity generating industry. Whether this includes Gabčikovo is unclear because formally it was built with Hungary, and both countries would have to agree to any sale. Moreover Hydro Quebec and/or Bayernwerk may or may not be interested. Nevertheless, private enterprise is soon certain to find other attractive propositions in the energy generation field in Slovakia or elsewhere in the region.

THE LOSS OF DEMOCRATIC CONTROL IN GERMANY

This chapter concludes with a review of the impact of privatization on the energy sector in Eastern Germany. It shows how the ex-GDR local authorities were defeated in their bid to keep full control of their energy policies by a combination of resource constraints, the corporate search for profits and paradoxically legal pressures to meet German and EC environmental regulations by 1996.

In August 1990, immediately after German unification, in the so-called German Electricity Contract, three of West Germany's largest electricity generating companies – RWE-Energie, PreussenElektra and Bayernwerk – took a major stake in the East German electricity supply industry, which was highly dependent on brown coal for power generation. The Treuhand made over to them 75 per cent of former national utility Veag, which controlled the high voltage network and the brown coal mines, and 51 per cent of the regional utilities. The other 25 per cent of Veag was given to five medium-sized West German utilities. The new structure, which was due to come into effect at the beginning of 1991 remained, however, provisional as there was no agreement on price.

The carve-up by the three large multinationals was contested by over 150 East German local authorities, not willing to have their energy options limited. In July 1991, 123 communes (later to be joined by a further 35) complained to the German constitutional court that the takeover restricted their ability to produce their own electricity.

This conflict can be viewed from two angles. From the point of view of the Treuhand and the large companies, only they had sufficient resources to restructure the network and power stations. The towns' argument had two elements – that they, and not Western companies, had the right to produce power for themselves and, second, that they would do so on a more environmentally sound basis. Before 1949 when the communists took over, the municipalities had been responsible for energy and they argued that this right had been unconstitutionally taken away from them. Moreover, just before the former GDR ceased to exist, the 'Local Constitution Act' had defined electricity supply 'as a local community task'.[31]

None of the arguments was straightforward. The three large utilities combined public and private capital. Just under two-fifths of the shares in Bayernwerk are held by one of Germany's major natural resource companies, Veag AG, and the rest by the state of Bavaria. Some 70 per cent of the equity of RWE-Energie was in private hands, while the other 30 per cent was held by 64 West German communes with 60 per cent of the voting rights. Though this structure has been described as anachronistic, RWE-Energie has been unable to remove it. PreussenElektra was a full subsidiary of Veba AG, a multi-billion DM energy company.

The Treuhand gave the ex-GDR communes the 49 per cent balance of the regional utilities. This was not so much a nod in the direction of democratic control, but an acceptance of the key role local authorities play in Germany as the owners of roads and paths. The utilities have to obtain a concession from the relevant local authority before laying their cables underground. The stake however did not give the communes the full right to determine which company could supply their area, for the 1990 contract also stipulated that the GDR regional utilities should take 70 per cent of their electricity from Veag and the municipalities should take 70 per cent of their needs from the regional utilities, thus strictly limiting their own potential for supply and integrated planning.

A senior official of the federal German environment ministry, who has to remain anonymous, said the government supported the large West German companies for several reasons. With the establishment of a Single Market in the EC in 1993, the Bonn government was anxious to strengthen the international competitive position of its large power companies. Moreover as they had strong historical links with government they were able to influence the decision.

The other reason was environmental. With strong regulations on air emissions in force in Germany, expensive FGD was the quickest method to reduce pollution and only the large companies had sufficient resources. To introduce end-of-pipe methods and modernize the supply network was expected to cost up to at least DM40 billion ($27 billion),[32] the lion's share of which could only be met by the large companies. The changes also had to be made quickly. In order to comply with German and EC regulations, many of East Germany's electricity and district heating plants either have to be closed or modernized by the end of 1996.

Greenpeace said the ecological advantages of local authority control would have included more widespread use of combined heat and power (CHP) in district heating, rational energy planning and a greater political will to conserve energy.[33] It could also have reduced costs, as the losses in purely local distribution would probably have been less than those from long-distance lines.

All the utilities involved said that, until the case was resolved, they had insufficient security to justify any long-term investment. Of the 6,700 towns and districts in Eastern Germany, just under half refused to sign power contracts until the court passed judgement on the case. The constitutional court, though, delayed making a decision. This strengthened the hand of the large utilities, as only they had the resources to meet the 1996 deadline. A quick decision by the court would have allowed more time for the development of local initiatives. The decrease in electricity demand (by about a third) in the early 1990s would have allowed the communes sufficient flexibility to have prepared their own environmentally safer systems for the generation, supply and use of electricity. Though the exact reasons are unclear, in late 1992, Eastern Germany's electricity consumption showed the first rise since unification: consumption in October 1992 was 2.2 per cent higher than in October 1991, putting extra pressure on the communes to settle.

As the court delayed, the communes and the utilities sought individual compromises during the course of 1992. For example, Leipzig and RWE-Energie agreed to set up a joint municipal utility for electricity and district heating, with the city of Leipzig taking the major share. Frankfurt am Oder on the Polish border meanwhile set up its own utility to build a gas-fired CHP (combined heat and power) plant, for electricity as well as district heating. Dresden came up with another solution, which gave the regional utility an exclusive concession contract, but also allowed for the city to take over part of its own electricity supply in the future.[34]

Eventually in December 1992, an out of court settlement was reached, allowing the local authorities to supply, from their own sources or elsewhere, a maximum of 30 per cent of their requirements. The West German utilities were guaranteed 70 per cent of the electricity market for the next 20 years, in return for job guarantees in the brown coal mining industry. With hindsight it might be said that the court case and its settlement meant that Germany missed a major opportunity to experiment with a locally controlled (and potentially environmentally friendly) supply and conservation of energy.

THE VISIBLE HAND

COUNTRIES IN TRANSITION

The move by the countries of Central and Eastern Europe to establish a free market resulted in their euphemistic categorization as 'countries in transition', rather than the more honest 'middle-income developing'. The term was presumably intended to be a label that combined a little of the third world, with a recognition that the region was also quite different due to its legacy of central planning and communism. In so far as the transition was from being state- to privately-owned and managed, it was a reflection of what is slowly happening. If instead, as with most of the other such designations, it was based on GDP per head, then it did not mirror reality. For the CEE countries were not in transit from being relatively poor to being relatively rich, industrialized, and western; to suggest otherwise was a hoax.

It might also be said that creating this label was about as far as the international community had come by 1993, in adjusting to the changed circumstances since 1989. Politically over these four years the world was preoccupied with the Arab Gulf, the disintegration of Yugoslavia, and the break-up of the USSR. Economically it was concerned with a recession, which was mild compared with that which had occurred east of the Elbe. This lack of a substantive response may indicate that little has really changed, and that the terms 'communist' and 'in transition' were just convenient labels for a group of countries which were and are likely to remain on the by-roads of the industrialized world.

Indeed the desire of these former Moscow satellites for a closer political and economic relationship with Western Europe was rebuffed by an EC divided within itself, and generally more concerned with protecting its own economic interests than looking outwards, except across the Atlantic. Few commentators recognized that giving the region a closer and more equal political relationship with the EC would also have given it additional economic stability and helped its transition at little monetary cost.

However, such an invisible hand needed to be complemented by a more visible presence if it was to curb pollution. Direct comparisons of the cost of restructuring the former GDR and the sums being spent in the rest of the region highlight its relative poverty, the failure of its restructuring programmes and the miserliness of the West.

Drastic steps were required if Central and Eastern Europe was not to drown in a political and economic quagmire, at least partly of the West's making. These should have embraced not only well-directed technical and infrastructural aid and risk-reducing measures to stimulate foreign investment, but also a clear commitment by the governments of the region to sustainable restructuring. This chapter elaborates these steps and makes other suggestions.

With hindsight it might be said that, in 1990, governments' perceptions of the process and progress of restructuring were essentially ideological. The generally right of centre politicians who took charge in 1989 and 1990 believed that capitalism would intrinsically succeed, where communism had failed. By 1993, their views had begun to change. Jacek Siwicki, one of Poland's first post-1989 ministers, was reported as saying that errors were made in forecasting the process of East European transition. Bringing about economic regeneration 'has to be a managed process. You need a surgeon on the battlefield. You cannot leave it all to the markets'.[1] Nonetheless, it has to be added that even if there had been a wider recognition of capitalism's warts in 1990, the desire for democracy and its historical identification with the apparently successful Western market economies would still have meant its adoption, though possibly in a more restrained way.

TURNING THE CORNER?

In late 1992 and early 1993, there was a spate of optimistic forecasts that Poland had turned the economic corner. 'Poland seems to be the only country in which some return to aggregate positive growth may have taken place in 1992', according to Michael Bruno, who subsequent to writing this was offered the post of the EBRD's chief economist. He continued, 'In all of the countries [of the region] there is a sharp difference between the contraction in the large state-owned enterprise sector and the buoyant and expanding small scale private trade and service sector. Only in Poland may the relative weights of the two sectors have tilted the aggregate result in the desired direction'.[2] Hungary was expected by some to follow Poland in 1993.

Even if these forecasts turn out to be true they were based on narrow premises. They ignored the steep decline in GDP in the first three years of the decade, and took their base as the low point in the transition process. Manufacturing for the local market remained at a low ebb. In addition, by assuming that the private sector was the dynamo, governments dismissed the public sector, which could have and in some cases was providing the basis for a more sustained upswing.

Moreover, while the upturn may have meant Poland was turning a corner economically, this was not necessarily true in environmental terms. Poland's national environmental policy, agreed in 1990, said, 'The policy of sustainable development means on the one hand, a manner of consumption and production, which, in a sustainable manner, preserves the qualities and resources of the environment, and on the other hand, active protection of natural habitats'. To emphasize the point, the statement continued 'Both these approaches towards a sustainable development policy are appropriate in Poland'.[3]

Such a policy was drafted at the high point of ecological influence and when it was still believed that the introduction of the free market would make a major contribution to environmental restructuring. By 1993, it seemed unreal. From an environmental point of view, virtually no fundamental changes had occurred in the way the economy was managed. The transition left unturned many of the economic and social structures inherited from communism. Whilst most of the old coal-fired power stations continued to pollute, the governments were encouraging foreign companies to build new nuclear power stations. This removed any incentive to use energy more efficiently or generate it from renewable sources. The old factories producing cars and washing machines were taken over by domestic and/or foreign consortia, which adopted Western-style promotion methods to sell more, undermining moves to reduce vehicular emissions and phosphate-containing water discharges. Yet within the lifetime of these installations, governments would probably have to take stringent measures to decommission the nuclear reactors, curb the emissions of greenhouse gases, and protect the physical fabric and quality of towns and rivers.

The recession threatened deindustrialization in some areas. On the one hand this could have created a clean slate upon which to build an environmental nirvana. On the other hand, for governments to have seriously adopted sustainable development as a policy, they would have had to carry the bulk of the population politically, and generally they did not even make the attempt. Most firms also did not consider environmental issues important: profits, higher wages and paying debts were their top priorities. Private capital was drawn to the most profitable areas, which environmentally were usually those where it was least needed.

There were only a few instances of local concerns investing in new environmental products and services – they included Rafako in Poland and Foron in Eastern Germany.

Financial auditing of firms took precedence over environmental auditing. Cheaper and known obsolete technologies were preferred to new clean ones. End-of-pipe installations were preferred to integrated solutions. Radical environmental policies which would have enabled the region to overtake the West and provide an economic and environmental infrastructure for the 21st century were considered inappropriate. Thus zero import duties on turbines for small hydroelectric power plants, costly royalties on the exploitation of non-renewable resources, road charging and tax breaks for households investing in energy saving were all rejected, partly because there was no Western example to follow.

State-funded environmental investments were also restricted, ostensibly to curb budget deficits. While environmental and infrastructure projects such as developing renewable energy sources and modernizing public transport were rejected as 'too expensive', governments turned a blind eye to the rising incomes of private entrepreneurs and gave tax breaks and investment incentives to foreign investors. Foreign aid portrayed the same imbalance – tiny sums were granted to conserve biodiversity and the natural environment, and hundreds of millions for structural adjustment.

SUSTAINABLE RESTRUCTURING

Leading up to the Earth Summit at Rio de Janeiro in mid-1992, one question from many leaders in the third world was why the industrialized nations hypocritically expected much more from them, in environmental terms, than they did from themselves. The third world, in this instance, was expected to take a range of steps to promote sustainable development, while the industrialized countries were allowed to continue to vandalize the earth. Central and Eastern Europe was seen as falling between the two groups of countries. Trade sanctions were increasingly seen by public opinion in the first world as the most appropriate tool to gain compliance.

Sustainable restructuring is a modification of the term sustainable development. It means the process of restructuring economic activity so that it does not adversely affect the ecological system. Quite insufficient consideration has gone into the policies needed to move from today's non-sustainable economies to ones which are based on the precautionary principle (which places the proof of not harming the environment on the potential polluter) and which do not wantonly destroy the earth's natural resources. At a minimum, they would have to cover:

- setting raw material prices to cover the full costs of exploiting non-renewable resources;
- the adoption in practice as well as in theory of the polluter pays principle (PPP);
- the integration of macro and micro economic and environmental activities, using lifecycle analysis of products, a critical examination of energy use, and a rapid move to best available (clean/low waste) technology;
- appropriate environmental investments; and
- cleaning up the environmental abuses of the past.

CEE governments rather than using the creativity and upheaval of the quiet revolutions as the opportunity to leapfrog the economic and environmental mistakes of the West, often copied them. By 1992, the perception of the late 1980s that economic and environmental change were two sides of the same coin gave way to the view that the environmental role of government was to clean up the mess made by industrialists. In other words, the clear pro-active environmental remit of the quiet revolutions was replaced by a retro-active approach.

At the first Environment for Europe conference, held at Dobris Castle in Czechoslovakia in June 1991, the ministers agreed that 'advantage must be taken of the transition to market economies and the restructuring of these economies to introduce ecological aspects ... from the very beginning'. It went on to talk about the need for 'projects of economic assistance, joint ventures and other forms of western co-operation in central and eastern European countries [to be] screened with regard to possible negative impacts as well as possible profit for the environment' as well as 'urgent assistance' for the region's 'ecological disaster areas'.[4]

Two years on, there were few signs that these recommendations had been followed. Rather than put ecological sustainability at or even near the top of the agenda, governments had allowed the market to come up with expedient and piecemeal responses. Companies increasingly offered technical fixes in profitable areas such as catalytic converters, incinerators, FGD, nuclear reactors, and water filters. Where profits were absent, so were the changes.

It is still too soon to say whether the second Environment for Europe conference, held at Lucerne in Switzerland in April 1993, will be heeded any more than the first. It was a lower key event than the Czech meeting, but reportedly with more documentation. The Environmental Action Programme for Central and Eastern Europe (EAP) agreed by ministers at the meeting contained a range of policy recommendations for integrating environmental factors into the process of economic restructuring. Its stated aim was to remove the most dangerous threats to health with practical short-term measures, which governments would be able to carry out with their own resources. The authors, principally at the OECD and World Bank, wisely also incorporated longer-term guidelines, which in the hurly-burly of the early 1990s were often missing from discussions.

In spite of considerable preparatory work, the EAP would seem to have largely ignored the region's economic difficulties. It 'is overly optimistic about the positive impact of market reforms and industrial restructuring on the environment ... in the absence of effective environmental policies, industrial restructuring may look quite different [from that] expected in the EAP's baseline scenarios'.[5] In particular, no new funds were agreed – the EAP would seem to have anticipated that economic instruments (particularly pollution charges) supplemented by debt for environment swaps, other bilateral agreements and market prices for energy would be sufficient to curb emissions. How they were also expected to stimulate the introduction of sustainable alternatives, including wind, solar and/or water power, organic farming, eco-tourism, or even more advanced manufactures such as fly-wheel/electric cars, triple glazed windows or heat pumps, was unclear.

The final section of this chapter looks at some of the measures which need to be taken to support the common process of economic and environmental change. Their main goal is to enhance the process of economic restructuring to establish and nurture a much stronger bond between it and environmental rehabilitation.

More appropriate policies for economic restructuring

Economic policies in the early 1990s necessarily involved trial and error. None of the existing economic models, from 19th- or 20th-century Europe or from the third world, provided a satisfactory framework for the shift from central planning to the free market, though some may have contained certain useful elements or approaches to avoid. Yet more or less by default the hands-off approach of governments meant that their core policies were *laissez-faire*.

As the decade wore on, policies were needed to help overcome the deficiencies of this off-the-shelf free market model bought from the multilateral banks and a number of Western governments. This suit left much to be desired when applied to a hybrid economy. In particular, it did not take sufficient account of the constraints facing the new governments (such as the social and economic legacy of communism and ministerial muddle) or of the risks of investing in a regional rough-house.

An industrial policy along the lines taken by several of the South-East Asian countries would have been a useful framework. This model was quite the opposite of the free market hot house, making considerable use

151

of state controls and subsidies. Generally the governments adopted an industrial strategy (to support private and state-owned industries they expected to carve out a global role), an exchange rate policy (to encourage exports and savings), a preference for licensing over foreign investment (to acquire technology), and where necessary price supports and subsidies. They also emphasized factors such as capital accumulation and an educated workforce.

Privatization was not the panacea it was believed to be, though in some cases it was a useful adjunct. A recent World Bank report from Poland (see pages 58 and 59) suggests that at least some state-owned enterprises were quite able to finance their own diversification into export markets. This process could be accelerated by splitting the large combines into smaller units, which would compete with one another, price at arms length, react more rapidly to events and breed new managers.

As in South-East Asia, the most likely winners, by sector, should have been commercialized as state-owned corporations and then restructured with the help of their own retained earnings, bank loans, pro-active public loans and where appropriate private investment. EBRD involvement and partial rather than full privatization would have reduced the risk for the domestic or foreign investor. Strong anti-monopoly laws and concrete hard budget constraints would have helped identify the winners.

The enterprises likely to succeed fall into two groups. The first were those based on existing industries. Examples included meters for water, gas and electricity, some fertilizers and other bulk chemicals, some steel products, textiles and clothing, telephones and telecommunications equipment, light electrical engineering products, energy efficient boilers, filters, battery-driven buses and rail wagons and coaches. Not all these would be appropriate for one country. The second category covered new fields requiring research and development, either by local institutes or companies, or foreign investors. Examples included low-input farming, filters, biological waste water treatment systems, heat pumps and radiator valves, and pollution monitoring equipment.

Product development was probably the easiest part of the change. The hardest was marketing – this incorporated market research, pricing, promotion, distribution, stock and financial controls and after-sales service; these were nearly all 'foreign' concepts to the state-owned enterprise and to many of the new entrepreneurs.

The weakest state-owned plants should have been left to fend for themselves in the private sector. That would have given their managers and workers an immediate incentive to diversify into new areas, rather than cling to the familiar and compete with the expected winners. Some would become insolvent and close, others would succeed in new areas. However the producers of military goods, which were without any markets, needed special help in adjusting to the post cold war era.

The slow progress in reforming the banking system was one of the major weaknesses of the hybrid economy. Restructuring the banks would have helped both state-owned firms to modernize, privatized firms to diversify and new businesses (particularly new manufacturing firms) to gain a foothold on the competitive ladder. In the early 1990s, creditworthy concerns were usually at the bottom of the pile, as most banks' top priority was securing earlier non-performing loans to established industry. Resolving these issues was unlikely to be easy. Banks had to be assisted in reducing the support given to insolvent clients and encouraged to evaluate and underwrite new commercial risks. Ultimately more generous support to viable or potentially viable concerns would have helped generate fresh work opportunities, which in turn could have helped reduce unemployment and permitted the government to close of some of the worst polluting dinosaurs.

The EBRD to be truly effective had to stop pretending that it was possible to be both active in the former communist countries and simultaneously a merchant bank in the traditional sense. None of the furore over Jacques Attali's presidency addressed this absolutely key issue. The bank needed to broaden its activity from being purely reactive to proposals from Western companies to being pro-active. This change of emphasis would involve financing feasibility studies, and gathering support from foreign investors for potentially bankable joint venture projects. This process might even have helped persuade some of the more timid Western companies to invest. Being pro-active might have meant taking a bigger equity stake than a traditional merchant bank function would have required, but at least in the early years, the bank had too few customers.

Local priorities included restructuring the heavy industrial and energy sectors, but those of the EBRD did not. One reason was political. The EC, which held a 51 per cent share of the bank's capital, was reluctant to agree to projects in areas such as steel, textiles or fertilizers, as they would threaten its own industry.[6] Indeed by its lack of action in these sectors, the bank would seem to have taken the view that such enterprises were not worth saving and should close.

The bank has disappointed in other commercial ways: most of its lending was conditional upon Western participation in a private or soon to be privatized company. Thus loans to the vast majority of state-owned enterprises, irrespective of their activity or profitability, were not sanctioned, though paradoxically state-owned enterprises from the West were allowed to partner them. For a project to be bankable, it had to be geared to the export market rather than supplying domestic consumers. Some capital was channelled to existing local banks in an attempt to increase the EBRD's responsiveness to local needs, but the volumes involved were small.

The bank also needed to re-examine its own disbursement procedures. In 1991, the merchant and development banking divisions together disbursed only $75 million and in 1992 only $90 million, though approved project loans/equity stakes were six times greater. For instance disbursement of the bank's first loan, to improve the efficiency of district heating operations in five Polish cities, which had been approved in June 1991, had not started by October 1992, as the borrowers were unable to meet the EBRD's loan conditions. This was because the Polish cabinet had refused to allow an increase in district heating charges (for social reasons) in late 1992. In these circumstances, the municipal authorities which were the borrowers could not charge full market prices, as the bank required, for their hot water and steam.

It would seem that the bank's charter required a major revision. As with much of the rest of the foreign assistance, its lending procedures were geared primarily to meeting the needs of Western investors, rather than their likely partners. New possibilities could include the funding of pre-feasibility and feasibility studies, a greater degree of public consultation, helping potentially profitable state-owned enterprises to restructure, and a soft loan capability for district infrastructure projects.

In fact, the district dimension to economic regeneration did not receive the top priority it deserved. The Phare programme assisted in pilot projects for fostering small and medium-sized enterprises in Smoljan and Burgas in Bulgaria, and in Poland through the Struder programme for 'structural development in selected regions'. The Smoljan region is remote, with problems of access, pollution around the mines, and a general lack of business know-how; Burgas is more developed but unemployment is 10 per cent and rising. For Bulgaria, the EC allocated about $30 million through the Bulgarian Ministry of Industry – three-quarters for financing appropriate credit, credit guarantee and equity schemes and a quarter for training and other programmes, to be run by regional development agencies. These amounts need to be multiplied by a factor of 5 or 10 or even 20 in order to cover other parts of the region.

The Struder programme was providing $75 million in aid over three years (to 1995) to four districts in Poland, where unemployment was high and yet there was 'good development potential'. The five voivodeships selected were: Walbrzych in Lower Silesia, a heavy industrial centre on the Czech border; Łódź – once Poland's textile hub; Rzeszów, which developed on the back of the defence industry; and the rural Olsztyn and Suwalki provinces in the north-east. Struder will support regional development structures, training and advisory services and small infrastructure projects.

Trade would have been more useful than aid. It was the best means of helping successful enterprises accumulate the resources they themselves needed to restructure. However, in several of the principal sectors, where Central and Eastern Europe had a comparative advantage (again much of its heavy industry and textiles), the EC was reluctant to allow significant access. Indeed, according to Leon Brittan, the EC Commissioner for External Economic Relations, in 1992 the EC enjoyed a $1.3 billion trade surplus with the chief CEE countries.[7] Even where the EC had accepted limited import quotas in the initial association agreements, the Commission in Brussels subsequently tried to impose more restrictions. For example in 1993 anti-dumping duties were imposed or threatened for some steel items and fertilizers, while bans were imposed on some meat products from all of Central and Eastern Europe due to an outbreak of foot and mouth disease in Italy, that was traced to ex-Yugoslavia.

The association agreements need to be renegotiated to give the region far greater access to West European markets. The precondition for this, as for changes at the EBRD, was a sea-change in political attitudes within Western Europe. Just as Central and Eastern Europe needed to restructure economically and environmentally, the other side of the iron curtain needed a parallel shift in attitude.

Achieving environmental goals

Until recently, there was little acknowledgment of the importance of a clean and safe physical environment in either the theory or practice of capitalism. At its most basic, both the individual state and the international community failed to price essential public goods and services (such as clean air, water and land) according to their true cost of maintenance. In Central and Eastern Europe, under communism, the degradation of these environmental raw materials reflected their low or non-existent prices, the priority given to production and the lax implementation of environmental laws.

While PPP (discussed in Chapter 6) was the official basis in the West and in theory under communism for internalising the costs of maintaining the health of the environment, in practice it has certain weaknesses. Its primary focus is current pollution not its past consequences. Subsidies are often given by governments, though strictly speaking PPP is a no-subsidy approach. It does not cover the cost to subsequent generations of using (and thus destroying) non-renewable natural resources, only the emissions and discharges (if any) associated with their processing. Nor does it cover threatened pollution, such as the risk of radioactive leaks from nuclear power plants. Moreover, the short-term view taken by most businesses meant that any investment made to reduce their payments for the use of the environment usually resulted in end-of-pipe technology rather than a rethink in the processes used.

To be even partially effective as a tool, PPP required emission charges that were high enough to induce polluters to limit their use of the environment and efficient monitoring by an independent agency to ensure that the laws were followed. In the past this was not done in Central and Eastern Europe, while in the West the application and impact of PPP was mixed. Therefore, on the one hand, it was difficult to expect the CEE countries to adopt such policies wholeheartedly, as it would have put them at a competitive disadvantage. On the other hand, if they had genuinely believed in sustainable restructuring, such policies were necessary.

Associated measures should include taxing the use of non-renewable resources, such as oil, as well as iron and coal. The tax would reflect the notional cost of using a resource which could not be replaced; a higher price would discourage its use and improve the efficiency with which it is used. In turn such a tax would also provide an incentive for the development of less resource-intensive alternatives. Furthermore, in so far as the tax increases the cost of metal and hydrocarbons used in the manufacture of capital equipment, the cost of labour relative to capital would decline. This in turn could boost employment levels.

Transport policy was one area where charging cars and trucks their true environmental cost could have helped the region leapfrog over the West. Many commentators accept that in recent years Western governments have under-charged vehicles for the use of public roads (particularly in urban areas). This lopsided pricing policy resulted in the rundown of public transport. Central and Eastern Europe has the opportunity now to avoid this blunder by making all vehicles and their drivers pay the full costs of using the road and its surrounding environment. At the same time, governments should invest in new buses, trams and trains. Such a combination of policies would help preserve the urban fabric, reduce the emissions of nitrogen oxides and carbon dioxide and provide the region with a significant economic and environmental gain no longer on offer to the West.

Tradeable permits, along the lines engineered at Chorzow (see Chapter 6), are also a valuable tool which could have been more widely considered. Their main advantages over emissions charges are flexibility and presumed cost efficiency. Other economic instruments where environment and finance ministries (both East and West) should be holding hands are refundable deposits and charges on products linked with non-point pollution such as high-sulphur diesel fuel, fertilizers and packaging.

One small improvement was the growing use of environmental assessments. In Poland, they have been required for major projects since mid-1990. After completion, they were examined by the Environmental Impact Assessment Commission, which included NGO representatives; this made recommendations and the Ministry took the final decision. However, the submissions were not public, as they belonged to the enterprise which paid for them. Moreover, due to the shortage of trained environmental consultants, they were often prepared by the staff of the local ecological department, acting in a personal capacity.[8] Hence they hardly constituted an unbiased evaluation of competing technologies.

Furthermore, quite insufficient attention was being given to compliance. It would seem that governments were advised by the World Bank to focus on making the rules and standards less stringent and thus in line with typical Western practice and so easier to enforce. In fact, the habit of non-compliance endured with its practices of buying time and a reprieve, as well as of politicking for exceptions. The continuing existence of a social network of ex-communist party bosses in enterprises and in government helped enterprises avoid action, whether for economic or environmental reasons. Under-staffed and under-equipped local enforcement offices, and the lack of governmental resources, compounded the difficulties. Even in 1993, most factory emissions were not being independently monitored on a regular basis, so a complete picture of environmental crime could not be built up.

One of the main themes of the EBRD, as originally conceived by the French in the late 1980s, was to improve environmental conditions; it was an emphasis that the British and the Americans apparently rejected in favour of helping private enterprise. The mandate remains, though in a truncated form. This is the obligation to monitor all investments from an environmental angle. Projects with a major environmental impact (such as pulp and paper, non-ferrous metallurgy) require a full environmental assessment, while those with a lesser impact require a partial assessment. The main emphasis is on compliance with local laws. To what extent the bank goes further is hard to fathom, but it would seem that projects involving the use of asbestos, PCBs, CFCs or other clearly life-threatening materials are likely to be rejected. Other less tangible environmental requirements such as waste or product recycling and energy efficiency are unlikely to be made formal conditions of the loan or equity stake; with so few appropriate applications for loans, the bank's top priority has been to find bankable projects.[9]

It was the general desire of governments in the region to adopt EC environmental regulations. Most EC legislation is in the form of directives, which set environmental objectives, but leave the detailed standard-setting to individual governments. Adopting EC goals, for example a 60 per cent reduction in sulphur dioxide emissions by a specific year, might provide an initial framework for action, but little else. Adopting best Western practice would perhaps have been a better alternative, if such a compendium of laws, regulations and their applications had been available.

Sustainable restructuring would in any case have required more. In mid-1993, Greenpeace International identified a number of steps investing companies (whether domestic or foreign) should take, to ensure that the impact of their activities on the environment was minimal. They were aimed at fostering clean technology, and raising the amount of corporate information entering the public domain.

For Central and Eastern Europe, Greenpeace proposed that these steps take the form of contractual clauses (see Box 8.1) between the government and the investor. They could also be used by the EBRD to advance environmental change. Their incorporation in any agreement was likely to require lengthy negotiation, as most were in advance of existing practice in Western Europe. The typical investor was likely to see them as infringing its freedom of action and requiring the disclosure of commercially sensitive information. Nevertheless they provided a useful negotiating goal for the region's environmental ministries, particularly where, as in Poland, they were collaborating with the privatization agency. In due course, companies that agreed, say, to carry out regular environmental and/or energy audits on their subsidiaries in the region were likely to want to publicize the results.

One benefit of the Greenpeace clauses is that they challenge the inertia in the market economy from the grass roots direction. At a macro-level, governments should supplement this data with national environmental and energy accounts. Material and energy balances are already published by some countries in the region, putting them ahead of many developed countries of Western Europe. It would not be difficult for these to be modified to show the efficiency with which materials are used and the extent to which natural assets are being destroyed, and hence pinpoint areas for action.

Between mid-1990 and the end of 1991, considerable governmental and corporate resources were spent on preparing guidelines covering corporate investment in the region. These were agreed in Budapest in November 1991 (see Chapter 6). It is tempting to ask whether, now they have been promulgated, they are also being monitored.

Environmental investments

As in the economic sphere, the piecemeal approach prevailed in the environmental arena. In the early 1990s, multibillion dollar investments were necessary for the physical restructuring of Upper and Lower Silesia,

Box 8.1 *The Greenpeace contractual clauses*

For governments to incorporate standard environmental clauses in all privatization contracts in Central and Eastern Europe would allow them to set minimum standards of environmental behaviour and partially compensate for an inadequate regulatory system. They could progressively cover all enterprises as privatization progressed.

Greenpeace believes that ideally such measures should be embodied in law as the clauses seek to establish the public responsibilities of the privatized company in the environmental sphere. To be successful, they would need to be monitored by a competent body and the media, just as financial behaviour and accounts are watched.

The clauses were drawn up for Greenpeace International by the Centre for International Environmental Law in Washington, USA, and were published in *Open borders – broken promises* in English and Polish in May 1993. They include the following.

- The public's right to environmental information about the site, the enterprise's past operations, and the company's proposed operations. This requires the publication of audits, assessments and data or estimates relating to environmental discharges.
- Public participation in investment decisions, negotiations and performance – this could take the form of an annual public meeting when the buyer announces the results of the various audits.
- An initial environmental audit, prior to purchasing, and an annual environmental and energy efficiency audit.
- A periodic evaluation, comparing the site in question with other similar operations of the same company.
- Environmental impact assessment where appropriate.
- Joint, several and strict lifecycle liability.
- Support for local conservation and training in environmental laws for NGOs and government officials.
- Enforcement – allowing a ministry or member of the public to sue in an independent court on behalf of the environment.
- Compliance with environmental laws.
- Implementing the precautionary principle through clean production methods, using the best available technology. The precautionary principle means that where there are threats of environmental damage, lack of full scientific certainty shall not be used as a reason for preventing cost-effective measures to prevent environmental degradation.
- Transfer of obligations to buyers' successors.

northern Bohemia, and a number of the larger hot spots. In addition, multimillion dollar investments were needed for desulphurization, sewage works and land reclamation. To ensure the available finance was spent cost effectively, local authorities and governments needed to identify priorities. By 1993, a few had even begun to draw up plans.

The energy demonstration projects in the Czech Republic and elsewhere (see Chapter 7) were a positive example. Ideally such public funds should be channelled through a local sustainable restructuring corporation, whose goal would be to rebuild an area's physical infrastructure on an energy-efficient basis. To be successful, the corporation would have had to be armed with wide-ranging powers to amalgamate land ownership, rehabilitate degraded land, close down major polluters, and assist in restructuring those remaining. In terms of fostering energy efficiency, on the one hand it would need to foster the co-generation of power and heat and district heating, using renewable sources wherever possible. On the other hand, it would have to embrace public transport, and incentives for reduced energy consumption in public and private buildings and by industry. This would include reducing pipeline leakages and other losses in energy distribution, building and pipeline insulation, and recycling.

The German government took a less daring but more generous approach. In March 1993, it agreed to provide DM15 billion ($9 billion) over the following five years to clean up the Halle–Leipzig–Bitterfeld triangle, because of the slow progress in privatizing and attracting investors to the district. Perhaps because it could not admit failure, the Treuhand claimed that it had no figures on 'the current state of privatization in this special region'.[10] Nevertheless, it conceded that of the six pilot projects – Buna, Leuna, Chemie Bitterfeld, Hydrierwerke Zeitz, Filmfabrik Wolfen and Stickstoffwerke Piesteritz – only the latter had been privatized; and that was a week after the announcement by the federal government of its support for the clean-up.

By contrast, in Poland and the Czech Republic the sums provided to the Silesia/north Bohemia areas seemed minute. The World Bank granted an $18 million loan for environmental management to Poland in 1990 (see Box 6.1). In 1992, Phare allocated $3.6 million for an air monitoring system and the preparation of a longer-term regional plan. Sums of a similar size had been provided for rural conservation in the Carpathians on the borders of Slovakia, Poland and Ukraine, and in the Danube delta in Romania. Poorly funded marine conservation programmes were also being developed for the Black and Baltic Seas and the Danube river basin.

One painless way of increasing the volume of available finance would be for the West to give more support to Poland's debt for nature Ecofund. Similar programmes could be run in Hungary and Bulgaria.

Western creditors need to consider converting a part of their debt into local funds for use in sustainable restructuring.

Stimulating local public awareness and involvement

Since the revolutions, most environmental pressure groups have been drowned in the cacophony of competing public priorities, particularly rising unemployment and economic growth. Many of the NGO leaders of the communist era were absorbed into government, either directly or indirectly, depleting their ranks of experience. This was said to be one reason why, as under communism, some groups, at least in Czechoslovakia, were under the influence of environmental ministries.[11] Others spent time fighting among themselves. Some groups were also compromised as under communism they had fervently espoused the free market as an environmental cure-all, only to see it flounder in the early '90s.

It was this lack of a strong and independent political force arguing for sustainable restructuring which was a major reason for the slow pace of change. Local groups lacked information, resources, organizational skills and the political clout to develop meaningful alternatives. NGOs needed reliable information about the best environmental practice in the West. Such a catalogue would have given them and concerned public opinion a concrete lever to show governments and companies that environmental change was possible and had been realized in this place or that.

There has been some support for environmental NGOs from Western governments, aid agencies and their colleagues in other countries, but it was insufficient. Various agencies supported the Budapest regional environmental centre, but it failed to live up to its earlier promise, soon becoming out of touch with its grass roots.

Tomasz Żylicz, former Director of Economics of the Ministry of Environment in Poland, noted in 1991 that 'it would be unfair to completely disregard the environmental lobby. Occasionally they file complaints, organise on-site happenings, give embarrassing media interviews – yet without any serious effect due to the low social awareness'.[12]

Yet on industry's side, the position was also fairly weak. Żylicz, talking about the 'developers', said that 'there [were] hardly any involved in environmental debates in Poland. In 1990, a number of voivodes [the heads of provinces], acting on behalf of suburban coal-fired greenhouse owners, filed complaints about the excessive level of emission charges. Apart from that, industry has stayed rather quiet except for lamenting about its financial predicament'.[13]

Moreover, in spite of fine words, both governments and the multilateral banks were reluctant to encourage a real public debate on their environmental policies. The EBRD held a closed session in Warsaw in early 1992 with regional NGOs which criticized its support for the car industry. While its infrastructure projects were subject to public consultation, credits to companies were not. Presumably this was deemed inappropriate because it could force concerns to divulge commercially sensitive information. The World Bank, which was a far larger source of public funds, had no means of gaining popular feedback on its projects.

Given this lack of formal and informal channels for communication, it is hardly surprising that the environmental NGOs at the Budapest meeting mentioned above responded with a critical resolution, which emphasized the need for more information and public participation in investment decisions. With the banks and multinational corporations crafting the East in the image of the West, it was also appropriate that the NGOs stressed the importance of building upon 'the existing positive [environmental] heritage', in terms of protecting wild areas, a good public transport system, the reuse and recycling ethic, and organic farming. As John Hontelez, Chairman of Friends of the Earth International said, these were all points missed by the mainstream conference delegates.

ALL CHANGE

After 70 years, the 1917 Russian Revolution ended up parodying its original objectives. What of the quiet revolutions of 1989? Just as the Bolsheviks were forced to turn in on themselves due in part to invasion and then rejection by the West, there is the danger that the quiet revolutions will also fail. This time, though, the invasion and rejection are commercial and the result rising unemployment. The iron curtain has been pulled back, but the Western attitudes which prevailed during the cold war have not.

Pressures by European Community leaders for the CEE countries to renew their ex-Soviet ties and to fund their own restructuring miss the point of the revolutions, perhaps intentionally. The people of Central and East European want to become part of the West and the West has to learn to respond. Quickly.

Politically it has begun to do this in little ways, such as town twinning, but much more could be done by all parts of the community – NGOs and governments, multinationals and small businesses, shops and utilities, universities and schools, cities and villages.

Since the Second World War, the West has created an economic model which many other countries have wanted to follow. Central and Eastern Europe was and is no exception. However, Western institutions (such as the EC and the multilateral banks) have found it nearly impossible to respond to this aspect of the quiet revolutions for several reasons. First, it is unclear if the model can be so easily copied, as it was founded on the worldwide exploitation of non-renewable natural resources. On the one hand, these resources are no longer available in such quantities and at such low prices, and on the other hand, it is now clear their use has had and will have a worsening impact on the environment. In addition, there is the West's meanness. Both require the West to rethink its priorities.

A Bill Clinton Fund modelled on the Marshall Fund would be helpful if democratically controlled, by governments as well as by the potential recipients. The peace dividend is still waiting to be used. It would be a firm sign of commitment and help provide the infrastructure and environmental investments that are needed.

To be productive, such a fund would need to be accompanied by a thorough reappraisal by the West of where it too was going. In this, the Earth Summit was only a precursor. If the industrialized countries could begin to develop their own programme of sustainable restructuring, it would be much easier to encourage those who now want to follow in their consumerist footsteps to do the same. Such a process is long overdue, to tackle both the global and the local environmental implications of what some would call economic over-development. Though the West may have been the winner of the cold war, if it does not soon begin to change its treatment of the environment, it could become the ultimate loser.

REFERENCES

CHAPTER 1

1. Personal communication with author.
2. Jerzy Kurbiel, Water Pollution Control, '*Conference on environmental business opportunities in Poland in {the} 1990s'*, Newark, New Jersey, 16 April 1991.
3. J Famielec, K Gorka, G Mojzesz-Wlazly, 'Economic losses due to environmental pollution in Poland and the Cracow region', *Environmental and economic aspects of the industrial development in Poland*, Kraków Academy of Economics, Kraków, 1991.
4. Jürgen W Möllemann (Federal Minister of Economic Affairs), 'Investment the key to new world markets', *The European*, 4 October 1991.
5. Dr Jan Cerovsky (Chief Scientist, State Institute for Protection of Monuments and Nature Conservation), Czechoslovakia, *Environmental status reports Volume 1 1988/89*, International Union for the Conservation of Nature (IUCN)/World Conservation Union East European Programme, 1990.
6. Misha Glenny, *The Rebirth of History*, Penguin, Harmondsworth, 1990.
7. Dr Angheluta Vadineanu (Secretary of State, Department of Environment), Romania, *Environmental status reports Volume 2 1990*, International Union for the Conservation of Nature (IUCN)/World Conservation Union East European Programme.
8. *Warsaw Voice*, Warsaw, May 1991.
9. Gerhard Pohl, *Economic consequences of German unification, twelve months after the big bang*, mimeograph, World Bank, Geneva Office, October 1991.
10. 'Benefits for Russia will take time', *Financial Times*, 25 March 1993.
11. William Ryrie (Executive Vice-president of the International Finance Corporation), 'Throwing money at Poland could do more harm than good', *Financial Times*, 5 January 1990.
12. *Conservation and Change in Eastern and Central Europe and the USSR, Min-*

isterial statements addressed to IUCN members, autumn 1990, IUCN/World Conservation Union, Switzerland, 1990.

13. *Ministerial statements*, IUCN/World Conservation Union, as above.

14. Personal communication with author.

CHAPTER 2

1. J Borkiewicz, E Mieczkowska, A Aleksandrowicz and J Leitmann, *Environmental profile of Katowice*, unpublished draft, August 1991.

2. Jolanta Matiakowska, Eco-Alarm, Silensian Ecological Foundation, Katowice, 1990.

3. Michael Beleites, *Pechblende: der Uranbergbau in der DDR und seine Folgen* (*Pitchblend: uranium mining in the GDR and its consequences*), Berlin, 1988.

4. James Winpenny (Overseas Development Institute, London), 'Do market forces befriend the environment? The case of economic reform and environmental policy-making in Hungary', European Association of Environmental and Resource Economists, Third Annual Meeting, Kraków, June, 1992.

5. J Winpenny, as above.

6. *Sustainable Development in Czechoslovakia, a blueprint for transformation*, Hubert Humphrey Institute of Public Affairs, University of Minnesota, November, 1992.

7. *Elbe*, Greenpeace, Hamburg, 1990.

8. *Environment statistics in Europe and North America*, Economic Commission for Europe, United Nations, New York, 1987.

9. 'Waste by type, Table 39', *Environmental Protection 1992*, Ministry of Environment, Warsaw, 1992, taken from *The environment in Europe and North America: Annotated Statistics 1992*, United Nations, New York, 1992.

10. Alphons A C Uijtewaal Amador, 'Buried pesticide waste hazard [in] Poland', *Waste Management and Research*, No 10, 1992.

11. *Setting environmental priorities in Central and Eastern Europe*, discussion document on analytical approaches, Environment for Europe, Washington, DC, 3 December 1992.

12. *Threatened ecological regions in Poland in the years 1982 and 1990*, Main Statistical Office, Warsaw, 1992.

13. J Borkiewicz and others, as above.

14. J Borkiewicz and others, as above.

15. *Setting environmental priorities*, as above.

16. J Borkiewicz and others, as above.

17. *The state of environment in the Katowice industrial region*, Katowice Voivodeship Department of Ecology, Katowice, 1990.

18. *Bytom: environmental degradation*, Bytom Solidarity Committee, Bytom, Poland, 1990.

19. Personal communication with author.

20. J Borkiewicz and others, as above.
21. *Setting environmental priorities*, as above.
22. Pal Stefanovits, 'Agricultural production and the environment', *Ambio*, Vol 13, No 2, 1984, pp 99–100.
23. 'Choking the unborn', *The Guardian*, 26 March 1993.

CHAPTER 3

1. Personal communication with author.
2. Town guide.
3. Zbigniew Landau and Jerzy Tomaszewski, *The Polish Economy in the Twentieth Century*, translated by Wojciech Roszkowski, Croom Helm, UK, 1985.
4. Charles Jelinek-Francis and Eva Klvacova (Ministry of Privatization, Czech Republic), 'Privatization in Czechoslovakia, 1991 country report', Second Annual Meeting on Privatization in Central and Eastern Europe, Ljubljana, November 1991.
5. Iza Kruszewska, *Poland – a local authority perspective*, photocopy, Ashford, UK, November 1990.
6. Maciej Nowicki, 'Crisis in Eastern Europe', Annual Conference of the (UK) National Society for Clean Air and Environmental Protection, Brighton, 1990.
7. Adam Zwass, *The Economies of Eastern Europe, in a time of change*, Macmillan, London, 1984.
8. 'LDC Growth Strategies Misfire in the East', *Wall Street Journal Europe*, 5 July 1991.
9. Maria Sierpinska, 'The necessity of introducing raw material saving and energy saving projects to Polish industry', *Environmental and Economic Aspects of Industrial Development in Poland*, editor Kazimierz Gorka, Kraków Academy of Economics, Kraków, 1991.
10. *Ecological reconstruction: basic guidelines for ecological recovery and development in the new Länder*, Federal German Ministry of Environment, November 1991 (English translation).
11. *Czech and Slovak Federal Republic: Joint Environmental Study*, World Bank, Washington, DC, November 1991.
12. Istvan Jakab (Deputy Director, Borsod Chem), Untitled paper on attitudes to the environment, Conference on the Environment, Industry and Investment in Central and Eastern Europe, Budapest, November, 1991.
13. Tomas Żylicz (Director of Economics, Ministry of Environment), 'Environmental reform in Poland: theories meet reality', *European Environment*, February, 1991.
14. 'Production or destruction', *The Voice of Solidarity*, March–May 1988 (a translation, based on an article in the Polish weekly *Technical Review*).
15. Leszek Preisner, *Sulphur mining in Poland*, Working Paper No 47, Centre for Resource Studies, Queen's University of Kingston, Canada, May 1991.

16. *Development and the Environment: World Development Report 1992*, World Bank, Oxford University Press (OUP), 1992.

CHAPTER 4

1. 'Poland and Privatisation', *Mergers and Acquisitions International*, Financial Times Newsletters, London, June 1991.
2. 'The challenge of development', *World Development Report 1991*, World Bank, OUP, 1991.
3. 'Economic growth – explaining the mystery', *The Economist*, London, 4 January 1992.
4. Gregory Jedrzejczak (School of Management, University of Warsaw) and Henryk Sterniczuk (University of New Brunswick), 'Privatization in Poland, 1991 country report', Second Annual Meeting on Privatization in Central and Eastern Europe, Ljubljana, November 1991.
5. *Privatisation: Learning the lessons from the UK experience*, Price Waterhouse, London, July 1989.
6. 'We need an untainted market economy, and we need it now', Vaclav Klaus' philosophy on dynamic reform, *Transition*, World Bank, Vol 2, No 8, September 1991.
7. *Privatization in Poland: Program and Achievements*, Ministry of Privatization, Warsaw, September 1991.
8. Lajos Csepi (Managing Director, State Property Agency) and others, 'Privatization in Hungary, 1991 country report', Second Annual Meeting on Privatization in Central and Eastern Europe, Ljubljana, November 1991.
9. 'Capitalism or bust', *The Economist*, 8 February 1992.
10. 'Slow Cure Not Quick Fixes', *The Guardian*, 20 September 1991.
11. Brunon Synak (Department of Sociology, University of Gdańsk), *Polish Society: Integration and Anomie* (draft), photocopy.
12. 'The Poles are frightened of privatization', *Gazeta Wyborcza*, 17 January 1992.
13. *Successfully managing investments in Eastern Europe*, Deloitte Touche Tohmatsu International, London, 1992.
14. Prof Dr Helmet Sihler (President and Chief Executive Officer, Henkel), 'Development strategies of a chemical specialities company', High-level meeting on cooperation and sustainable development in the chemical industry, UN Economic Commission for Europe, Warsaw, March 1992.
15. 'Wanted: People for Top Jobs', *Warsaw Voice*, 15 March 1992.
16. 'Privatising East Germany', *The Economist*, 14 September 1991.
17. G Jedrzejczak and Henryk Sterniczuk, as above, p 6.
18. 'Lingering in ruin', *Warsaw Voice*, 3 May 1992.
19. 'Dreams about departure', *Gazeta Bankowa*, Warsaw, 26 April 1992.
20. *Economic Survey of Europe in 1992–3*, United Nations, New York (taken from 'Moscow needs own Marshall plan', *Financial Times*, 14 April 1992).

21. 'Nynex pulls out of Hungary', *East European Markets*, Financial Times Newsletters, London, 2 October 1992.
22. G Jedrzejczak and Henryk Sterniczuk, as above.
23. 'Japan holds off in eastern Europe', *Financial Times*, 25 May 1990.
24. Charles Jelinek-Francis and Eva Klvacova (Ministry of Privatization, Czech Republic), 'Privatization in Czechoslovakia, 1991 country report', Second Annual Meeting on Privatization in Central and Eastern Europe, Ljubljana, November 1991.
25. 'Don't build a welfare wall', *The European*, 12 July 1991.
26. S Collins and D Rodrik, *Eastern Europe and the Soviet Union in the World Economy*, Institute for International Economics, as reported in 'Eastern Europe and the World', *The Economist*, 6 July 1991.
27. Personal communication with author.
28. 'Throwing money at Poland could do more harm than good', *Financial Times*, 5 January 1990.
29. 'Catalysts, not saviours', *The Economist*, 21 September 1991.
30. 'More promises than cash', *Wall Street Journal*, 9 February 1992.
31. Stuart M Butler, *Central Europe's Mass-Production Privatization*, US Heritage Foundation, 1991.
32. Josef Marek (Prague Ecology Centre), 'National Report on the Czech Republic', Friends of the Earth West Goes East Conference, Sofia, January, 1992.
33. 'Credit takers paid only 500 million dollars', *Nowa Europa*, 26 February 1992.
34. 'A changing Europe', *EBRD annual report 1991*, London, 1992.
35. 'Growing pains at the Eurobank', *The Economist*, 28 March 1992.
36. Personal communication with author.
37. 'EC paid programs fuel reform in former east bloc', *Wall Street Journal*, 22 February 1993.
38. G Oprescu (Council of Reform) 'Privatization in Romania, 1991 country report', Second Annual Meeting on Privatization in Central and Eastern Europe, Ljubljana, November 1991.
39. 'Grim prognosis for East European recovery', *Financial Times*, 1 May 1991.
40. 'Eastern Europe seen heading for Thirties-type depression', *Financial Times*, 2 December 1991.
41. 'A new economic order eludes eastern Europe', *Financial Times*, 6 April 1992.
42. 'Polish state industries perform strongly', *Financial Times*, 17 January 1993.
43. 'Dynamic state sector bucks conventional wisdom', *The Guardian*, 9 January 1993.
44. 'Obstacle Track from Trade to Production', *Review of Commerce*, Poznan, September 1991.
45. 'Private business failures in first two months of 1993', *BBC Survey of World Broadcasts (Eastern Europe)*, Reading, UK, 15 April 1993.
46. Sanjay Dhar, 'Public enterprise restructuring: Achilles' heel of the reform

process', *Transition*, Vol 3, No 3, World Bank, Washington, DC, March 1992.
47. 'Czechoslovak voucher scheme opens doors for western investors', *PlanEcon Business Report*, 4 March 1992.
48. Jouko K Leskinen (Vice-chairman of Neste Oy and Chairman of the Chemical Industry Federation of Finland), 'Conditions and requirements for Western investment as seen by the business community', High-level meeting on cooperation and sustainable development in the chemical industry, UN Economic Commission for Europe, Warsaw, March 1992.
49. *Reforming the economies of Central and Eastern Europe*, OECD, Paris 1992.
50. 'Troubled times for industry', Hungary supplement, *Financial Times*, 30 October 1991.
51. 'Bankruptcy in Hungary rises', *Financial Times*, 10 April 1992.
52. Eugenio Lari (World Bank Director Europe and Central Asia), International conference on privatization, foreign direct investment and environmental liability, World Bank, Warsaw, May 1992.
53. 'Ex-DDR: Wenig Arbeit, viel Natur?', (Ex-GDR: less work, more nature?) *Tages Zeitung*, Berlin, 7 August 1991.
54. Personal communication with author.
55. G Pohl, Economic Consequences of German Unification: twelve months after the big bang, Mimeograph, World Bank, Geneva, October 1991.

CHAPTER 5

1. B Kaminski, *Conservation and Change in Eastern and Central Europe and the USSR*, Ministerial statement addressed to IUCN members, IUCN/World Conservation Union, Switzerland, 1990.
2. Personal communication with author.
3. *Setting environmental priorities in Central and Eastern Europe*, Environment for Europe conference, Washington, DC, 3 December 1992.
4. Eugenio Lari (World Bank Director Europe and Central Asia), International conference on privatization, foreign direct investment and environmental liability, World Bank, Warsaw, May 1992.
5. 'Development and the environment', *World Development Report 1992*, World Bank, OUP, 1992.
6. Personal communication with author.
7. *Basic Guidelines for Ecological Recovery and Development in the New Länder*, Federal German Ministry of Environment, Bonn, 1991.
8. Personal communication with author.
9. Federal German Ministry of Environment, as above.
10. 'Environmental pollution reduced in 1992', *BBC Survey of World Broadcasts (Eastern Europe)*, Reading, UK, 3 December 1992.
11. 'Crash clean-up', supplement on Saxony, *Financial Times*, 1 September 1992.

12. 'Recessionary waters [are of a] better class', *Gazeta Wyborcza*, 30 March 1992.
13. *Ecological recovery and development concept Leipzig/Bitterfeld/Halle/Merseberg*, Rheinland Technical Inspection Service (Tüv), commissioned by the Federal German Environment Agency, Köln, December 1991.
14. 'Environmental spending in 1992', *BBC Survey of World Broadcasts (Eastern Europe)*, Reading, UK, 18 February 1993.
15. Personal communication with author.
16. *National Environmental Policy*, Ministry of Environment, Warsaw, May 1991.
17. 'Development and the environment', as above.
18. Ruth Bell, 'Privatization and the environment in Central and Eastern Europe: obstacles and opportunities for environmental gain', Milan Preparatory Commission for the Earth Summit, September 1991.
19. 'Lingering in ruin', *Warsaw Voice*, 3 May 1992.
20. Personal communication with author.
21. Wojciech Stodulski, *Environmental liabilities in privatization through liquidation in Poland, 1990–1*, Institute for Sustainable Development, Warsaw, May 1992 (photocopy).
22. Kazimerz Gorka and Grzegorz Peszko (Kraków Academy of Economics), 'Privatization, environmental liabilities and credit insurance funds for foreign investments in Central and Eastern Europe', Third Annual Conference of the European Association of Environmental and Resource Economists, Kraków, June 1992.
23. Wojciech Stodulski, as above.
24. 'Development and the environment', as above.
25. E Lari, as above.
26. *Preliminary report on the social and economic situation in 1992*, Central Planning Office, Warsaw, February 1993.
27. *Bulgaria: environmental strategy study*, Joint report of the government of Bulgaria, the US government and the World Bank, Washington, DC, November 1991.
28. *Setting environmental priorities*, as above.
29. 'Where the devil says goodbye', *The Sunday Times (colour supplement)*, London, 22 April 1990.
30. 'Scrapped factories "will feed" E Europe's steel industry', *Financial Times*, 4 September, 1990.
31. 'Privatisation in Eastern Europe', *The Economist*, 14 April 1990.
32. 'List of investment projects in the scope of environmental protection', Conference on Environmental Business Opportunities in Poland, Promasz, Newark, New Jersey, April 1991.
33. Tomasz Żylicz (Director of Economics, Ministry of Environment), 'Financing Environmental Protection in Poland: the Past and the Future', Seminar on Poland's Debt for Environment Swap, Poznan, November 1991.
34. Personal communication with author.

35. *Environmental business opportunities in Poland*, Prospectus Publications, Canada (from information provided by the Ministry of Environmental Protection), and the Ministry of Environment, Warsaw, January 1991.

36. Jonathan Plaut (Director Allied-Signal and Chairman of the Environmental Committee of the US Council for International Business), 'Environmental evaluation and assessment', Conference on the environment, industry and investment decisions in Central and Eastern Europe, Budapest, November 1991.

37. Personal communication with author.

38. 'ABB loses battle for Polish boiler maker', *Financial Times*, 14 January 1993.

39. 'For Czechs, good water is no longer hard to find', *Wall Street Journal Europe*, 8 March 1993.

40. 'EBRD issues its guidelines for environmental consultants', *Development Business*, No 355, United Nations, New York, 30 November 1992.

41. *The state of the environment: damage and remedy*, Ministry of Environment, Warsaw, 1991.

42. *National Environmental Policy* of Poland, May 1991, as above.

43. *The environment in Eastern Europe*, IUCN East European Programme, Switzerland, 1991.

44. 'Power plant modernisation to cut pollution', *Petroleum Economist*, July 1992.

45. 'Both ends of the pipe', survey on the Environment, *The Economist*, 8 September 1990.

46. 'Environmental Policy Issues, Environment for Europe', International Conference on Privatisation, Foreign Direct Investment and Environmental Liability, Warsaw, May 1992.

47. *The state of the environment*, as above.

48. *Development Business*, United Nations, New York, January 1993.

49. *Environmental business opportunities in Poland*, as above.

50. Tomasz Zylicz (Director of Economics, Polish Ministry of Environment), 'The Greening of the Post-Communist Europe?', Second Annual Conference of the European Association of Environmental and Resource Economists, Stockholm, June 1991.

51. Piotr Glinski and Grzegorz Peszko, *Polish National Report for Global 2000*, Austria, May 1992.

52. Jeff Cole (Programme Specialist, Ministry of Environment), 'Poland's Domestic vs International Investment Priorities', International Ecological Fair, Poznan, November 1991.

53. S Sitnicki, Conference on the Environment, Industry and Investment Decisions in Central and Eastern Europe, Budapest, November, 1991.

54. Stefan Kozlowski (Ministry of Environment), 'Opening address', High-level meeting on co-operation and sustainable development in the chemical industry, Warsaw, March 1992.

55. 'Waste is Falling On Us, Sewage will Poison Us', *Gazeta Wyborcza*, 4 November 1991.

56. 'Swedish invasion', *Warsaw Voice*, 10 November 1991.
57. 'The Packaging Board Industry in Eastern Europe', Credit Suisse First Boston, the Second Packaging Board Conference, Brussels, November 1991.
58. 'Projecting car emissions' (a summary of a report prepared by Earth Resources Research for the Worldwide Fund for Nature), *Acid News*, June 1991.
59. 'Eastern Europe is a major opportunity for oil industry', *Oil and Gas Journal*, 21 October 1991.
60. 'Czech villagers reject US scheme', *EEE*, Financial Times Newsletters, September 1992, p 13.
61. Personal communication with author.
62. *Setting environmental priorities*, as above.
63. *Setting environmental priorities*, as above.
64. E Lari, as above.
65. *Setting environmental priorities*, as above.
66. Tomasz Zylicz (Director of Economics, Polish Ministry of Environment), 'What Environmental Policy For a Successful Industrial Restructuring?', High-level meeting on cooperation and sustainable development in the chemical industry, Warsaw, March 1992.
67. *Poland, the Waste Invasion*, a Greenpeace Dossier, October 1990.

CHAPTER 6

1. 'Environmental Policy Issues', International Conference on Privatization, Foreign Direct Investment and Environmental Liability, Environment for Europe (background note), Warsaw, May 1992.
2. *Economic Instruments for Environmental Protection*, OECD, Paris, 1989.
3. 'Survey on Industrial Investment and Environmental Issues, Preliminary Results', International Conference on Privatization, Foreign Direct Investment and Environmental Liability, Environment for Europe (background note), Warsaw, May 1992.
4. Dr-Ing Heiner Bonnenberg (Treuhand Director of Environmental Protection), 'Treuhand's handling of environmental problems on industrial sites to be privatized', International Conference on Privatization, Foreign Direct Investment and Environmental Liability, Warsaw, May 1992.
5. Personal communication with author.
6. *Ecological recovery and development concept Leipzig/Bitterfeld/Halle/Merseberg*, Rheinland Technical Inspection Service (Tüv), commissioned by the Federal German Environment Agency, December 1991.
7. Ruth Greenspan Bell (Assistant General Counsel, Water (Effluent Guidelines), Environment Protection Agency, Washington), 'Industrial privatization and the environment in Poland', *Environmental Law Reporter*, February 1992.

8. Conference on the environment, industry and investment decisions in Central and Eastern Europe, Budapest, November, 1991.

9. R Bell, *Environmental Law Reporter*, as above.

10. R Bell, 'Integrating environmental concerns into the privatization process – general considerations', International Conference on Privatization, Foreign Direct Investment and Environmental Liability, Warsaw, May 1992.

11. R Bell, *Environmental Law Reporter*, as above.

12. Personal communication with author.

13. Jim Sherer (Advisor to the Czech Ministry for the Environment), *Privatisation and Environmental Issues: Compliance with Environmental Laws and Clean-up of Past Contamination*, photocopy, early 1992(?).

14. Istvan Jakab (Deputy Director, Borsod Chem), Untitled paper on attitudes to the environment, Conference on the Environment, Industry and Investment in Central and Eastern Europe, Budapest, November 1991.

15. Lajor Bokros, (Chairman and CEO, Budapest Bank), 'Spontaneous privatization in Hungary, 1991 Country Report', Second Annual Meeting on Privatization in Central and Eastern Europe, Ljubljana, November 1991.

16. Lajor Bokros, as above.

17. J Kindler and others (Budapest University of Economic Science), 'National Report on Hungary', Friends of the Earth West Goes East Conference, Sofia, January 1992.

18. 'Communism's dirty legacy', *International Herald Tribune*, 14 May 1992.

19. Personal communication with author.

20. 'Continental AG talks with Czechoslovakia over pollution issues', *Wall Street Journal*, 6 November 1992.

21. Dr Eva Kruzikova (Advisor to Czech Deputy Minister of Environment), 'Privatization and environmental liability, the experience of the Czech Republic', Conference on Privatization, Foreign Direct Investment and Environmental Liability in Central and Eastern Europe, Warsaw, May 1992.

22. Personal communication with author.

23. *Economic tools for environmental protection*, Ministry of Environment, Czech Republic, Prague, January 1992.

24. Personal communication with author.

25. G Peszko and W Stodulski, 'National Report on Poland', Friends of the Earth West Goes East Conference, Sofia, January 1992.

26. Personal communication with author.

27. Boguslaw Fiedor (Professor, Oskar Lange Academy of Economics, Wroclaw), 'The use of funds for financing environmental cleanup', International Conference on Privatization, Foreign Direct Investment and Environmental Liability, Warsaw, May 1992.

28. *The state of the environment in Poland: damage and remedy*, Ministry of Environment, Warsaw, 1991.

29. Daniel Dudek (EDF), Zbigniew Kulczynski (Warsaw School of Economics) and Tomasz Zylicz (Director of Economics, Ministry of Environment), 'Implementing Tradeable Rights in Poland: a case study of Chorzow',

Third annual conference of the European Association of Environmental and Resource Economists, Cracow, June 1992.

30. Personal communication with author.
31. Personal communication with author.
32. John E Marrow (Coopers & Lybrand Deloitte), 'Eco-Fund: a new source of project finance', International Ecological Fair, Poznan, November 1991.
33. 'Conclusions and statement of guiding principles', Conference on the Environment, Industry and Investment Decisions in Central and Eastern Europe, Budapest, November 1991.
34. 'Conclusions and statement of guiding principles', as above.
35. *The Business Charter for Sustainable Development: principles for environmental management*, International Chamber of Commerce, Paris, 1991.

CHAPTER 7

1. Edward Krapels, 'The commanding heights: international oil in a changed world', *International Affairs*, London, January 1993.
2. Miroslaw Dakowski, 'Energy control – a challenge for [the] Polish economy', Conference on global collaboration on a sustainable energy development, Copenhagen, April 1991.
3. M Dakowski, as above.
4. *Energy Operations Policy*, EBRD, London, March 1992.
5. 'Bulgaria far from solving energy equation', *Financial Times*, 24 March 1992.
6. 'Hungary's energy use down in 1991', *East European Energy Report*, Financial Times Newsletters, June 1992.
7. Mohamed Hafiz-Khodja and Rabea Ferroukhi, 'Eastern Europe in transition: energy use and the environment', *OPEC Bulletin*, March 1992.
8. Charles Movit (PlanEcon, Washington), 'East Europe's energy trade takes new shape', *Oil and Gas Journal*, 3 June 1991.
9. 'Electricity in the Slovak Republic', prepared by SEVEn, in *Energie für die Slowakei*, a report by the Austrian Ecology Institute for the Worldwide Fund for Nature (WWF), Vienna, Austria, March 1992.
10. Jeremy Russell, *Energy and environmental conflicts in East/Central Europe: the case of power generation*, Royal Institute of International Affairs (RIIA), Energy and Environmental Programme, London 1991.
11. Douglas Gyorke, Morton Blinn and Thomas Butcher, 'The Krakow clean fossil fuels and energy efficiency project', The 85th annual meeting of the Air & Waste Management Association, June 1992.
12. *OPEC Bulletin*, as above.
13. 'IEA predicts Eastern Europe expansion in nuclear, oil and gas', *European Energy Report* (EER), Financial Times Newsletters, 6 March 1992.
14. J Russell, as above.
15. *Poland Environmental Strategy*, World Bank, Washington, 1992.

16. 'When will there be a programme for energy?', *Rzeszpospolita*, Warsaw, 17 July 1992.
17. *Poland Environmental Strategy*, as above.
18. 'Nuclear plants and our fears', Interview with Otto Lendvai and Dr Gyorgy Pethes of the Nuclear Atomic Energy Committee, *Review of the Ministry of Environment*, No 1, Budapest, 1992.
19. *Summaries of programmes approved by October 1992*, Phare, EC Commission, Brussels, 1992.
20. 'West rescues East's nukes', *Petroleum Economist*, June 1992.
21. *Energy Operations Policy*, as above.
22. *Summaries of programmes*, as above.
23. 'Czechoslovakia', *Power in Europe*, Financial Times Newsletters, 14 August 1992.
24. J Russell, as above.
25. J Russell, as above.
26. 'Amoco unit acquires two blocks covering 2.7 million acres in Poland', *Oil and Gas Journal*, 12 October 1992.
27. P J Kowalik, *Bio-energy potential utilization in Poland*, Gdansk, undated.
28. J Russell, as above.
29. *Let's save the Danube now!*, flyer from SZOPK (The Slovak Union of Nature and Landscape Protectors), Bratislava, late 1992.
30. *Let's save the Danube now!*, as above.
31. Franz Schmitt, 'The development of the electricity industry in the former GDR', *Perspectives in Energy*, Moscow, 1991.
32. F Schmitt, *Perspectives in Energy*, as above.
33. *Kommunalisierung der Energieversorgung in der neuen Bundesländern*, (*The municipalization of energy supply in the new Bundesländer*), Greenpeace, Berlin, undated.
34. 'German communes fight back', *Power in Europe*, Financial Times Newsletters, 30 January 1992.

CHAPTER 8

1. 'Caught out by a turning tide', *Financial Times*, 8 April 1993.
2. Michael Bruno, 'Stabilisation and the macroeconomics of transition – how different is Eastern Europe?', *Economics of Transition*, Vol 1, No 1, 1993.
3. *National Environmental Policy*, Ministry of Environment, Warsaw, November 1990.
4. 'Conclusions', Environment for Europe conference, Dobris Castle, Czechoslovakia, June 1991.
5. Grzegorz Peszko (Poland's Green Federation and Kraków Academy of Economics), *The use of economics to develop environmental policy*, a discussion paper for Environment for Europe ministerial conference, Lucerne, April, 1993.
6. Personal communication with author.

7. 'East Europe calls EC's bluff over free trade', *Financial Times*, 16 April 1993.
8. Personal communication with author.
9. Personal communication with author.
10. Personal communication with author.
11. *Sustainable Development in Czechoslovakia, a blueprint for transformation*, Hubert Humphrey Institute of Public Affairs, University of Minnesota, November, 1991.
12. Tomasz Żylicz, 'The Greening of the Post-Communist Europe? Yes, but not quite', European Association of Environmental and Resource Economists, Second Annual Conference, Stockholm, June 1991.
13. T Żylicz, as above.

Index

47; alumina refinery 82–3; biomass potential 140; chemicals 28–9; coal and pollution 133, 134; coal the main fuel for domestic heating 34; cost of environmentally safe technologies 87–8; cost of restructuring 147; dangers of working and living in uranium mining area kept quiet for security reasons 19; electricity and district heating plants 144; electricity consumption 145; electrochemical industry 28; energy consumption 127, 139; environmental groups 72; factories selling to, badly hit 10; impact of privatization of energy sector 143; importance of coal as main fuel for power generation 132–3; infrastructure and appropriate resources 49; insolvent industrial enterprises 66; manufacturing output 57; new Bundesländer 39, 51, 53, 73; new company registrations 61–2; 'new economic system' 33; non-point pollution sources 23; number of registered cars 96; oil refineries 31; opposition groups 37; Phare in 56; private capital invested in 12; response to liability 110–11; sulphur dioxide received in Poland from 21; Western car companies the largest investors 97; world leader in emissions per head 19; see also Black Triangle; Halle; Leipzig; Treuhand

EBRD (European Bank for Reconstruction and Development) 85, 86, 90, 131, 147, 152, 153–4, 155, 158; credits to companies 162; disbursement of first loan, to improve the efficiency of district heating operations 154; energy operations policy 128–9; infrastructure projects 161; initial years 55, 88; nuclear power advisory group 137, 138; one of the main themes 157; selected bankable projects 11

EC (European Community) 94, 119, 142, 146–7, 153–5 *passim*, 162; Common Agricultural Policy 69; Czech, Hungarian and Polish goods to conform with rules 69; environmental protection standards 124; environmental regulations 134, 144, 157; firms 91; imports from 11, 68; industries locating in the countries of Central and Eastern Europe 123; new Bundesländer immediately incorporated 39; short-sightedness of 52; Single Market 144; steel exports from Czechoslovakia to 14; steel industry in 83; see also Phare

ecological issues 118; mess left by communism 6, 16, 18; one of Europe's worst 'hot spots' 23; 'police' 94; poor record 71; severe threats 22

economic assistance see aid

economic growth 41, 127, 161; falling rates 33

economic instruments 75, 104, 112–22

Economist, The 42–3, 45, 53, 54, 56, 83

ECSC (European Coal and Steel Community) 84, 85

EDF (Environmental Defence Fund) 120, 122

EFTA (European Free Trade Association) 124

Elbe 21

electrical products 29

Électricité de France 138

electricity 7, 31, 34, 128, 133, 138; centralized control of generation 127; cost of 99; environmentally safer systems for generation, supply and use 144–5; forecast rises in use 137; inefficient production 129; price reportedly tripled 83; relatively cheap 98; restricted ability to produce 143; supplied to industry 81; see also hydroelectricity

Electrolux 111

emissions: airborne 21, 23, 36, 74, 79,
126, 134; charges for 13, 113, 93,
114–15; 156, 161; curbing some of
the worst excesses 72–7;
disorganized, hydrogen sulphide
36; factory 6, 157; falling/
increasing 100; fines 13; fugitive,
unmeasured 35; industrial 4, 21;
PPP and 155; progress in reducing
134; regulations 122; relative to
GDP, quite high 20–1; rise in some
emission levels 96–7; technologies
for reducing 134, 135; vehicle 20,
120, 148; water 3, 36; world
leaders 19; *see also under various
headings, eg* carbon dioxide;
hydrocarbons; nitrogen oxide;
sulphur dioxide

employment 3, 49, 156; full 12; rapid
gains 44

energy 13, 30, 36, 88, 90, 124;
allowing prices to rise to market
levels 77; conservation of 127, 130,
145; consumption of lignite mining
7; efficiency of production and
consumption 127–32; electrical,
coal-based 7; excessive reliance on
narrow range of sources 127;
forecast increase in demand 140;
heavy users 82; insolvent and
obsolete sector 102; intensity per
unit of GDP 32; losses 128–9;
political emphasis on 31; prices 43,
77, 129; renewable 87, 127, 140–2,
160; sources of 132–42; subsidies
80; switch-on 126

Engels, F 29

engineering 28, 91; *see also* under
individual companies

enterprises and companies 40; likely to
succeed 152

entrepreneurs 10, 12, 48, 55

environment: abuse of, in the cause of
production 37; achieving goals
155–8; adjunct to regulations 105;
attempt to shift responsibility for

78; basis for control 104; benign
products 102, 113; clean and safe,
little acknowledgment of the
importance of 155; cleaning up
abuses of the past 150; communist
governments and 27; consequences
of the market economy 70–103;
controls on dumping process waste
in the sea 100; costs 86, 98–100,
106; damage 15, 85; degeneration
after Second World War 28–38;
EC protection standards/regulations
124, 134, 144, 157; escape clauses
64; expenditure 13; experimenting
with change 104–25; guidelines
and codes of conduct 123–5; lax
implementation of regulations 100;
legislation 15, 77, 92–4, 99;
liability 105–12; likely failure of
free market to bring substantial
improvements 15; low-penalty
rules 100; minimisation of adverse
impact 124; poor 6; pressure   .
groups 161; protection 13, 52, 77;
radical policies 149; reducing the
impact of economic activity on 13;
threats to 3, 102, 105; use and
abuse of 19–23; widespread
devastation 11; *see also*
environmental degradation;
environmental funds;
environmental groups;
environmental laws; infrastructure;
investment; pollution;
restructuring

Environment for Europe conferences
(1991, 1993) 150

environmental degradation 7, 16, 19,
71; continuing 101; economic
instruments to try to prevent 75;
incineration often a cause of 114;
increased 97; industrial 8; progress
in tackling 6; raw materials 155;
result of coal combustion 134;
rising, opposition to 72; severe 92

environmental funds 75, 90, 113, 117,
116–20; national 90

183

environmental groups: Bulgarian 9, 26, 79; Czech 1, 130, 132, 161; East German 72; Hungarian 8, 26, 142; Polish 3, 26, 80; Slovak 98
Environmental Impact Assessment Commission 156–7
environmental laws 92; failure of 34–6; lax implementation of 14; on waste and recycling 102; stringent, on emissions and waste disposal 10; stronger, introduction and enforcement 103; strict enforcement sometimes impossible 94; weak administration of 15
Environmental Protection Fund 116
Esso 98
eutrophication 21
exchange rates see foreign exchange
ex-communists 41
expectations 43; and reality 7, 10
expenditure 13, 75–6, 81; 'non-essential' 33
exports 14, 37, 66, 100

feedstock 31, 34
fertilizers 30, 56, 74; anti-dumping for 155; chemical 23; high-sulphur 156; less use of 73; manufacture 34; nitrate 21, 26; residues 21
FGD (flue gas desulphurization) scrubbers 76, 85, 87, 90, 91, 122, 134, 135, 144, 150; upgrading 88
Fiat 85, 116
Fiedot, Boguslaw 116
filters 85, 150; more efficient operation of 74–5
finance 46, 131; development of a framework for doing business 52; local, availability of 11; reforms 45, 65; see also banks
fines 13, 112, 122; enterprises allowed to sidestep payment 114–15; low level of 35; ways to avoid paying 14
Finnish bilateral aid programme 77
fiscal policies 66
fixed incomes 11
fluorescent tubes 80

fluoride 20
fluorine 23, 82, 99
fly tipping 96
food: falling demand 73; lower prices 73; processed 66, 96, 100; storage 96
foot and mouth disease 155
foreign exchange 14, 37, 46, 66
foreign investment 13, 55, 63, 64, 102, 106; conference on 107; direct 4, 54; environmental conditions for 15; fostering 12; low levels of 39; nationalism influence on attitudes towards 11; and official assistance 52–6; policy 92; projects needing, to reduce environmental damage 85
forests 62, 92; erosion channels in 23; fertilized 37; intensification of production 116; rain 37, 123
France 123, 135; farmers 68
Frankfurt am Oder 145
free market 4, 40–6, 161; difficulties of introducing 13; environmental trends of transition to 71–103; insufficient acknowledgement of intrinsic weaknesses 11; likely failure to bring substantial improvements to environment 15; limited breadth of 33; move to establish 146; nascent, interaction with rest of world 51; passage to 16; rules 41; satisfactory framework for shift from central planning to 151; supported as a general concept 41; unbridled 67; weaker rates of exchange 14
freight 96
fridges 91
Friedman, Milton 41
Friends of the Earth International 162

gas 30, 114, 132, 139–40; airborne 83; dependence on imports 127; emissions 21, 74, 114; methane 29; natural 31, 81, 121, 122

heavy industry 14, 28, 32, 33, 35, 62; insolvent and obsolete sector 102; mineral-based 29; political emphasis on 31; priority to 30

heavy metals 3, 23, 74, 82, 84, 99; accumulation in the soil 25; chemical cleaning of brown coal to remove 91; high levels 21, 25

Henkel 48

Holoubek, Michal 1

Hontelez, John 162

Hoogovens units 135

'hot spots' 6, 22, 25, 111, 158; ecological, one of Europe's worst 23

housing: acute shortages 60; blocks poorly insulated 129–30; communist governments made impressive improvements in 36; new 131; see also heating systems; Thion

Hume, Ian 59; see also World Bank

Hungary 35, 51, 64, 83, 113–14, 147; agricultural liquid wastes 22; biomass potential 140; budget deficit 66; capitalist comparison 71; chlorine in soil 23; coal the main fuel for domestic heating 34; communist government 8, 141, 142; comparative advantage 100; cost of environmentally safe technologies 87; currency convertibility 46; debt 160; energy 129, 131, 132, 133, 139, 140; environmental funds 116; environmental liability 111–12; foreign investment in 54, 63, 66; goods have to conform with EC rules 69; 'goulash communism' 33; 'hot spot' areas 25; import agreements 41, 68; income levels 57; industrial output 57; infrastructure and appropriate resources 48; insolvent industrial enterprises 66; major polluters 30, 84; National Atomic Energy Committee 135; nuclear power 135, 138; number of cars brought

into 96; oil refineries 31; Phare in 56, 90; private capital invested in 12; privatization 63, 90; protests against higher petrol prices 43; regulations on car testing 97; signs of modest growth in industrial production 59; State Property Agency 44; subsidies 45, 65; sustainable environmental development 14; uranium mining 19; water supply 21, 26, 119; see also Budapest

hybrid economy 66–9, 153

hydroelectricity 132, 140–2; zero import duties on turbines for small plants 149

hydrocarbons 20; aromatic 26; chlorinated 21, 28; volatile 23; substantial reduction in emissions 121

IAEA (International Atomic Energy Authority) 82

ICC (International Chamber of Commerce) 124

IEA (International Energy Agency) 134

IMF (International Monetary Fund) 10, 11, 42, 52, 57; imposed limits for budget deficits 49, 50; stabilization policies 56, 66

immunity disorders 99

imports: cardboard and plastic boxes 102; cheap ready made clothing 61; cheaper, from developing countries 102; coal 81; consumer goods 68; foreign capital 52–3; foreign goods 95; gas 127, 137, 139; liberalization of 96; new and second hand cars 96; oil and gas 127; partially dependent on 34; rising 97; rising tide from the West 57; secondary raw materials 101; shrimps 99; tariffs and quotas on 64; waste 9, 100–1; water 86; zero duties 149

improvements 102–3; failure to bring 15, 77–94; rate of savings 49

parliamentary elections (late 1991) 40–1; percentage of prices market determined 65; Phare in 56, 90, 154; price liberalization 45; private capital invested in 12; privatization 39, 62–3, 67, 92; projects linked to the Baltic 91; recycling 102; rehabilitation of district heating in five cities 88; response to liability 106–10; restructuring of steel industry 3–4, 84–5; *Review of Commerce* (Poznan) survey 61; Russian, Belorussian and Ukrainian tradespeople in 60; Six Year Plan (1950–55) 31; social and economic legacy 46–7; steam and hot water consumption 81; still a communist society 46–7; strikes against higher energy prices 43; US-based firms looking to invest in 91; value of production lost due to sickness and other environmental causes 6; voivodeships 80, 93, 94, 115, 117, 121, 122, 161; waste water that needed treatment 119; water supply 119; world's first oil well 29; *see also* Black Triangle; Gdańsk; Katowice; Kraków; Lódź; NFEP; Rafako; Silesia; Solidarity; Szczecin; Vistula; Warsaw

political instability 15

pollution 13, 18, 24, 72, 123, 154; abatement equipment 121; charges 35, 116; coal and 133–5; continuing 102; control equipment 76, 87; curbs conditional upon availability of local resources 124; current 109; development of 27–38; energy generation 81; industrial 81, 119; lack of control technology 9; non-point 21; overlapping concentration of heavy industry and 22; progress in curtailing 46; reducing 67, 75, 121; solid fuel 133; water 23, 70, 76, 100, 106; *see also* air pollution; PPP

Porcelana Walbrzych 48

Portugal 71

poverty 4, 7, 9, 11; spiralling 49

power generation *see* power stations

Power International 138

power stations 19, 26, 30, 36, 93, 122; coal-fired 20, 87, 88, 127, 128, 135, 140; gas-fuelled 140; lignite-fired 6, 7, 34, 76, 90, 99, 135; local 133; private gas-fired combined-cycle 140; thermal 8, 81; trade between steel mill and 122; water discharges and solid waste from 126; *see also* FGD; nuclear power

PPP ('polluter pays' principle) 15, 16, 104–5, 112, 116, 150, 155, 156

Prague 22, 71, 97; stock exchange 63

precautionary principle 124–5, 142

PreussenElektra 138, 143

Price Waterhouse 44

prices: coal import 81; consumer goods 65; differential 112; domestic fuels 127; dumped 57; energy 43, 77, 129; falling 65; freeing 45, 48; higher 130; impact on water discharges 81; inherited subsidized 126; low 32, 33, 57; market, introduction of 134; natural resource 77; petrol 43, 114; rising 11, 65; stabilization 52; subsidized 32; sudden shift to real rather than artificial 67; undercutting 96

privatization 10, 14, 40, 42–5, 77, 78–80, 109–10; agencies 106, 110; bank 65; capitalist 39; complications of speeding up 50; consequences of 59–69; contracts 159; controversial 50; difficulties 16; first wave of 112; further factor in delaying 64; impact on energy sector 143; large-scale 112; main method of promoting 52; mass 63, 107; nationalism influenced attitudes towards 11; opposition to 47; partial rather than full 152; pressures on new governments to introduce 102; progress in 62–4;

Index compiled by Frank Pert